Preliminary Edition Notice

You have been selected to receive a copy of this book in the form of a preliminary edition. A preliminary edition is used in a classroom setting to test the overall value of a book's content and its effectiveness in a practical course prior to its formal publication on the national market.

As you use this text in your course, please share any and all feedback regarding the volume with your professor. Your comments on this text will allow the author to further develop the content of the book, so we can ensure it will be a useful and informative classroom tool for students in universities across the nation and around the globe. If you find the material is challenging to understand, or could be expanded to improve the usefulness of the text, it is important for us to know. If you have any suggestions for improving the material contained in the book or the way it is presented, we encourage you to share your thoughts.

Please note, preliminary editions are similar to review copies, which publishers distribute to select readers prior to publication in order to test a book's audience and elicit early feedback; therefore, you may find inconsistencies in formatting or design, or small textual errors within this volume. Design elements and the written text will likely undergo changes before this book goes to print and is distributed on the national market.

This text is not available in wide release on the market, as it is actively being prepared for formal publication. Accordingly, the book is offered to you at a discounted price to reflect its preliminary status.

If you would like to provide notes directly to the publisher, you may contact us by e-mailing studentreviews@cognella.com. Please include the book's title, author, and 7-digit SKU reference number (found below the barcode on the back cover of the book) in the body of your message.

Converting Shoppers to Buyers

The Power of Shopper Marketing and Promotions

Preliminary Edition

Jean Marc Rejaud and Renee Azoulay

Fashion Institute of Technology

Bassim Hamadeh, CEO and Publisher
John Remington, Acquisitions Editor
Jamie Giganti, Project Editor
Casey Hands, Associate Production Editor
Jess Estrella, Senior Graphic Designer
Alexa Lucido, Licensing Associate
Natalie Piccotti, Senior Marketing Manager
Kassie Graves, Vice President of Editorial
Jamie Giganti, Director of Academic Publishing

Printed in the United States of America.

ISBN: 978-1-5165-2682-6 (pbk) / 978-1-5165-2683-3 (br)

SP Book Project v. 1.9

Learning Outcomes

Through this book, the reader will be able to do the following:

- Formally understand the role and function of sales promotion and its evolution into shopper marketing
- Effectively integrate sales promotion and shopper marketing into the communication objectives and strategies of a marketing campaign
- Define shopper marketing objectives
- Define shopper marketing consumer target
- Engage shopper marketing-focused research and analysis to inform shopper marketing consumer target, strategies, and tactics decisions
- Define the appropriate retailers target for any sales promotion/shopper marketing campaigns
- Develop effective campaign ideas for sales promotion/shopper marketing
- Execute a shopper marketing campaign idea
- Select the right promotion tactics
- Create the proper mix of communication channels for any sales promotion/shopper marketing campaigns
- Select and manage the key metrics and KPIs to use for tracking the implementation and results of sales promotion/shopper marketing campaigns

Contents

Chapter 1: The Evolution of Sales Promotion into Shopper Marketing

Learning Objectives

After completing this chapter, you will be able to do the following:

- Clearly and correctly define and differentiate sales promotion and shopper marketing
- Identify and explain how shopper marketing logically evolved from sales promotion
- Explain why shopper marketing is growing
- Understand how shopper marketing is effectively used by winning businesses and brands
- Start analyzing the application of shopper marketing by any brand or business

Introduction

What Is the Chapter About?

Sales promotion is all about short-term sales through gifts and incentives. Shopper Marketing is all about marketing to and building a relationship with the consumer every time he or she shifts to a shopping mindset . . . and doing this over time.

Why Is This Important?

Shopper marketing is the natural evolution of sales promotion into a more mature and disciplined marketing communication method.

In the end, this is still about selling products and services but with a more thorough, holistic, and long-term perspective.

Key Terms

- **Sales promotion:** Marketing and communication activities that change the price/value relationship of a product or service perceived by the target customer, thereby (1) generating immediate sales and (2) altering the long-term brand value (Accessed at Sales Promotion – by Tony Yeshin (Author) – 2016)

- **Shopper marketing:** Marketing to the shopper; a full spectrum of marketing and communication activities designed to generate sales once the shopper is in the mindset to buy

- **EPOS:** Electronic point of sale; back-end computer system that tracks and stores what each consumer purchases. Uses scanners at the cash registers in the store

- **Strategy:** A roadmap; a plan that creates and directs shopper marketing initiatives

- **Omnichannel:** A multi-channel sales approach that provides the customer with an integrated shopping experience. Channels include retail stores, online stores, mobile stores and apps, telephone, TV, direct mail, and any other method of transacting with a customer (Accessed at https://www.emarsys.com/en/resources/blog/what-is-multichannel-marketing)

- **LTV:** "Lifetime value" is a metric that represents total profit (or loss) estimated to result from an ongoing business relationship with a customer over the life of the relationship

- **Big data:** The term used to describe the dramatic and exponential growth and use of information

An Expert's Perspective

Mike Ryan—Client Service Director at Tracy Locke (1)

What is sales promotion for you?

Sales promotion is the back end of brand marketing (which is to create awareness of a brand/product), and sales promotion helps pull it through the whole cycle to purchase.

What is shopper marketing?

[Shopper marketing] is more holistic, across more channels and more elements of the consumer shopper journey

What are the biggest challenges for shopper marketing professionals?

Resources are very challenged because everyone is trying to find growth. There are not as many resources as there used to be, but people are finding more value in pooling resources, whether with a retailer or another brand.

The most important thing is a clear understanding of the retail and shopper barriers—what is inhibiting growth—and making sure to align it with the sales and marketing members, and aligning on what the objectives are.

Key Concepts

Sales Promotion

What is traditionally meant by the term *sales promotion*?

Strategic Definition:

"Sales promotions are marketing and communications activities that change the price/value relationship of a product or service perceived by the target, thereby (1) generating immediate sales and (2) altering the long-term brand value." (Accessed at Sales Promotion – by Tony Yeshin (Author) – 2016)

As Renee Azoulay, Professor of Marketing Communications at FIT explains, sales promotion "is all about delivering incentives to consumers and trade."

There are key elements to a sales promotion, and these elements differentiate a "promotion" from an "advertisement":

- **Inducement:** There needs to be some type of *inducement* to buy; for example, "Get a free make up bag when you buy $50 worth of cosmetics."
- **Required action:** Typically, there is an action or behavior required by the target customer; for example, "**Buy one** and get one free" or "**Sign up** for our newsletter and get a chance to win."
- **Impact on the purchase**: Sales promotions are meant to drive purchase. Said another way, while sales promotions can work to enhance a brand's image, their main purpose is to generate a sale.
- **Measurability:** Promotions should be measurable. The way to support that a promotion resulted in sales is to set up way(s) to measure it.
- **Time:** There are a beginning and an end to a promotional campaign. Unlike an advertising campaign that may be seen for an extended period of time without a beginning and end date, a promotional campaign requires a start and end date. There are legal reasons why this is true as well as cost issues. For example, if an offer is for a free cosmetic bag, it would likely be too costly for a free bag to be given to customers forever. Additionally, there is a customer-motivation justification as formal start and end dates add pressure on the target consumer to "act now."
    - See the following example:

STORES • PREFERRED CUSTOMERS • CUSTOM FRAMING

TAG YOUR LATEST MASTERPIECE ON SOCIAL MEDIA
#BLICKFRAMING & #BLICKPRINTING

FAMILY-OWNED AND SERVING ARTISTS SINCE 1911

In this example, Blick Art Materials offers a 50% off custom framing and painting to acquire new customers. The strength of the offer is reinforced by the large font used for the 50% Off.

Importantly, promotional spending is on the rise. In fact, it is greater than advertising spending. Total promotions spending in the US reached $633.4 billion in 2013, more than double the total advertising spending of $263 billion. (Accessed at http://thepomoblog.com/index.php/borrell-big-spike-in-promotions-spending/)

Figure 1: U.S. Total Promotions Spending vs. Ad Spending, 2000 – 2013

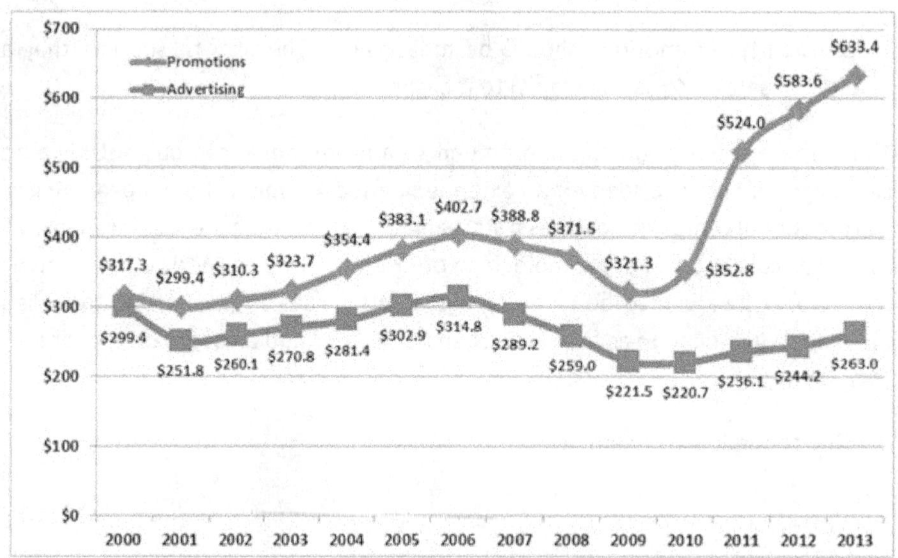

The bottom line here is that consumers have accepted sales promotion as part of buying-decision criteria and are in fact always looking for "best deals." Part of this is due to the decline in consumers' purchasing power and less available disposable income. This, in turn, has made consumers more price sensitive and responsive to promotional activity.

The increase in promotion spending has its roots in a number of factors:

- **Competition intensification:** The fight for market share has intensified, so companies are looking for ways to "maintain an edge." Said another way, brand categories and the brands themselves are saturated, making it difficult to maintain sales. The addition of "generic" brands has also added to the set of options within a category.

- **Retailers dictate the market's moves more and more:** Retailers in and of themselves have become powerful promoters and use promotions both on brand names as well as their own private label brands.

- **An accelerating trade concentration:** The trade (comprised of retailers, wholesalers, and distributors) has become more concentrated and powerful, thereby increasing their demands on the manufacturers to help increase their margins and foot traffic (traffic into their store locations).

- **The fear of slowing sales:** Under the pressure of their shareholders, companies are more concerned about negative sales trends, so they focus on short-term results that are often achieved by price promotion.

- **Media costs escalation:** In this context, companies are exploring alternative ways to meet their objectives.

- **The electronic point of sales revolution:** The availability of electronic point of sale scanner technology (EPOS) means it is easier to execute promotions and accurately measure their performance.

The proliferation of promotion spending and significant changes in the marketplace discussed later in this chapter has led to the evolution of traditional sales promotion into a discipline that is focused on marketing to the shopper, also known as *shopper marketing*.

Shopper Marketing

Shopper marketing is, in fact, marketing to the consumer as he or she shifts to a shopping mindset after having engaged in research and some analysis on his or her needs and how to satisfy those needs. The idea of marketing to the shopper encompasses a full spectrum of activities designed to generate sales once the shopper is in this mindset, so this is much more than a simple incentive such as a coupon or gift.

At its genesis in late 2004, shopper marketing was defined by companies such as Nestle as "understanding how our target consumers behave as shoppers in different channels and formats and leveraging this intelligence via strategies and initiatives that result in a balanced benefit for all stakeholders

- our brands, our key retailers, and the mutual shopper." (Accessed at Shopper Marketing: Profiting from the Place Where Suppliers, Brand Manufacturers, and Retailers Connect by Daniel J. Flint (Author), Chris Hoyt (Author), Nancy Swift (Author) – 2014)

From this initial definition, which is focused on understanding and gaining intelligence on the consumer, shopper marketing has broadened dramatically both in its scope and financial commitment made by companies. Financially, for example, spending on shopper marketing more than doubled, moving from representing 6 percent of marketing spending by Consumer Packaged Goods (CPG) manufacturers in the US in 2012 to 12.9 percent in 2017.

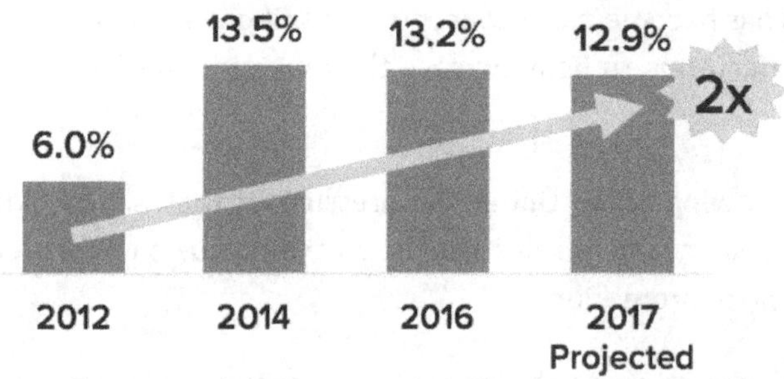

(Source: 2017 Marketing Spending Industry Study—Cadent Consulting Group)

A more recent report from the Association of National Advertisers (ANA), conducted in partnership with market research firm GfK says that "between now and 2020, investment in Shopper Marketing is expected to increase 5.8 percent to $18.6 billion, outperforming the growth of total brand marketing spending." (Accessed at https://www.ana.net/content/show/id/40812)

In terms of the broader scope shopper marketing entails, it has grown to include the creation of meaningful and memorable brand experiences in the retail environment. It is maturing to include a far more sophisticated and holistic understanding of "marketing" to shoppers. In that context, Tracy Locke—a major shopper marketing agency—defines the discipline of marketing to the shopper as "using design thinking to craft brand experiences that create value at every relevant touch point. From in-store merchandising, digital/social/mobile applications and retailer initiatives to local marketing, packaging development, and content creation, our purpose is to get consumers and shoppers to buy into your brand and purchase your product." (Accessed at https://www.theipm.org.uk/members/tracylocke.aspx)

Expanding upon this definition, Adam Drake—Associate Creative Director at Tracy Locke(2)—adds that shopper marketing is about "understanding how the consumer exists within the retail space" and gaining an "understanding of shopper behavior and how to create memorable and enticing campaigns to bring" the consumers to the store.

This holistic definition is broader in scope in that, not only is it meant to focus on the actual shopping stages of the purchase process, but also to do so using a more focused marketing and marketing communications angle.

The traditional definition of sales promotion with its gifts and incentives naturally flows into this idea of "marketing to the shopper" as it becomes one of the methods used to "get consumers to" actually "buy into your brand and purchase your product" at the actual or virtual store. The traditional sales promotion activities are now *one part* of the puzzle because gifts, incentives, and special retail displays have to support the total brand experience in the store, which leads up to and accomplishes the sale.

To be able to deliver successful shopper marketing campaigns that achieve such a paradigm shift, it is necessary to understand the specific dynamic changes that have shaped this evolution.

Market and Marketing Evolutions

From an overall perspective, it is safe to say that the changes in the marketplace have driven the explosion of the shopper marketing discipline. A key driver for the growth of shopper marketing rests on the need for significant data that leads to insights and business intelligence (e.g., who is the target audience, what is the shopper behavior, what are the barriers to purchase?) So, what we have is a demand by marketing professionals for data or information in order to accomplish shopper marketing coupled with an explosion on the offer side that is fueled by digital data access.

This significant need and "hunger" for information, along with specific fundamental marketplace changes, have amplified the emergence and growth of sales promotion and its morphing into marketing to the shopper, "shopper marketing." These fundamental changes are outlined in the following section.

Power Shift

Consumers vs. Brands

The consumer has gained significant power. In the past, the manufacturers "ran the show." With the emergence of the Internet and other digital capabilities, consumers have real power to learn about brands, make educated choices, and provide feedback. Not only can they better understand and formulate their needs through online research, guides, peer advice, and videos, but they can also compare options and prices in real time. Moreover, they can do this anytime, anyplace, 24/7—this is significant power!

Importantly, the increased ability of the consumer to constantly jump between in- and out-of-store activity, as well as offline and online, amplifies the need for creating promotional campaigns that are more than a one-time deal and cover all shopping-related activities. For example, when consumers engage in "showrooming," they check the actual product in which they are interested in the store and then purchase it online at a cheaper price. Or they can also practice "webrooming" where consumers check online first for all information, characteristics, and prices of the products they are interested in, and then, once they have made the purchase decision, they go to the selected store to purchase the actual product. In both cases, the brands have to provide dynamically-adjusted offerings and activities that help manage the consumer through all those moves and shifts to be sure that this consumer will end purchasing with them.

Additionally, social media has enabled consumers to interact en masse with each other, with the brand and with the retailer—again, giving such consumers more power.

Digital video and tutorials provide consumers with access to information that can sway the purchase decision. These changes put pressure on the manufacturers who have to provide timely and relevant information, answers, and incentives. *As a net result, the shift in power to the consumer has removed power from the manufacturer.*

The following charts illustrate this quite well, showing how product reviews and YouTube played a key role in the way Millennials found information for beauty products in 2016.

US Beauty Consumers—Sources of information, by generation, January 2016

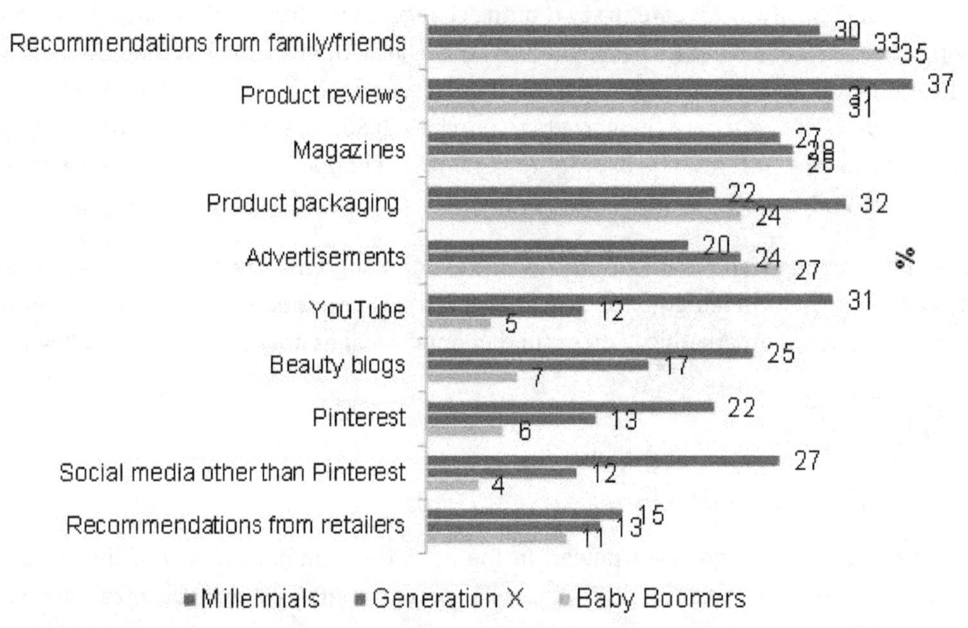

Source: Lightspeed GMI/Mintel

In this shift of power to the consumer, manufacturers' abilities to persuade and influence consumers on their websites and social media pages have weakened. As illustrated by the chart, consumers are relying on independent digital sources of information from bloggers, vloggers, peers, family, and friends for their advice on products and services.

Most Trusted Sources of Information When Making Purchase Decisions According to Internet Users in North America, July 2015
% of respondents

Source	%
Friends & family	81%
Online reviews	76%
Third-party experts	70%
Websites	67%
Articles & news	63%
Videos	63%
Marketing materials	55%
Online bloggers	55%
Social	49%
Advertising	47%

Note: n=300 ages 18+; "extremely" or "somewhat" trust
Source: Expertcity, "2015 Consumer Trust Survey," Sep 29, 2015
201135 www.eMarketer.com

Once again using the US beauty market as an example, the graph clearly indicates that while beauty brands are getting better at managing their social media presence, 65 percent of the first-page organic search results on beauty brand searches on YouTube are with vloggers.

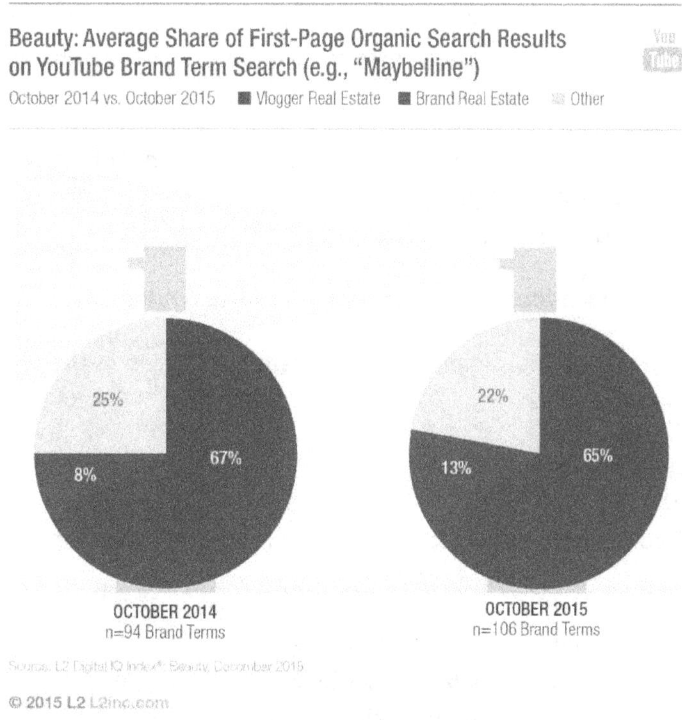

Similarly, social media was used for many purposes for shopping for beauty products in the US in 2016, with a clear predominance for heavy beauty buyers.

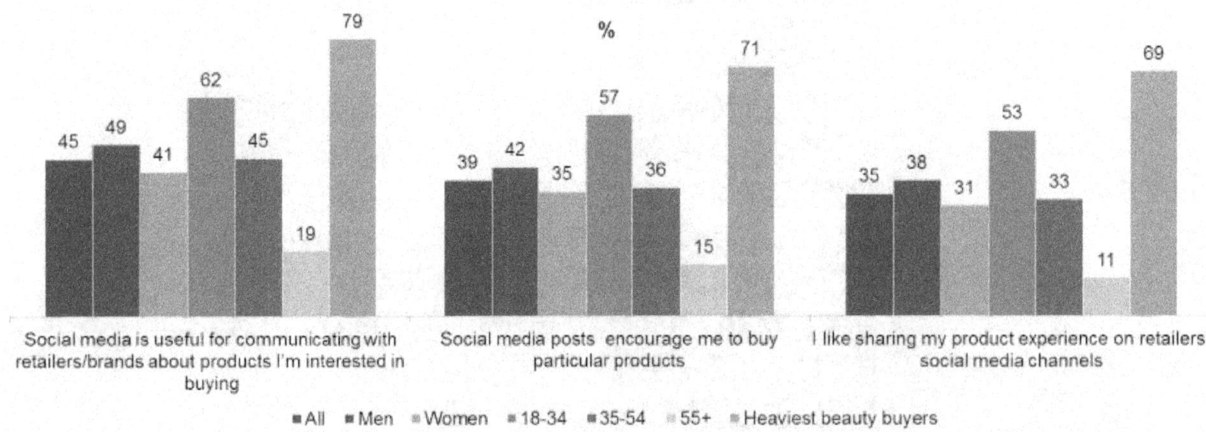

Source: Lightspeed GMI/Mintel

Retailers vs. Manufacturers

There has been a sizeable shift of power from manufacturers to retailers as well. This trend is expected to continue as retailers flex their muscles and use EPOS (electronic point of sale) systems to determine:

- which products deliver the greatest profits, and
- which offers result in the greatest profit margins.

In simple terms, EPOS systems employ scanner technology that tracks purchase transactions. When you make a purchase at the store and the item is scanned at the register, this information is fed into a computer system. More about this later.

The following statistics demonstrate this point in terms of sales volume. Retailers outsell manufacturers by a substantial margin.

1. In 2016 (2016 Forbes Global 2000),
    a. the top ten food companies in the world generated $425.6 billion in sales, and
    b. the top ten household/ personal care companies in the world have generated $261.9 billion in sales
2. By contrast, over the same period, the top ten retailers in the US (starting with Walmart) have generated $1,019.37 billion in sales (National Retail Federation 2017), or 2.4 times the top ten food companies' worldwide volume and 3.9 times the top ten household/personal care companies' worldwide volume.

Retailer growth is evident in all industries and all categories. For example, Amazon.com reached the $100 billion sales mark in 2016 (2016 Forbes Global 2000) and is expanding rapidly into many industry segments (fashion, groceries, etc.) for its retail strategies.

The fact that retailers are outselling manufacturers points to the power shift away from manufacturers and onto retailers. However, it is the use of the EPOS systems and resulting data analytics that is fueling the power shift. The retailer is able to maximize profits by analyzing purchases, product placement, and promotional offers.

In addition, retailers have created an additional revenue stream with private label (generic) brands. These brands have a higher profit margin for the retailer because the retailer manufactures the product and thereby removes the middleman, i.e., the manufacturer. For example, CVS, the drugstore chain, produces a generic baby shampoo with the "CVS" label on it. The manufacturer Johnson & Johnson manufactures Johnson & Johnson baby shampoo. Both products are shampoos for babies, and they compete on the shelf at CVS. This again puts pressure on the manufacturer to have to compete with a store/generic brand, more often than not at a much lower price point, of course. Since the acceptance of private label, generic brands have increased in the minds of consumers, and manufacturers are forced to contend with this more today than in the past.

The net result is a highly challenging competitive environment putting manufacturers in a very weak negotiating position with their retailers.

Manufacturers are therefore under pressure to provide the retailers "more of everything" including sales promotion, discounts, and/or special offers. The manufacturers are expected to deliver these offers not only to the retailers themselves but also to the consumers of those retailers in order for their products to be put on the shelves in the first place and to be able to stay there. Another reason the manufacturer has to deliver these offers is simply to have the retailers pay attention to their products.

This situation has also generated a highly competitive environment between retailers, which are all under the pressure of e-commerce and, in particular, Amazon. This is clearly pushing the retailers to fight on price and offers to keep customers coming to their stores.

The net effect is a cumulative pressure that requires both manufacturers and retailers to be even more disciplined and strategically driven in their sales promotion and shopper marketing campaigns. The importance of proper disciplined planning and extensive use of information accessible through trackable digital interactions has become necessary to succeed. For these reasons, a full shopper marketing approach (not just with price off, gifts, and incentives) and a formalized creative process will stack the deck in favor of developing the most effective campaign idea using the best sales promotion techniques and communication activities.

A Formal Discipline Requiring Strategic Planning and Effective Creative Process

Sales promotion has historically been tactical in nature with a short-term sales focus. For example, if a company saw it had low earnings for a quarter, the answer was a short-term solution of offering a coupon to the consumer who bought the product. The result in that scenario oftentimes was successful, in that the short-term lack of sales was rectified with a sales boost. However, the question is posed: What happened to the sales of that brand after the coupon? (i.e., Did the sales slump again?). The answer here is yes; oftentimes sales went back to the level achieved before the coupon was used.

Since historically the sales promotion discipline was all about finding the right gift or incentive, promotional campaigns were tactically built around such gifts or incentives. This was and still is mainly bottom-up driven, where the gift selection/incentive dictates the campaign setup. There was (and still is) no strategic foundation for the campaign nor was there any real creative process to create such a campaign. For example, if the promotion idea was to give a gift to the consumer for the purchase of the product, the emphasis was on the amount that could be spent on buying the gift and less on the "worthiness" of the gift in the eyes of the target customer. The focus was not on how to motivate the target customer to become loyal to the brand; the focus was on making a one-time sale.

That is why there is an abundance of literature and guides on sales promotion, mainly focused on gift options and directories of gift providers or store display providers.

Over time, promotion books have evolved to include a more strategic perspective, e.g., *Sales Promotion Essentials: The 10 Basic Sales Promotion Techniques and How to Use Them* by Don Schultz or *The Sales Promotion: How to Create, Implement and Integrate Campaigns that Really Work* by Roddy Mullin. Both are excellent books but are outdated in that neither one integrates strategy and digital marketing or the necessity of a formal creative process.

First, understanding that all marketing communication methods have gone through maturation stages that resulted in more formal planning processes with specific steps, including a formal creative process, is important. The creative process starts with the client brief and ends with the creative outputs. These processes are fluid in nature, being refined, improved, and expanded as the marketers become increasingly familiar with them. These processes and steps are required by the clients and the brands to ensure their marketing money is spent wisely—on the right target, with the right message at every stage, with the proper incentive, and through the proper channels. Clearly, the name of the game is strategy. Solid strategy drives success.

Strategy is so important because the dramatic rise in promotional activity has resulted in too many messages; good strategy breaks through the clutter. It also drives high levels of customer involvement, which in turn results in sales and alteration of long-term brand equity. Additionally, strategic thinking improves product differentiation by planning messages focused on customer needs and addressing those needs over time.

Importantly, strategy involves commitment and time. It is part of the role of shopper marketing practitioners to help clients resist the urge for short-term promotional activity.

The discipline of marketing to the shopper is, in fact, the mature expression of sales promotion with the application of a formal step-by-step, disciplined planning process and a formal creative process. This means that such processes focus on shopper insights and behavior and what they expect as inputs, with integrated shopper marketing campaigns and communications as the outputs.

The creative process is a shopper-focused campaign of "big ideas." These big ideas are identified through an iterative and formal creative process including a number of steps, such as brainstorming for unique ideas. This can be equated with how advertising focuses on consumer and awareness insights as the input and on advertising communications elements as the output.

While, of course, shopper marketing continues to use gifts and other types of incentives, the selection of such gifts or incentives is now driven by their appropriateness for the target audience and proper reflection of the target consumer's purchase behavior.

A Key Component of Marketing Communication Requiring Integration

Sales promotion, and now shopper marketing, is a marketing communications method that is part of the promotional mix, in addition to advertising, public relations (PR), direct marketing, personal selling, and word of mouth. Each of these components has a particular purpose for moving a target from the "I-do-not-know-you/I-don't-buy-you" stage to the "I-will-buy-you" stage.

Advertising is focused on creating awareness big and fast; public relations on generating and maintaining goodwill from all stakeholders for your products or services (starting with your consumers); direct marketing on generating an immediate response from your target; personal selling on generating an actual purchase from your consumer while this person is in the actual or virtual store; word of mouth on spreading the word; and, sales promotion or shopper marketing on boosting your sales from your baseline and hopefully doing so over a longer period of time.

In that context, integration has many requirements:

Shopper Marketing Campaign Integration from Within

First, the shopper marketing campaign components have to work together toward the same goals. The boost of sales generated by shopper marketing will come from a marketing continuum, i.e., "marketing" to the shopper from the outside of the actual or virtual store to the inside of the store and finally to the product itself on the shelf.

The key to this activity is to generate more shoppers purchasing your product, or the same shopper purchasing more often, or the same shopper purchasing more products from you. The idea is to generate incremental sales, that is, more sales than you had before and more than the amount you spent on the shopper marketing campaign.

Shopper Marketing as Part of Integrated Marketing Communications

Secondly, not only do the shopper marketing activities have to be integrated at all stages of the shopper marketing communication process (from outside the store to inside the store and finally to the product location in the store), but they also have to be integrated into the overall marketing communication campaign of a brand or product by aligning with any advertising, public relations, direct marketing, personal selling, and word-of-mouth communication elements of the campaign.

Through their specific roles and purposes (awareness for advertising, liking for public relations, sales boost for sales promotion and shopper marketing), all communication methods aim at achieving the same overall marketing objective for the same target customer.

In that context, all marketing communication methods in a campaign have to have the same foundation in terms of value proposition, positioning strategies, and brand identity/message. This would include the overall look and feel of the campaign in terms of design and copy. It could also be argued the same major selling idea should be the foundation of an overall campaign, just expressed and applied differently depending upon the marketing communication method.

With this in mind, it is important to note that shopper marketing professionals cross the line into advertising, PR, and the other marketing disciplines. Importantly, promotion professionals need to be brought into in the planning process much earlier so that integration with the other disciplines can be achieved. As a result, promotion professionals benefit from having more knowledge of a variety of marketing communication methods, including advertising, PR, and direct/interactive marketing, as well as from having the ability to think strategically and plan well.

Offline and Online Integration for Shopper Marketing

Finally, digital technology is adding another layer of integration requirements.

- Digital is not another communication method but another communication channel, another way to deliver the shopper marketing campaign to the target audience.
- Digital is becoming *the* major communication channel or medium for the US market and will continue to grow as such.

US Total Media Ad Spending, by Media, 2016-2021
billions

	2016	2017	2018	2019	2020	2021
Digital	**$71.60**	**$83.00**	**$93.75**	**$105.44**	**$117.53**	**$129.26**
—Mobile	$46.70	$58.38	$70.05	$82.31	$93.01	$102.31
—Desktop/laptop	$24.90	$24.63	$23.70	$23.13	$24.52	$26.95
TV*	**$71.29**	**$71.65**	**$71.93**	**$72.22**	**$74.03**	**$74.17**
Print	**$26.02**	**$24.30**	**$23.12**	**$22.61**	**$22.38**	**$22.26**
—Magazines**	$12.70	$12.44	$12.38	$12.30	$12.23	$12.16
—Newspapers**	$13.33	$11.86	$10.74	$10.31	$10.15	$10.10
Radio* **	**$14.33**	**$14.36**	**$14.41**	**$14.43**	**$14.46**	**$14.49**
Out-of-home	**$7.52**	**$7.67**	**$7.78**	**$7.86**	**$7.94**	**$8.02**
Directories**	**$4.25**	**$4.08**	**$3.95**	**$3.87**	**$3.80**	**$3.72**
Total	**$195.01**	**$205.06**	**$214.94**	**$226.44**	**$240.14**	**$251.92**

*Note: numbers may not add up to total due to rounding; *excludes digital; **print only, excludes digital; ***excludes off-air radio and digital*
Source: eMarketer, Sep 2017

230236 www.eMarketer.com

Whether it is for advertising, public relations, direct marketing, personal selling, word of mouth or shopper marketing, digital communication should be used if appropriate to the target audience. Depending on the unique media consumption of the target audience, plans should incorporate both offline and/or online channels in such a way that they complement and reinforce one another. For example, TV could be used as an offline channel for awareness and social media as an online channel for building knowledge and liking the product as well as for stronger relationships between the consumers and the brands. The key is that they work together to direct consumers from one to another, with the ultimate goal of moving toward a purchase.

With shopper marketing, the scope of digital assets is expanding again dramatically as virtual or augmented reality or digital displays (just to name a few) are creating additional communications channels to drive shoppers from outside to inside the store (even a virtual store). These need to be properly integrated into the campaign as well.

The Explosion of Shopper Data through Digital Capabilities

Digital analytics and big data have transformed the marketing decision-making landscape across all aspects of marketing, including promotion.

Areas in Which US Marketing Executives Use Marketing Analytics to Make Decisions, Aug 2015, Feb 2016 & Aug 2016
% of respondents

	Aug 2015	Feb 2016	Aug 2016
Customer acquisition	36.6%	43.6%	42.4%
Customer insight	-	46.4%	40.5%
Digital marketing	-	36.7%	39.1%
Customer retention	30.7%	38.1%	35.0%
Branding	26.5%	30.8%	34.5%
Social media	30.7%	29.4%	33.3%
Segmentation	29.2%	31.8%	31.0%
New product or service development	20.2%	25.3%	29.2%
Promotion strategy	29.2%	28.7%	28.2%
Product or service strategy	20.2%	21.8%	25.5%
Marketing mix	31.5%	31.5%	24.8%
Pricing strategy	21.8%	21.5%	24.8%
Multichannel marketing	16.3%	20.8%	19.9%

Source: Duke University's Fuqua School of Business, "The CMO Survey: Highlights and Insights" commissioned by American Marketing Association (AMA) and Deloitte, Aug 23, 2016

215629 www.eMarketer.com

The growth of data available primarily through digital technology has led to an explosion of shopper profile, behavior, and transaction (purchase) data. This explosion of information provides unique and robust opportunities to gain a detailed and accurate understanding of consumers and their purchase patterns. These patterns can be used by manufacturers and retailers to understand barriers to purchase, as well as to create more effective campaigns. The truth is in the numbers, and the numbers are there! Shopper marketing campaigns are using this data in many ways, such as offering personalization or real-time reporting.

The Contribution of Shopper Marketing in Building Customer Lifetime Value (CLV)

While sales promotion has, by nature, a short-term view on sales, shopper marketing has a "longer" view because it focuses on all the shopping stages of a consumer, not just on giving gifts or incentives at the final stage to boost sales. It also encompasses long-term thinking.

As mentioned before, shopper marketing also has to be an integral part of any integrated marketing communications plan, which by nature has to be long-term in its ambitions and, like many other marketing communication disciplines, needs to help build customer lifetime value.

According to the Harvard Business Review, customer lifetime value (CLV) is the amount of profit a company can expect to generate from a customer for the time the person (or company) remains a customer (e.g., x number of years) (Harvard Business Review 2014).

While shopper marketing is focusing on the final stages (shopping stages) of the purchase process in order to increase purchase frequency, upselling and cross-selling into larger package sizes, multiple units, and related products, it is aimed at doing this every time and over time, thus helping build CLV.

We also know that shopper marketing has to align with and reinforce the brand or product value proposition and positioning, leading to greater brand equity.

Shopper marketing is by nature focused on building customer lifetime value, but it also incorporates an omni-channel strategy.

An omni-channel strategy is one where the consumer has a homogenous experience with a brand or a product across all appropriate channels. If a consumer sees coherent and consistent personalized messaging and offerings in multiple places across multiple channels, he or she has a greater propensity to remember them, to reflect on them, and to act on them by making a purchase. This also implies that channels work together to generate more sales opportunities and to convert more of these opportunities into an actual purchase. This is where, for example, the click-and-collect offering comes into play in which a consumer can purchase online but pick up the product at the store for convenience and speed-of-product access reasons.

According to a 2015 study by IDC, omni-channel shoppers have a 30 percent higher lifetime value than those who shop using only one channel. (Accessed at https://www.thinkwithgoogle.com/marketing-resources/omnichannel/omni-channel-shoppers-an-emerging-retail-reality/)

Shopper marketing is at the core of the omni-channel evolution as it is aimed at marketing to the shopper across all appropriate "shopping-focused" channels. So, mechanically, it is supporting the shift to higher consumer lifetime values.

Here is an example from the Tracy Locke agency with Pepsi Cola on the benefits of going from a pure Sales Promotion mindset to a Shopper Marketing mindset as you conceive campaigns. Tracy Locke could have just "given" gifts and special offers like contest or coupons…But they did much more for their client with a much bigger and positive impact on sales and brand equity.

Case Study:
Bringing Shopper Marketing To Life

Case Study

2017 GOLD SHOPPER MARKETING EFFIE AWARD WINNER

"#Say It With Pepsi"

With young cola drinkers looking at the category in a whole new way, we helped differentiate Pepsi at shelf with #SayItWithPepsi - their biggest campaign in a decade. We designed over 200 custom emojis, placed them on millions of Pepsi bottles and got the word out with a "kitchen sink" campaign that turned every touchpoint into an opportunity for self-expression. By the end of the Summer, we had crushed every objective and had everyone talking

Competition:
Shopper Marketing Effie Awards

Ran in:
USA

Category:
Omni-Channel Shopper Experience

Brand/Client:
Pepsi / PepsiCo

Lead Agency:
TracyLocke

Product/Service:
Food and Beverage

Classification:
National

Dates Effort Ran:
May 15, 2016 - August 31, 2016

Program Origin:
Brand Driven

Credits:
Danielle Anastasi
Dan Cishek
Sabrina Diez
Christy Hanlon
Ben Loht
Matt Nevins
Jim Ryan
Rachel Seeger
Sarah Sims
Amy Spiridakis

Version: Original

#SAYITWITH
PEPSI

effie
awards

Executive Summary

The Challenge

Make Pepsi the relevant cola choice for a new generation of consumers

The Idea

With #SayItWithPepsi, we set out to interject the Pepsi brand into the cultural conversation by transforming every moment at-shelf into an opportunity for self-expression.

Bringing the Idea to Life

We over 200 custom emojis, placed them on millions of Pepsi single-serve designed bottles and got the word out with a "kitchen sink" campaign that included national TV, digital content, breakthrough retailer programs, hyper local OOH and a partridge in a pear tree!

The Results

Across retailers and priority accounts, sales of Pepsi single-serve products crushed expectations and #SayItWithPepsi swung share of Coca Cola to Pepsi's favor for an incredible [REDACTED] straight weeks.

Effie Awards Category Context

We set out to change the face of Pepsi and give consumers a new way to relate to the product and interact with each other through relatable, contemporary, socially-significant symbols: custom-created Emojis. Thanks to our Emojis, Pepsi became more than a drink choice. It became a way to express yourself and Say It With Pepsi.

State of the Marketplace & Brand's Business

State of the Marketplace & Brand's Business:

Consumers have gotten healthier habits. Colas have taken a hit. Particularly hard hit has been Diet Colas, as artificial sweeteners are perceived as just as unhealthy as regular sugar.

The entire CSD category has been experiencing declining sales, but regular Cola is actually growing in popularity and is the most sought-after choice for a consumer treat. Getting Pepsi to differentiate itself within the category was the goal.

At-shelf or in a cooler case, consumers are also bombarded by choices, from sparkling water to tea. When faced with so much mass choice, a friendly, playful icon is a welcome option. In a sea of labels, a smiling Emoji reaches out and entices a consumer to have a larger experience. Pepsi became the popular face that everyone wanted to have on hand.

Strategic Communications Challenge:

Summer has historically meant Pepsi. Road trips, picnics, BBQ's – all places where Pepsi was the beverage of choice. Coke's 20 oz. bottles, personalized with a consumer's name (the "Share A Coke" campaign), had consumers opting for Coke instead.

Taking back summer was Pepsi's priority for 2016. Getting retailers to drive sales of single-serve Pepsi products, which meant incremental merchandising units and coolers, was a challenge we needed to embrace. By giving Pepsi summer a new look - an Emoji that was either a fun character, or a symbol of summer like sunglasses or flip-flops – we created a new social currency. Suddenly, you were never taking a road trip or a vacation just with friends or family. You were taking Pepsi along. And thanks to a Big Idea, Say It With Pepsi, it was more like taking a close pal or the promise of an even better experience along for the ride, not just a beverage.

Shopper Segment

Like most brands, we were after the ever-elusive millennial shopper. Unlike most brands, this new generation was single-handedly shifting the perception of our category.

For years, shoppers had viewed Cola as a "do it all" beverage that could quench your thirst, accompany some popcorn or even join you at the dinner table. Thanks to millennials, those days are fading fast. This new generation of Cola drinkers

views brands like Pepsi as a "treat" - something fun and delicious to enjoy in moderation when the moment calls for it. It was important to understand that, regardless of whether or not they were loyalists or switchers, they were looking at us differently.

Objectives & KPI's

NATIONAL PROGRAM OBJECTIVES

1. Demonstrate the many ways that Say It With Pepsi drove commercial results across all retail outlets/channels nationally by surrounding shoppers/consumers with our campaign

Success Metrics:

- Volume Share: Hold TM Pepsi single serve value share flat to Coca Cola
- Volume Sales: In a declining category, hold volume sales flat versus trend
- Incremental Merchandisers: Secure and execute [REDACTED] merchandisers in large and small format retailers
- Execution Gaps: Close merchandising execution gaps against Coca Cola in the small format channel during program timeframe.

2. Demonstrate ability to surround consumers with regionally relevant Pepsi Emoji messaging to drive awareness

Success Metric:

- Deliver the contracted amount of OOH media impressions [REDACTED] amongst A18+ in priority Pepsi markets

RETAILER SPECIFIC PROGRAM OBJECTIVES

Demonstrate how Say It With Pepsi drove commercial results for specific customer partners across various channels (large format, small format, Foodservice) through customized shopper marketing programs

Success Metrics:

- TARGET:
  - o Objective 1: Secure incremental Pepsi merchandiser displays vs. YAG
  - o Objective 2: Exceed TM Pepsi historical mobile coupon redemption rate of [REDACTED]
- 7Eleven
  - o Objective 1: Drive incremental in-store traffic to 7Eleven locations across the country
  - o Objective 2: Drive Pepsi 20 oz. single serve sales performance vs. YAG

Pizza Hut: Drive incremental in-store traffic to Pizza Hut locations across the country

Shopper Insight

The Shopper Insight

Modern shoppers view cola as an enjoyable treat - not just "something to drink" - and Pepsi was uniquely positioned to capitalize on this shift by leaning into its famously fun brand equity.

Cultural Observation

Emojis had gone mainstream and were a readily acceptable and often used form of communication amongst both the young and young at heart. The most popular word of 2014 wasn't even a word at all - it was the heart emoji[1]. And with

over 90% of people using emojis, regardless of age or gender[2] we knew we were onto something big!

The Shopper Barriers:

With cola being perceived as more of an indulgence, it's not just as simple as "red vs. blue" anymore. Shoppers are considering the entire category more thoughtfully than ever, and Pepsi needed something to differentiate itself at-shelf that resonated with this new generation in a meaningful way. With emojis, we found a way for the Pepsi brand to speak their language (literally).

1 Global Language Monitor 2014 Annual Word of the Year Survey.
2 2015 Emoji Report

The Big Idea

With over 200 pop culture, emotional, sports and regional Emojis, Pepsi gets fun and personal, connecting with shoppers and offering up a new social way to connect and express yourself.

Bringing the Idea to Life

#SayItWithPepsi - Right Message. Right Time. Right Place.

Emojis were a fun and highly interactive way to connect to consumers without saying a word. To make this communication especially relevant, we contextualized it at a regional level, making sure we used the right cultural matchups to tell our story the right way for that part of the country. Throughout the campaign, our Emojis were relatable to the consumers they were reaching - through NFL and MLB teams, landmarks, foods and popular activities of a specific region - making consumers feel special with every Pepsi.

Small Format: Emojis added that surprisingly personal pop of fun that broke-through in cluttered small format environments. Through the use of traditional POS, combinations of bottles told fun, simple, summer-themed stories, and added unexpected spontaneity to what would otherwise be a routine shopping trip. To take shopping even further away from the same-old-routine, we used full store takeovers with unexpected POS elements (i.e. floor decals, pump toppers and inflatable displays).

Large Format and Grocery: In Large Format and Grocery stores we introduced innovative merchandisers that secured incremental space for Pepsi 20 oz. bottles. Our merchandisers were circular and shoppable from all sides. This drove consumers to seek out the Emoji that connected with them and to add it to their cart. Special dump bins which were clear allowed consumers to have fun "rummaging" for that special Emoji.

Target: At Target, we developed "My Pepsi, My Emoji" where consumers uploaded a selfie and we converted it into a Pepsi Emoji that could be customized. Consumers automatically received a Buy One, Get One free 20 oz. Pepsi coupon when they shared their Emoji with #MyPepsiMyEmoji.

7-Eleven: 7-Eleven shoppers are on the go and depend on GPS navigation, so we partnered with WAZE to drive consumers to 7-Eleven with geo-located messaging that had Emojis prompt them to stop in for a chance to win exclusive prizes. At the cooler, consumers were prompted to pick up a 20 oz. Pepsi and snap/share a photo for a chance to win.

Pizza Hut: Pizza Hut wanted to drive traffic - so we created #PizzaHunt. Our scavenger hunt had consumers looking for 20 oz. Pepsi featuring pizza Emojis, that they could bring to any Pizza Hut for a free personal pizza.

Foodservice: At Food Service locations, we wrapped fountain cups with Emojis that mirrored the design on our single-serve packaging. To drive awareness and encourage Emoji-cup orders, we took over menu board signage with videos that showcased our Emojis.

Co-Branded TV Spots & Content: We let our emojis do all the talking when we made them the stars of national TV spots for Little Caesars and the darlings of social media in content for Dollar General, Meijer and Circle K.

OOH: With OOH we could tell unique, celebratory stories that were highly visible and relevant to the target audience. Our buy extended across the country, however placements and creative varied greatly by market. By looking closely at demographics, we penetrated markets strategically with local and regional assets, thematics, emojis and messaging to truly engage with consumers.

So, yeah, #SayItWithPepsi was huge. But it didn't succeed simply because of its size. As you can see, the campaign worked because we obsessed about context on our way to delivering an incredibly personalized and localized brand experience all the way to the shelf.

Communication Touch Points - All

Digital/Interactive
- Pre
- Post
- Developed Retailer Site Content
- Digital Video
- Display Ads

Mobile/Tablet
- Pre
- During
- Post
- App
- Other

Packaging
- Pre
- During
- Post

Retail Experience
- During
- In-Store Merchandizing
- POP
- Sales Promotion

Sponsorship
- Pre
- During
- Post

Direct
- Pre
- During
- Post
- Retailer Specific
- In-Store Merchandizing
- Retail

OOH
- Pre
- Post
- Billboard
- Place Based
- Transit
- Other

Pricing
- During

Paid Media Expenditures

Current Year: September 2015 - August 2016
- $2-5 million

Year Prior: September 2014 - August 2015
- $2-5 million

Budget
- About the same as other competitors.
- More than the prior year's budget.

2016 Budget was up slightly when compared to 2015.

Owned Media & Sponsorship

- Packaging - Pepsi, Diet Pepsi and MAX 20 oz. bottles were wrapped with Emojis and #SayItWithPepsi
- Pepsi Social Media - Facebook, Instagram, Twitter, Snapchat
- Truck backs - Emoji signage was featured on the backs of Pepsi trucks
- NFL and MLB league sponsorships (created regionally relevant emojis based on Pepsi sponsored teams)

- Post
- Couponing

Social Media
- Pre
- During
- Post

Results

NATIONAL PROGRAM RESULTS

· Value Share: Against our goal of holding TM Pepsi single-serve value share flat to Coca Cola, we crushed our goal by not only holding flat, but by driving [REDACTED] consecutive weeks of positive single-serve share swing to Coca Cola[3] in a declining category - for the first time in [REDACTED].

· Volume Sales: Against our goal of holding volume sales flat versus trend ([REDACTED] for 12 weeks prior[4]), we over-delivered when the program drove a [REDACTED] volume lift versus the trend[5].

· Incremental Merchandisers: Against our goal of securing and executing [REDACTED] merchandisers in large and small format retailers, nationally - we beat our goal by [REDACTED] when we secured and executed [REDACTED] merchandisers[6] to support the program.

· Execution Gaps: Against our goal of closing merchandising execution gaps against Coca Cola in the small format channel during program timeframe, we dominated our competition when we installed merchandisers in [REDACTED] of store locations vs. [REDACTED] for the competition[7] who was also driving execution of a national summer program.

· OOH: Against our goal of delivering the contracted amount of OOH media impressions [REDACTED]amongst A18+, we eclipsed our goal by [REDACTED] impressions [REDACTED]when we delivered a grand total OOH impressions of [REDACTED] [8]

RETAILER SPECIFIC PROGRAM RESULTS

· TARGET:

o Against our objective of securing incremental Pepsi merchandiser displays vs. YAG, program drove a [REDACTED] increase in displays versus YAG[9]

o Against our goal of exceeding the TM Pepsi historical mobile coupon redemption rate of [REDACTED], we crushed our goal when [REDACTED] of coupon recipients redeemed our offer[10].

· 7-Eleven

o Against our objective of driving incremental in-store traffic, we drove a [REDACTED] navigation rate (beating the industry benchmark of [REDACTED]) and delivered [REDACTED] navigations[11] via our Waze partnership,

o Against our goal of driving Pepsi 20 oz. single-serve sales performance vs. YAG, Say It With Pepsi at 7-Eleven drove a [REDACTED] volume sales increase and a [REDACTED] velocity increase versus YAG[12]

· Pizza Hut:

o Against our objective of driving incremental in-store traffic to Pizza Hut locations across the country, we delivered in a huge way when consumers engaged with our Pizza emoji scavenger hunt and ran to Pizza Huts, redeeming [REDACTED] free pizzas[13]

3 IRI, June 12 – Aug 6, 2016 vs. Year Ago
4 Target provided information; June 12, 2016 through August 6, 2016
5 Waze program reporting; July 6, 2016 through August 5, 2016
67Exchange Data through 8-29-16
7 Pizza Hut POS Data; June 15, 2016 through August 7, 2016
8 Influencer Agency Analytics Report; June 15, 2016 through August 7, 2016
9 Pre-program: IRI MULOC Channels Dollar Sales; 1 Week Ending Feb 28, 2016 thru 1 Week Ending May 15, 2016 / Program: IRI MULOC Channel Dollar Sales; Launch to Date ending July 31, 2016
10 Pre-program: IRI MULOC Channels Dollar Sales; 1 Week Ending Feb 28, 2016 thru 1 Week Ending May 15, 2016

11 Program: IRI MULOC Channel Dollar Sales; Launch to Date ending July 31, 2016
12 PepsiCo Internal Information, including POLR order system and DX/Shopper Marketing ordering data
13 IRI Crowd sourced Collection audit "Wave 1"; Collection Period: 6/28 - 7/10/16
14 Vendor Media Affidavits; May 16, 2016 through June 12, 2016

Other Contributing Factors

National Brand TV

Application Workshop

Throughout this book, you will have formal application workshops and exercises with supportive tools to help you apply the information from each chapter to your particular case or assignment. You will also have access to lists of key decisions to be made or capabilities that you need to have in place at each step of the shopper marketing planning process.

For this first chapter, the workshop will focus on auditing your current sales promotion and shopper marketing management situation or the current situation of a brand or business of your choice. This will help you learn how you compare to a best-in-class score and where to focus on, particularly as you go through this book and its chapters.

Here is an example of the scorecard that you will be using:

Shopper Marketing Management - Performance Score Card - Students Version	
Performance Dimensions	**How strongly do you agree with each of the following statements?**
By analyzing a specific Shopper Marketing campaign for the selected brand or product, we can conclude the following:	*From Very (5) to Not At All (1)*
Foundations	
The brand seems to be using Customer Journey mapping and shopping analysis	-
The brand or product has formulated clear Marketing Objectives	-
The Marketing Value Proposition of the brand or product is formally defined	-
The Marketing Positioning Strategies of the brand or product are formally defined	-
Their communication objectives for the brand or product are formally formulated	-
Average Performance Score - Foundations	-
Sales Promotion/ Shopper Marketing Planning	
Shopper Marketing seems to be planned in full integration with the other marketing communications methods	-
The Shopper Marketing objectives seem to be formally defined	-
The Shopper Marketing objectives seem to be formally aligned with the marketing objectives	-
The Shopper Marketing objectives seem to be formally aligned with the communication objectives	-
The Shopper Marketing targets seem to be formally defined and aligned with our marketing targets	-
The expected shopper behavior changes seem to be formally defined in alignment with the shopper marketing objectives and targets	-
The Shopper Marketing campaign success metrics seem to be formally defined, measured and controled against defined benchmarks	-
Average Performance Score - Shopper Marketing Planning	

If you are a professional, go to this link (https://drive.google.com/file/d/0B80ePSvryN3aMm1JNEZObHM5aUE/view), download the Excel document and complete the performance scorecard for your brand or product, as instructed. This is a step-by-step process.

As you complete the performance assessment, you will be able to detect the key strengths and weaknesses of your shopper marketing planning process.

You are invited to use this baseline assessment to help you determine where to deepen your attention to some particular chapters as well as to track your progress as you apply the processes and best practices mentioned in this book.

If you are a student, go to this link (https://drive.google.com/file/d/0B80ePSvryN3abmNQT0x0OGVaXzQ/view), download the Excel document and complete the performance scorecard as instructed. This is a simplified version of the professional step-by-step scorecard that you will be able to use for a particular shopper marketing campaign of a brand or product of your choice for which, of course, you will have limited access to data and information.

As for the professional scorecard, as you have completed the performance assessment (to the best of your judgment and abilities based on the information, examples, data, etc. that you will be able to gather), you will also be able to detect the key strengths and weaknesses of the shopper marketing planning process for the selected brand or product.

Conclusion

Shopper marketing is a natural evolution of sales promotion by making it more strategic, planning-driven, and aligned with the marketing strategies of a brand or product. In fact, shopper marketing is the marketing maturation of sales promotion.

Just as marketing requires that you develop and know your marketing objectives, your marketing target and their behavior, your core proposition, and an aligned marketing mix, shopper marketing requires that you know your shopper marketing objectives, your shopper marketing target and their behavior, your core proposition, and an aligned shopper marketing mix. By applying such a disciplined approach to sales promotion, sales promotion has, in fact, become shopper marketing and is a far more impactful and effective marketing communication method for both short- and long-term purposes for any brand.

Furthermore, shopper marketing requires a complete integration with the marketing and the marketing communications strategies, ensuring that all efforts are aimed at the same ultimate objectives in a coherent, consistent and efficient way.

(1) 2017 Shopper Marketing Survey with shopper marketing agencies representatives – Conducted by Professor Jean Marc Rejaud

(2) 2017 Shopper Marketing Survey with shopper marketing agencies representatives – Conducted by Professor Jean Marc Rejaud

Chapter 2: The Evolution of Shopper Behavior

Learning Objectives

After completing this chapter, you will be able to do the following:

- Understand the core principles of consumer purchase behavior (also called consumer journey) and how these core principles remain valid in a digitally-driven world
- Identify specific new digital, mobile, and consumer trends that are impacting the shopping behavior, the consumer touch points, and, in relation, shopper marketing
- Articulate how the understanding of the shopping behavior of consumers (and all the possible touch points across a consumer journey) is critical to shopper marketing planning
- Understand how brands and businesses are properly integrating shopper behavior analysis and consumer journey mapping into the development of effective shopper marketing campaigns
- Start analyzing the consumer journey and related touch points of any brands and businesses for their shopper marketing activities

Introduction

What Is the Chapter About?

Over the last few years, multiple signs point to the fact that shopper behavior has changed.

New information and communication channels, as well as entertainment and productivity applications such as cloud-based software, have multiplied thanks to the digital revolution. The purchaser or shopper can now use more shopping pathways than ever before. The digital revolution resulted in a multitude of ways a consumer can navigate a purchase decision. For example, Facebook lets you ask for the opinions of your friends on a product or service that you have noticed; Google Search allows you to obtain information on that same product and its competitors in a way that most likely exceeds what a salesperson in the store could provide; companies such as Amazon empower you even more by providing the ability to check product ratings and make the purchase from the convenience of your home and receive the product on the same day as it was ordered, at a price that beats the competition.

So, things have changed.

What remains the same, however, is the core shopper behavior. A consumer still needs to first realize and identify the need, then find information on the available options, compare those options to make a purchase decision, make the actual purchase, and finally, second-guess if it was the right decision. For example, a consumer has to first realize he or she needs to eat, then find out what are the available food options, then decide what type of food to actually eat and where to buy it, then make the purchase, and finally re-consider if the choice made, was, in fact, the correct choice.

Why Is This Important?

The core principles of shopping behavior as described will remain intact; what is evolving is the shopping journey itself.

In this context, it is very important for marketers to recognize what has changed and not changed in the consumer behavior, particularly at the shopping stage, to properly plan for any shopper marketing campaign.

Key Terms

- **Pyramid of needs:** "Maslow's (1943, 1954) Hierarchy of Needs is a motivational theory in psychology comprising of five human needs levels. According to Maslow, people are motivated to achieve certain needs and that some needs take precedence over others (with the physiological-survival need as the most basic need). Once a level is fulfilled, the next level up is what motivates us, and so on."

- **Consumer purchase behavior process:** "A buying process describes the various steps (or stages) that a consumer will take to make a purchasing decision: A standard model includes the following steps: Needs and wants recognition, information search, alternatives comparison, purchase decision, and post-purchase behavior or dissonance." (Accessed at https://study.com/academy/lesson/what-is-the-buying-process-in-marketing-stages-lesson-quiz.html)

- **Customer journey:** The steps a customer(s) go through in engaging with a company, whether it be a product, an online experience, retail experience, or a service, or a combination of these. Each step is called a touch point and represents an opportunity for interactions with the customer

- **E-commerce:** Commercial transactions conducted electronically on the Internet

- **Digital Media:** "Digital media refers to audio, video, and photo content that has been digitally encoded. After the encoding phase, the digital media can be easily manipulated, distributed, and played by computing devices." (Accessed at https://docs.microsoft.com/en-us/windows-server-essentials/use/play-digital-media-in-windows-server-essentials#BKMK_1)

- **Content marketing:** "A type of marketing that involves the creation and sharing of online material (such as videos, blogs, and social media posts) for a brand that is intended to stimulate interest in its products or services." (Accessed at http://the-cma.com/news/content-marketing-advertising-whats-the-difference/)

- **Marketing Attribution:** "Attribution is the science of assigning credit or allocating dollars from a sale to the marketing touch points that a customer was exposed to prior to his or her purchase." (Accessed at https://www.convertro.com/faq/what-is-marketing-attribution)

An Expert's Perspective

While the tools (of the trade) have changed, the universal drivers of needs and wants haven't (and won't).

- Marty Glovin, Executive Vice President and Chief Marketing Officer at Marden Kane Digital Promotions

Key Concepts

Is There a New Shopper? (Yes and No)

As stated in the introduction of this chapter, at the core, a consumer goes through a set of stages before reaching the purchase decision. This process has not changed.

It is traditionally recognized that a consumer will go through five stages in the consumer purchase behavior process:

- **Needs recognition:** At this first stage, the consumer will realize that he or she has a need. This need could be spontaneous or induced by marketing stimuli which are driven by the attraction of gain or the fear of loss. In all cases, the consumer will realize that he or she has such a need and is fueled by the urge to satisfy it.

  The need can be of different natures, which can be understood by studying Maslow's Hierarchy of Needs (Maslow 1943).

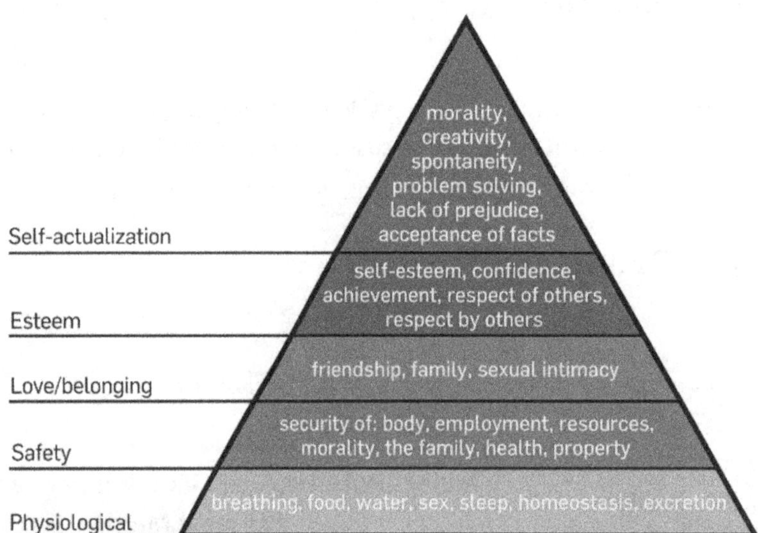

As the chart depicts, the needs hierarchy moves from the most basic of needs to the most advanced ones. As a marketer, it is important to understand and target marketing messages based on what needs a product or service (through its unique value proposition and positioning strategies) is aimed at satisfying.

In creating a successful offer, a shopper marketer needs to understand the need level that his or her marketing colleagues aim at for the concerned product or service, to determine the type of offer to be selected and whether it has to be a "rational" offer or an "emotional" offer.

Rational offers appeal to consumers' basic physiological and safety needs such as food and shelter, typically presented in a logical manner. These types of offers fall under the bottom two tiers of Maslow's Hierarchy of Needs.

For example, when Kellogg's has a discounted price or a "get-20-percent-more-for-the-same-price" type of offer for its cereal products, it aims at our rational-based safety needs (to be able to provide to our family).

Emotional offers focus on consumers' desires and feelings such as social status, prestige, power, recognition, and acceptance. These offers focus on the top three tiers of Maslow's Hierarchy of Needs.

For example, a product called Emode is a leading self-assessment company that is selling an IQ test. The marketer developed an emotional offer appealing to the emotion of a consumer of wanting to know how "smart" one is... Clearly a self-esteem need!

- **Information gathering:** At this second stage, the consumer will try to find information to better understand his or her need as well as identify possible solutions that will satisfy the need. The consumer will work to process the information and assess the pluses and minuses of each solution. Included in the information gathering stage is the identification of the possible shopping options. For example, if a consumer is hungry, the information gathering process will involve determining the type of food that might satisfy the need (e.g., pizza or a burger) as well as where the need can be satisfied (e.g., at Pizzeria #1 or Pizzeria #2).

- **Alternatives comparison:** Equipped with all the information that he or she has gathered and the insights he or she has on the pluses and minuses of each solution, the consumer will compare them (e.g., pizza vs. burger) to pick one that matches his or her purchase preference criteria the most. The consumer will then compare the shopping options (Example: If pizza, Pizzeria #1 vs. Pizzeria #2) for that solution, to once again pick the "best" one.

- **Purchase decision:** With the choices now made by the consumer for the preferred shopping option, now comes the time for the actual purchase decision. In fact, it is one thing for the consumer to "decide" which product or service to pick, and another to actually act on this decision and make the purchase. That is where sales promotion traditionally has played and continues to play a key role, i.e., to affect the ultimate purchase decision being made in the moment of truth in the store. Said another way, sales promotion works to influence the purchase decision at the moment the consumer is going to buy and can, in fact, sway a purchase choice to another product even if that product was not the one initially selected to be purchased. In fact, the power of sales promotion tactics is demonstrated by the statistics of impulse purchases:

  According to brandongaille.com, 40 percent of all consumer spending is impulse spending and over 90 percent of people who shop today make occasional impulse purchases that they didn't intend to buy initially (https://brandongaille.com/18-dramatic-impulse-buying-statistics/).

  What this is saying is that even though a consumer may have made up his or her mind on what product to buy, a successful shopper marketing campaign can sway that decision at the point of purchase or when the actual purchase is made.

- **Post-purchase dissonance:** Once the purchase is made, and depending on the level of involvement in the purchase, a consumer may question if he or she made the right decision and he or she will work to confirm the decision. This is done by re-evaluating the choices and comparing expectations of the product or service to what it actually delivers. Included at this stage would be posting product reviews and sharing with friends. As might be expected, a more expensive product purchase satisfying an emotional need might involve this fifth stage whereas a less costly product purchase satisfying a basic need might not.

As stated earlier, these five stages have been and continue to be active in the purchase behavior process. At times, consumers move through them quickly, and may not even realize it, but the consumer shopping behavior and purchase motivation stages have not changed.

What has changed though is the set of channels that the consumer uses to go through those stages. This change is driven by the emergence and the predominance of digital channels, which have significantly impacted the way consumers communicate, gather information, and make a purchase.

Specifically, the consumer is no longer going through a purchase process that is mono-dimensional where there is one direct path from needs recognition to purchase. Furthermore, the purchase process is no longer linearly controlled with one stage after another. This differs from the past when brands controlled and influenced the majority of the information to the consumer as well as the channels used to do so.

With digital technology, not only does the shopper have more ownership of his or her shopper behavior "movements" (much more of the shopping flow is directly under his or her control) but the shopper also has many more choices for information gathering, evaluation, and purchase options.

These changes are potentially creating a somewhat chaotic situation in which consumers might seem to be "going all over the place," back and forth and back again.

This apparent chaos led to new shopping path models such as the Purchase Fish by Resource Interactive/The Futures Company.

The purchase fish

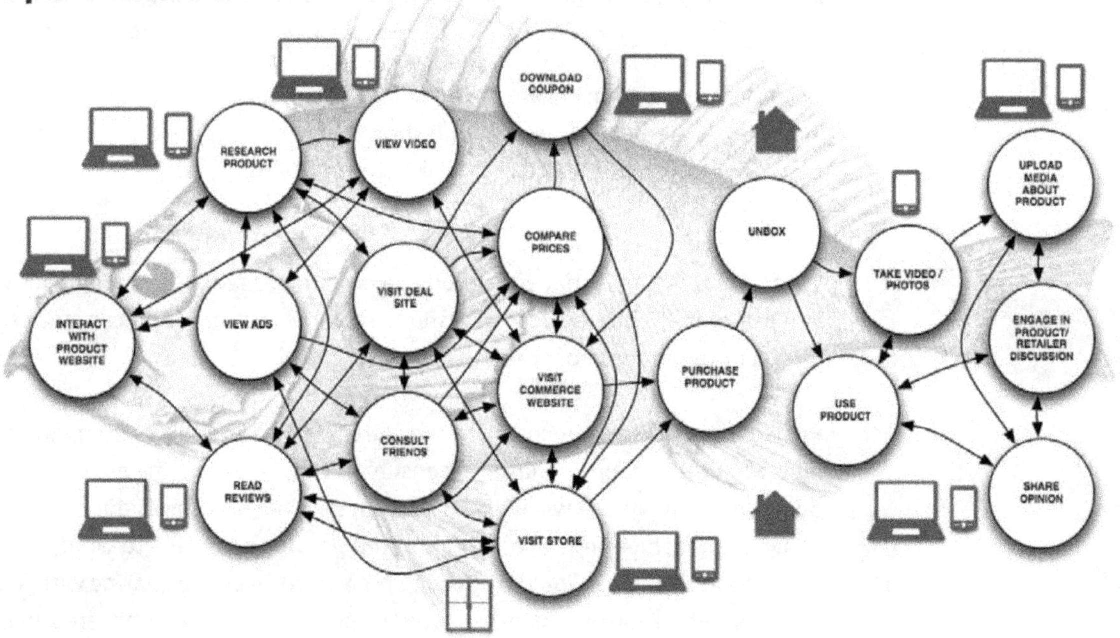

Source: Resource Interactive/The Futures Company

While there are multiple purchase path options to reach the purchase stage (with some back and forth), these options still align with the five main stages.

This is confirmed by the following information about the actual online customer journeys of consumers in the US.

According to the August 2017 Consumer Barometer statistics from Google for the US Market, 68 percent of the surveyed consumers in the US. engage in some research before any purchase and 72 percent of those individuals who engage research do it either exclusively online or through an offline/online combination. When research is engaged online, roughly one third (36 percent) do it through search engines, followed by the brand's website and retailer's website. Online research is also used for the alternatives-comparison stage in the consumer purchase process as more than half (53 percent) of those surveyed use online resources to compare selected choices. (Accessed at https://www.consumerbarometer.com/en/graph-builder/)

As the consumer moves from the information-gathering stage to the alternatives-comparison stage and then the purchase-decision stage, online research also plays a role in multiple forms. Once again, according to the August 2017 Consumer Barometer statistics from Google, 21 percent of those surveyed will research and purchase products online; 28 percent will research online but purchase offline, and 9 percent will research offline but purchase online. So many combinations are possible at this stage of the consumer purchase process and in many cases, online activity plays a role.

Finally, online activity is also very important for the last stage of the consumer purchase process. According to the same Google source, 45 percent of the purchasers having post-purchase activities share their experience on social media and 40 percent post reviews and ratings about the purchase online.

To be successful, a shopper marketer needs to have a more detailed understanding of the actual steps and channels that a consumer will use at each stage of the behavior purchase process. To do this, an important resource is marketing attribution.

According to Wikipedia, marketing attribution is defined as "the identification of a set of user actions ('events' or 'touchpoints') that contribute in some manner to a desired outcome, and then the assignment of a value to each of these events. Marketing attribution provides a level of understanding of what combination of events," (online or offline) "in what particular order influence individuals to engage in a desired behavior, typically referred to as a conversion." (Accessed at https://en.wikipedia.org/wiki/Attribution_(marketing))

For example, marketing attribution tools, such as Google Attribution 360, allow the marketer to identify the sequencing of touchpoints or events that a consumer goes through on his or her journey to purchase. Examples of online events or touchpoints are a digital ad, a paid-search ad, a direct visit to a company's website, an email, a social media ad, a social media post, or an organic search result. Offline events could be, for example, a store visit or a call to a brand's customer service department. In all cases, by using marketing attribution tools, a marketer can identify which particular touchpoint was first used by the consumer, which was used second, etc., up to the purchase being made. Included in the analysis would be post-purchase activity. Importantly, the touchpoints can easily be grouped into the five main consumer purchase behavior stages. This analysis will enable the shopper marketer to identify the specific stages and related touchpoints that should be used for the shopper marketing activities and when they should be used (at the point when the consumer formally shifts to a shopper mindset).

The acceleration of the purchase process

Another notable change in consumer purchase behavior is the fact that consumers are moving through the purchase stages more quickly. The reason for this is that consumers have increased amounts of information that can be accessed more rapidly. In addition, they have access to others' opinions to assist in making their own decision. The net result is that the consumer is more educated in both identifying the need and researching the possible solutions and purchase options. The speed of knowledge is quick and the level of emersion in the decision is deeper.

The result is that consumers are in an actual shopping mode more quickly. Again, this is because they become aware of their need more rapidly, along with the possible solutions, and are able to make quick comparisons. In essence, the information is compacted and the knowledge is concentrated into easily identifiable and accessible digital formats.

Compare this to the past, when a consumer was exposed first to a TV ad to become aware of his or her needs and potential product solution, followed by print ads to increase product knowledge and then, public relations activity to increase product appeal.

Clearly, this is no longer the case.

An online search result or digital ad directing the consumer to a website or video could convert the user from "interested" to "purchaser" in very little time.

Statistics from the US Bureau of Labor Statistics clearly confirms the acceleration of the purchase process.

The time dedicated daily to consumer goods purchase activities by individuals fifteen years and older in the US moved from 0.41 hours per working day in 2005 to 0.36 hours per day in 2016, or a 13 percent drop. (Accessed at https://www.bls.gov/tus/home.htm)

The change in shopping behavior, specifically the change in how the shopping process occurs, explains the emergence of shopper marketing and the role it plays. Shopper marketing is not just to boost sales at the store, the last stage of the shopper purchase process, but to manage the shopper experience across the shopping journey that starts and ends more rapidly and with more depth.

Because of this change, sales promotion had to become more strategic. It had to be more driven by the targeted consumer and his or her needs. It had to become shopper marketing.

A dramatic digitalization of shopping habits

There is clear market growth in the digital and ecommerce sectors as compared to traditional channels of purchase.

- According to eMarketer, ecommerce sales will grow every year by 14 percent to 16 percent from 2015 to 2021, to reach $790 billion in the US by 2021.

- According to the same source, traditional (non-ecommerce) sales will grow every year by only 1 percent to 2.5 percent from 2015 to 2021, to reach $4.9 trillion in the US by 2021.
- Consumers are also embracing omni-channel, where online and offline channels are combined by manufacturers, and especially retailers, to provide a seamless experience to their consumers across all channels.
- Consumers believe that it is important for brands to have physical stores, but the purpose of the physical store might be shifting. For example, more and more consumers are purchasing products online and picking them up at a store.
- All generations are now using online reviews and social interactions with brands to obtain information as they go through the stages of the purchase process.

Sources Used to Research a Product/Brand Before Purchase According to US Internet Users, by Generation, May 2016

% of respondents in each group

	Millennials (18-34)	Gen X (35-54)	Baby boomers (55+)	Total
Online product reviews	78%	72%	62%	69%
Retailer's website	57%	55%	54%	55%
In-store/in-person	51%	52%	57%	54%
Brand website	55%	53%	49%	52%
Word-of-mouth	50%	52%	33%	40%
News articles on the brand/product	21%	19%	22%	21%
Email interactions with brand	15%	19%	12%	15%
Social media interactions with brand	25%	16%	5%	14%
Other	4%	3%	4%	4%
Never research prior to buying	2%	4%	5%	4%

Note: among those who purchased consumer goods in the past 12 months
Source: Salesforce, "2016 Connected Consumer Goods Report," June 13, 2016

211956 www.eMarketer.com

Finally, consumers—led by the Millennials—are using their mobile smartphones, tablets, and laptops to make online purchases more and more frequently, shifting the ecommerce devices' universe away from the traditional desktop.

Devices Used to Purchase Products Digitally According to US Internet Users, by Age, Jan 2016
% of respondents in each group

	18-24	25-34	35-44	45-54	55-64	65+	Total
Laptop	75%	77%	71%	58%	55%	54%	63%
Desktop	39%	43%	44%	55%	53%	62%	49%
Smartphone	65%	63%	58%	31%	19%	9%	38%
Tablet	29%	39%	42%	20%	16%	8%	25%
Wearable	7%	12%	8%	4%	0%	0%	5%

Source: Bronto Software and Ipsos, "The Influence of Multi-Device Ownership on Ecommerce," April 21, 2016

209105 www.eMarketer.com

Accordingly, shopper marketers must increasingly leverage digital channels and devices (with a focus on mobile) as they are the preferred and most-often channels used to make purchases. Following this logic, since younger generations will become the major purchasing forces in the market and they are heavy digital shoppers responding to omni-channel communications, shopper marketing campaigns will achieve greater success if they work across communications channels in a coherent and integrated way.

A dramatic digitalization of media habits

- Just like commerce is digitalized, news and information consumption is becoming increasingly digitalized as well.
- According to eMarketer, while in 2014, TV, radio, and print represented 54 percent of the time spent by American adults consuming media daily; it has decreased to 50 percent in 2016 and is projected to decrease further to 47 percent by 2019 (eMarketer April 2017).
- By 2019, most the time will be spent on digital media with mobile representing more than half of that digital time, with people listening to the radio, checking social networks, or viewing videos. (Accessed at http://totalaccess.emarketer.com/chart.aspx?r=206490)

Share of Average Time Spent per Day with Major Media by US Adults, 2014-2019
% of total

	2014	2015	2016	2017	2018	2019
Digital	**42.8%**	**45.1%**	**46.7%**	**48.2%**	**49.3%**	**50.2%**
—Mobile (nonvoice)	**21.5%**	**23.7%**	**25.3%**	**26.7%**	**27.7%**	**28.5%**
——Radio	6.0%	6.8%	7.1%	7.3%	7.4%	7.5%
——Social networks	3.1%	3.7%	4.1%	4.5%	4.8%	5.1%
——Video*	3.0%	3.6%	4.1%	4.5%	4.8%	5.1%
——Other	9.4%	9.6%	9.9%	10.4%	10.6%	10.8%
—Desktop/laptop**	**18.6%**	**18.2%**	**17.8%**	**17.6%**	**17.4%**	**17.2%**
——Video*	3.3%	3.4%	3.4%	3.4%	3.4%	3.4%
——Social networks	2.2%	2.0%	1.9%	1.8%	1.7%	1.7%
——Radio	1.0%	0.9%	0.9%	0.8%	0.8%	0.7%
——Other	12.2%	11.9%	11.7%	11.5%	11.5%	11.4%
—Other connected devices	**2.7%**	**3.2%**	**3.6%**	**3.9%**	**4.2%**	**4.4%**
TV***	**36.7%**	**35.3%**	**34.5%**	**33.6%**	**32.9%**	**32.4%**
Radio***	**12.4%**	**12.2%**	**11.9%**	**11.8%**	**11.7%**	**11.6%**
Print***	**4.4%**	**4.0%**	**3.7%**	**3.5%**	**3.3%**	**3.2%**
—Newspapers	2.6%	2.3%	2.1%	1.9%	1.8%	1.7%
—Magazines	1.9%	1.7%	1.6%	1.6%	1.5%	1.4%
Other***	**3.6%**	**3.4%**	**3.1%**	**2.9%**	**2.7%**	**2.6%**

*Note: ages 18+; time spent with each medium includes all time spent with that medium, regardless of multitasking; for example, 1 hour of multitasking on desktop/laptop while watching TV is counted as 1 hour for TV and 1 hour for desktop/laptop; numbers may not add up to 100% due to rounding; *excludes time spent with video via social networks; **includes all internet activities on desktop and laptop computers; ***excludes digital*
Source: eMarketer, April 2017

225416 www.eMarketer.com

- The digitalization of media consumption is across all generations, but it is of course primarily driven by the younger generations. The eighteen to twenty-four-year-old generation already spends close to two times more time consuming digital media and doing so on a mobile device than their thirty-five to forty-four-year-old counterparts. Once again, as those generations reach purchasing power maturity, the media consumption shift to digital will accelerate.

Daily Time Spent with Select Devices/Media Among US Parent Internet Users, by Age, Dec 2016
hours

	18-24	25-34	35-44
Digital—smartphone	3.6	2.5	1.9
Online—desktop/laptop	2.5	1.9	2.0
TV—DVR/on-demand	2.3	1.3	1.4
Radio—streamed & AM/FM	2.3	1.7	1.5
Digital video	2.0	0.7	0.4
TV—live	1.9	1.7	1.6
TV—streamed	1.8	1.0	0.6
Digital—tablet	1.1	0.6	0.5
Print	0.5	0.3	0.3
Total	**18.0**	**11.7**	**10.2**

Note: 230 male parents and 1,129 female expectant parents or with children under age 5
Source: BabyCenter, "The Internet of Things Empowers Parents," April 28, 2017

226583 www.eMarketer.com

- For shopper marketing, the implication is clear: Use digital formats with a major focus on the use of mobile technologies and use them outside and inside the store.

All about customer engagement

Engagement is a big buzzword in marketing. It is all about "engagement." Engagement is interaction, in a meaningful way, to build brand commitment, and trust. A brand cannot just charm its customers; it must engage the targeted consumer by:

- providing valuable content around the product, and
- making the shopping experience positive and memorable.

This includes the information-gathering phase, the actual purchase transaction, the use of the product, and the post-purchase opportunities and feedback interactions.

To create this engagement and trust, content is king.

However, it takes more than good content to succeed in creating meaningful connections with customers. It takes the correct context as well. Put another way, good content is great context. Social media encourages social-based conversation (i.e., inside jokes, references, etc.). A company needs to have the correct voice and context in which it delivers its content or joins the conversation.

Part of this is looking at the conversation from the point of view of the customer; for example, will what is said offend anyone? Is it meaningful to the customers?

Part of creating meaningful communications with customers is opening the line of communication between the company and the consumer. Let the consumer know his or her thoughts and ideas are welcome. Even criticism can be accepted. Let them know what they say has value. Create a true two-way street whereby customers tell the company what they think and the company responds to their concerns.

This also applies to the communications that a company sends to its customers as they reach the last stages of the purchase process.

What a company is ultimately striving for is an ongoing relationship, and just like in any ongoing relationship, there is a give and take. That too exists in the social relationship. As the give and take broadens and deepens, the trust level between the two entities grows stronger. Stronger levels of trust result in higher levels of brand loyalty and sales.

Importantly, the give and take itself, the dialogue, heightens customer engagement. By providing consumers with interactivity, they are, by virtue of the exercise itself, engaging with the brand. That is precisely the goal of the dialogue: to spark customer engagement.

This importance of content creation and sharing is another key justification for any marketer to move from a traditional sales promotion approach to a shopper marketing focus. By definition, shopper marketing should create and support a positive interactive and highly integrated shopper experience.

As such, content creation, sharing, and two-way interactions also need to be formally integrated into the purchase process stages. These interactions and messages should be more directly related to the actual purchase decision and motivate action on the part of the consumer.

The shopper marketing discipline enables a brand to foster strong customer engagement throughout the shopping journey.

This means that promotions and offers must be integrated into the content that is delivered to the consumer. In fact, the offer needs to support the experience that you are trying to create for the consumer. There cannot be, anymore, a stand-alone offer that is disconnected from the product and the shopping experience that you are trying to create. It must support it.

Impact(s) on Shopper Marketing & Sales Promotion

- With the multitude of communications and interactions channels used by consumers, shopper marketing must be active in and through these multiple channels.
- The focus of the shopper marketing campaign needs to be digital and delivered across the various stages of the consumer purchase process.
- With the digitalization of media consumption, mobile technology is significant and should be the main component for delivery across digital channels.
- It is all about mobile, mobile, and mobile for shopper marketing, perhaps even more, with the intense use of mobile outside but also inside stores.

- Shopper marketing needs to continue to be focused on converting product research into purchase actions. This is necessary online and offline as well.
- With the shopping mode (making the purchase) happening faster than before, due to the digitally-led acceleration of the shopping stages, sales promotion must become more strategically aligned with the marketing and communication objectives, targets, and strategies behind a product or a service. This is, in fact, the purpose of shopper marketing.
- Shopper marketing must be part of and support the consumer experience throughout the shopping journey. And to do so, it should be part of the valuable content that a brand must create, share, and encourage interaction about for the consumer experience to be real and trustworthy.

Here is an example illustrating the positive impact that a proper understanding and integration of media consumption trends and shopping habits of the targeted shoppers can have on sales results and brand connection.

Case Study:
Bringing Shopper Marketing To Life

CASE STUDY

2016 SILVER SHOPPER MARKETING EFFIE AWARD WINNER

"SOUR PATCH WATERMELON SLURPEE CAMPAIGN

The SOUR PATCH KIDS were on a mission to become famous amongst teens. The problem: 7-Eleven's non-chocolate candy/gum sales were underperforming the rest of C-Store. To make SOUR PATCH KIDS famous with teens, they need to be associated with a brand teens already love...like SLURPEE. To meet this challenge, we first did a little sour/sweet snooping on social media. Guess what? #Opportunity! We saw what they were doing...listened to what they were saying...created what they wanted...SOUR PATCH Watermelon SLURPEE! Teens thirsting for an authentic experience slurped it up and they kept coming back all summer long!

COMPETITION:
Shopper Marketing Effies

Ran in:
USA

CATEGORY:
Shopper Experience

BRAND/CLIENT:
SOUR PATCH KIDS & SLURPEE/Mondelez International 7-Eleven, Inc.

LEAD AGENCY:
Phoenix Creative Co.

CONTRIBUTING COMPANIES:
T3 Ketchum TPN
Camelot Strategic Marketing & Media

PRODUCT/SERVICE:
Beverage, Canady, Gum

CLASSIFICATION:
National

DATES EFFORT RAN:
06/30/2015 - 08/31/15

CREDITS:
Kim Yansen
Steve McGowen
Heather Johnson
Abbey Ash
Laura Gordon
Maria Trujillo
Matt Schmertz
Tara Apisa
Mindy Rickert
Tim Jones

Effie Awards Category Context

Mondelez International developed a custom program with 7-Eleven that brought together TWO iconic brands-SLURPEE & SOUR PATCH KIDS-to create ONE sweet and sour sensation that created a cultural craze at 7-Eleven. The fully integrated program was designed to boost category growth and drive more SLURPEE sales.

It all started with a little sour/sweet snooping on social media...

- We saw what they were doing...
- Listened to what they were saying...
- Created what they wanted...SOUR PATCH Watermelon SLURPEE!

State of the Marketplace & Brand's Business

SOUR PATCH KIDS. Everybody loves them. They're sour. They're sweet. Then, they're gone. But, in 2014 at 7-Eleven, they were mostly...overlooked. While everybody loves running to 7-Eleven for snacks and refreshments, business was getting a little sour for SOUR PATCH KIDS candy and gum.

In the past, you could count on SOUR PATCH KIDS to always be among the most popular treats, but at 7-Eleven, Non-Chocolate candy sales were underperforming the rest of the Convenience channel, and gum as a category was shrinking compared to a year ago. As a result, SOUR PATCH KIDS brand sales were suffering as well (7-Exchange IRI ending 8/31/15).

Strategic Marketing Challenge

While everybody enjoys making the occasional run to 7-Eleven for snacks and refreshments, underperforming sales in our key categories made it apparent that consumers looking for a treat were becoming bored with the sweet selection at the tried and true convenience chain. Mondelez International and 7-Eleven needed a way to shake up consumers' perceptions and give them a reason to buy their SOUR PATCH KIDS at their local 7-Eleven store. To achieve this goal, we set out to make the SOUR PATCH KIDS famous with teens, revive Non-Chocolate Category candy sales, and drive gum sales.

To tackle this opportunity, we braced ourselves for a high degree of difficulty as our primary target audience is among the most resistant to traditional marketing. In addition, with so many digital and social distractions, breaking through and capturing their attention along the shopper journey would be a monumental achievement.

In short, our strategic challenge was to bring together TWO iconic brands-SLURPEE & SOUR PATCH KIDS-to create ONE sweet and sour cultural craze at 7-Eleven.

Objectives & KPIs

Believe it or not, Millennials are aging out and the nation's teenagers, Generation Z, are coming in! The Gen Zers are a breed of their own. They are the first generation to be raised in the era of smartphones and don't remember a time before social media. They crave information immediately and lose interest just as fast.

Knowing this, to start our journey, we looked at the target market for both SLURPEE and SOUR PATCH KIDS to understand the affinity and ultimately the brands' synergy.

- SLURPEE: Gen Z teen's ages 16–19
- SOUR PATCH KIDS: ages 13–24, with bull's-eye on ages 16–19

Generation Z was our sweet spot and our target audience!

Looking deeper, research showed Gen Zers value fun, friendship, and individuality in their lifestyles and actively seek out experiences that are authentic, fresh, and on trend all at the same time *(Ad Age, 2015)*. This not only aligned, but also seamlessly connected with our iconic brands.

- SLURPEE Brand Belief: You should be happy and life should be fun
- SOUR PATCH KIDS Brand Belief: We roll deep; mischief is more fun in groups

In the end, we knew whatever we did would have to break traditional molds and have enough true social swag to make a splash where Gen Zers live (online) in order to drive in-store sales.

Reminder: Entrants will copy their answers into the entry form in the online entry area for judging purposes – this document will not be uploaded for judging. Use this form to draft your responses and collaborate with team members.

Shopper Segment

OBJECTIVES	MEASUREMENT TOOL
Grow SOUR PATCH KIDS brand sales at 7-Eleven by at least 5% to drive category sales lift needed *(Business)*	**7-Exchange IRI ending 8/31/15**
Place 5,000 SOUR PATCH KIDS candy displays in 7-Eleven stores by the week prior to the launch of SOUR PATCH Watermelon SLURPEE *(Business)*	**7-Exchange IRI ending 8/31/15**
Make SOUR PATCH Watermelon SLURPEE a Top 3 selling SLURPEE flavor during the promotional time period *(Business)*	**7-Exchange IRI ending 8/31/15**

Shopper Insight

While it would be cool to be able to say we had to hire a Sherpa, scale a mountain and seek the wisdom of a crazy-bearded hermit to obtain the insight that led to the big idea, the simple answer was, we got it by listening.

By looking and listening to what our target audience was doing, we noticed a trend popping up all over social media. Teens and young adults were enjoying SOUR PATCH KIDS with their SLURPEE drinks and sharing their creations on Facebook, Twitter, Instagram, Vine, Snapchat and other social platforms with the tags #slurpee and #sourpatchkids. They loved the two brands together...and it showed! #Opportunity!

The Big Idea

Two iconic brands-SLURPEE and SOUR PATCH KIDS-coming together for the ultimate candy/beverage mash-up...SOUR PATCH Watermelon SLURPEE! #Brainfreeze!

Bringing the Idea to Life

Mondelez Internationl and 7-Eleven took the SOUR PATCH KIDS...captured them in a SLURPEE...and challenged teen shoppers to “Catch Them While You Can” with a shopper experience they just couldn't miss!

This full-scale integrated campaign took over 7-Eleven stores nationwide and engaged shoppers in and out of store. The surround-sound support of SOUR PATCH Watermelon SLURPEE began on 6/30 with a major media outreach push to announce the exclusive SOUR PATCH Watermelon SLURPEE, along with a social campaign that had teens showing their SOUR PATCH SLURPEE selfies all summer long.

The campaign came to life in-store with the central idea of “letting the kids run wild.” We created signage that brought excitement into the candy and gum aisle with shelf talkers and wobblers, grabbed consumer attention by the SLURPEE machine with translites and flavor cards, drove traffic into the store with eye-catching window banners, pump signage and more! We truly let the kids run wild! In addition to using these elements, we let the stores “run wild” too. Each store received several die-cut SOUR PATCH KID window banners for exterior windows to draw in shoppers to the store.

But this wasn't enough-we needed to slow shoppers down. To do so, we placed impactful SOUR PATCH KIDS floorstands with a life-size-die-cut SOUR PATCH KID on each display in-stores, along with SOUR PATCH KIDS front-end trays to drive impulse purchase at checkout.

To gain further engagement, can't-miss billboards were placed strategically in select cities across the country trumpeting the arrival and availability of the one-of-a-kind flavor experience!

Knowing that our Generation Z target audience is averse to sticking to the status quo, we knew the SOUR PATCH Watermelon SLURPEE launch would have to break traditional molds, challenging us to create a far-from-average media strategy. With this in mind, we focused on Gen Zers by using a combination of traditional tactics and social media to reach the target where they consume the most content. We opted to “tease” the never-been-done sour candy and SLURPEE combination through digital channels to feed their curiosity, increasing their appetite to try this brand-new flavor. The teaser was then followed by a full-blown earned-media PR campaign.

Reminder: Entrants will copy their answers into the entry form in the online entry area for judging purposes – this document will not be uploaded for judging. Use this form to draft your responses and collaborate with team members.

A day prior to the launch, targeted outreach to national and local media with news of the newest SLURPEE flavor was conducted. A press release, coupled with "reveals" on social media channels, was distributed the day before launch to ensure fans heard and shared the news, driving traffic into stores for the Fourth of July holiday. Within hours of the announcement, numerous national and local online, print and broadcast media covered the news with fun mentions-among them the *Huffington Post, Refinery29, Food & Wine Magazine's* blog *FWx and The New York Daily News.* We secured broadcast coverage in six key SLURPEE markets including Los Angeles, New York, Washington, D.C., Detroit, and Denver.

We also worked with Food Network for a Snapchat integration on the "Discover" page to tell the story of SOUR PATCH Watermelon SLURPEE. "Discover" gives users quick "shareable" bites of information, perfect for the Generation Z target that are always on the go.

At launch, the program secured 286 placements, garnering 557.4+ million impressions. Efforts around promoting SOUR PATCH KIDS Day secured 238 placements and 344.3+ million impressions, unheard-of results for a newly created program. Overall, the program secured 524 placements that generated over 900 MILLION IMPRESSIONS!

In addition, the brands worked with Relativity Media for a joint 7-Eleven and SOUR PATCH KIDS integration in the movie *Summer Forever,* a teen-targeted digital film starring popular social influencers. The integration attracted the attention of teens with store appearances by the stars and private screenings for select fans in Los Angeles and New York, engaging social media posts from the stars, and a 10-city promotional tour.

Reminder: Entrants will copy their answers into the entry form in the online entry area for judging purposes – this document will not be uploaded for judging. Use this form to draft your responses and collaborate with team members.

Path to Purchase Communications & Marketing Components

Pre	During	Post
Retail Experience	**Retail Experience**	**Retail Experience**
-POP	-POP	-POP
-In-Store Merchandising	-In-Store Merchandising	-In-Store Merchandising
Print	**Direct**	**Social Media**
-Retailer Specific Publication	-Email	
Digital/Interactive	**Digital/Interactive**	
-MFR/Retailer Website	-MFR/Retailer Website	
-Developed Retailer Site Content	-Developed Retailer Site Content	
-Digital Video	-Digital Video	
-Gaming	-Gaming	
-Other	-Other	
PR	**Pricing**	
Social Media	-Trade	
	-Couponing	
	Mobile/Tablet	
	-In-App or In-Game Ad	
	-Display Ad	
	-Location-based Communications/Real Time Marketing	
	Shopper Involvement	
	-Consumer Generated	
	Event	
	Guerrilla	
	-Street Teams	
	OOH	
	-Transit	
	-Billboard	
	PR	
	Trade Comm./Promo	
	Social Media	

Paid Media Expenditures

September 2014 - August 2015

- $1-2 million

September 2013 - August 2014

- Not Applicable

Budget

- About the same as other competitors.
- More than prior year's budget.

Owned Media & Sponsorship

- Mondelez International Corporate website, Mondelez International Facebook, Twitter, and Instagram pages
- 7-Eleven Facebook, Twitter, and Instagram pages, 7/10 LA Store takeover event, 7/25 NY street team store event, 7-Eleven Slurpee truck stops

Reminder: Entrants will copy their answers into the entry form in the online entry area for judging purposes – this document will not be uploaded for judging. Use this form to draft your responses and collaborate with team members.

Results

It was a total sweep for sour and sweet! Teens thirsty for an authentic, new experience slurped up the SOUR PATCH Watermelon SLURPEE, SOUR PATCH KIDS candy and gum, and kept coming back for more!

During our program, which ran from 6/30/15 to 8/31/15, the SOUR PATCH Watermelon SLURPEE was one of the best-selling SLURPEE flavors in their 50-year history and SOUR PATCH KIDS brand sales took off:

OBJECTIVES	RESULTS	MEASUREMENT TOOL
Grow SOUR PATCH KIDS brand sales at 7-Eleven by at least 5% to drive category sales lift needed *(Business)*	• SOUR PATCH KIDS brand sales grew 82.6% in unit sales • STRIDE SOUR PATCH KIDS Gum grew 51.4% in unit sales • The candy category for 7-Eleven grew 15.5% in unit sales	7-Exchange IRI ending 8/31/15
Place 5,000 SOUR PATCH KIDS candy displays in 7-Eleven stores by the week prior to the launch of SOUR PATCH Watermelon SLURPEE *(Business)*	• The program secured a 24% increase over what was forecast in incremental displays	7-Exchange IRI ending 8/31/15
Make SOUR PATCH Watermelon SLURPEE a Top 3 selling SLURPEE flavor during the promotional time period *(Business)*	• For the first time ever at 7-Eleven, a limited-time offer SLURPEE become the #1 SLURPEE seller	7-Exchange IRI ending 8/31/15

Other Contributing Factors

Summer, the time period during which our program ran is traditionally the biggest time of year for SLURPEE, candy, and gum sales. Additionally, the yearly, much hyped and anticipated 7-Eleven Day observance also fell within our program's time period. While both of these factors could have impacted the results, the results we saw clearly and exponentially exceeded the typical seasonal boost in sales that would be expected.

Reminder: Entrants will copy their answers into the entry form in the online entry area for judging purposes – this document will not be uploaded for judging. Use this form to draft your responses and collaborate with team members.

Application Workshop

Throughout this book, you will have formal application workshops and exercises with supportive tools to help you apply the information from each chapter to your particular case or assignment. You will also have access to lists of key decisions to be made or capabilities that you need to have in place at each step of the shopper marketing planning process.

For this chapter, the workshop will focus on having you audit the consumer journey and the current touchpoints along that journey for a brand or product. By engaging the analysis, you will be able to identify any customer journey changes and the touchpoints gaps (if any) and plan for new appropriate touchpoints along the journey. This will allow you to identify which touchpoints should be under the shopper marketing umbrella and planned as such.

Here is an illustration by Smart Insights of the customer journey audit that you will be using:

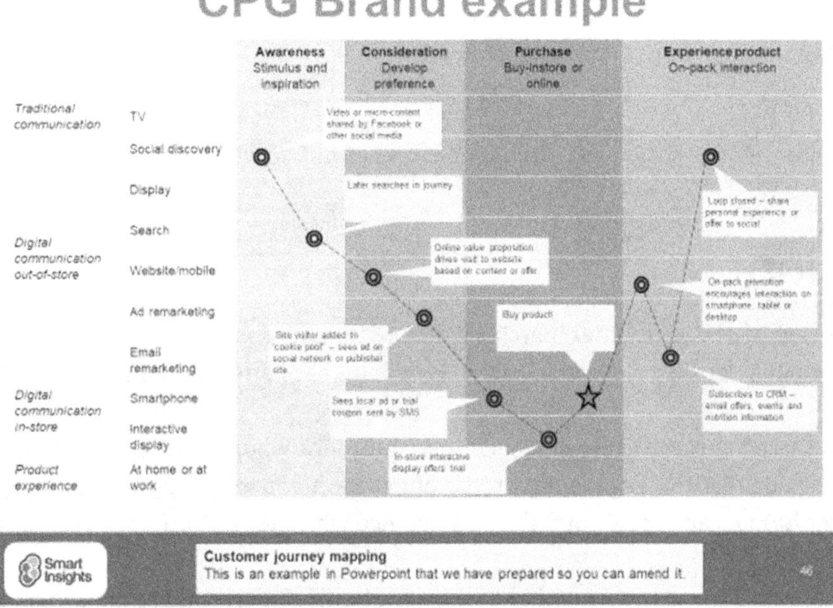

If you are a professional: Look at your own product or brand and download this tool (https://drive.google.com/file/d/0B80ePSvryN3aazltUmc4RUhRdDQ/view?usp=sharing) to map the customer's steps within the five consumer purchase behavior stages that you think your customer goes through. For each step, identify if you have a touchpoint. If yes, describe what the customer needs at that stage and what is your actual touchpoint. If there are none, still describe what the customer needs at that stage and indicate there is no touchpoint. Follow the instructions from the mapping tool to complete this exercise. At the end, you will be able to come to some key conclusions on your touchpoints management approach so far:

- The consumer steps with the proper touchpoints
- The consumer steps with the wrong touchpoints
- The consumer steps with no touchpoints

From all the consumer's steps and touchpoints, you will define which one(s) should fall under shopper marketing.

If you are a student: Look at a selected product or brand of your choice and download this tool (https://drive.google.com/file/d/0B80ePSvryN3aazItUmc4RUhRdDQ/view?usp=sharing) to map the customer's steps within the five consumer purchase behavior stages that you think the customer goes through. For each step, identify if you know that they have a touchpoint. If yes, describe what you think the customer needs at that stage and what is the actual touchpoint proposed by the product or brand. If none, still describe what you think the customer needs at that stage and indicate there is no touchpoint. Follow the instructions from the mapping tool to complete this exercise. At the end, you will be able to come to some key conclusions on touchpoints management approach for the product or brand so far:

- The consumer steps with the proper touchpoints
- The consumer steps with the wrong touchpoints
- The consumer steps with no touchpoints

From all the consumer's steps and touchpoints, you will define which one(s) should fall under shopper marketing.

Conclusion

The understanding of the consumer purchase behavior, the consumer purchase journey, and the touchpoints within that journey are critical to the development of effective shopper marketing campaigns.

A shopper marketing campaign will engage the consumer when he or she starts morphing into an actual shopping mode. For the engagement to be effective, it has to be applied at the right touchpoints through the right formats and media in the right sequence with the right offers/messages at each point.

This can only be achieved by formally and very specifically understanding the shopping behavior and consumer journey of a shopper target.

Chapter 3: The Transformative Digitalization of Shopper Marketing and Sales Promotion

Learning Objectives

After completing this chapter, you will be able to do the following:

- Understand how sales promotion and shopper marketing evolved under the pressure of the digital and mobile revolution
- Identify specific digital and mobile trends that are relevant to shopper marketing and explain how they are impacting shopper marketing
- Understand how brands and businesses are properly integrating digital and mobile into winning shopper marketing campaigns
- Begin analyzing the appropriateness of the shopper marketing digitalization strategies employed by any brands and businesses

Introduction

What Is the Chapter About?

This chapter focuses on the specific ways the digital revolution impacts how the shopper makes the purchase decision, as well as how companies surround their target customer with sales messages and promotional activity. The traditional forms of communication to sell products and services, namely television, radio, direct mail, and promotional tactics such as coupons, have been replaced by carefully crafted multi-channel personal messages designed to sell using information gathered about the customer.

Why Is This Important?

Key to the success of a brand is the company's ability to harness the paradigm shift caused by digital technology. There is no longer one message for all people delivered at a stagnant one moment in time.

Selling is a fluid, ongoing, evolving series of messages using real-time data and two-way interactions between seller and buyer throughout the shopping journey.

Key Terms

- **IP address:** A numerical label assigned to each computer or mobile device connected to a computer network that uses the Internet protocol for communication. The IP address enables a company to specifically identify each device. (Accessed at https://en.wikipedia.org/wiki/IP_address)

- **IP targeting:** The process of targeting Internet offers and advertising to specific households based on their Internet protocol address location.

- **Geo-targeting:** The process of targeting Internet offers and advertising to a group of IP addresses in a geographic area.

- **Location-based marketing:** Associated with the GPS and location detection capabilities of mobile phones, location-based marketing enables a marketer to detect the location of a specific mobile phone and deliver pertinent messages via push notifications, text, or email to the phone's user.

- **Cookie:** A short program that is stored by the Web browser on a system's hard drive that enables to know which websites a computer visited.

- **Behavioral targeting:** Technique that allows advertisers and publishers to analyze a user's previous web browsing behavior to customize the types of ads the user receives. (Accessed at https://www.tubemogul.com/glossary/)

- **EPOS:** EPOS (Electronic point of sale) systems manage the check-out and cashier system of a store and store valuable purchase information that can be transferred to databases.

- **Mobile wallet:** A mobile wallet is a way to carry credit card or debit card information in a digital form on a mobile device. Instead of using the physical plastic card to make purchases, a purchaser can pay with a smartphone, tablet, or smartwatch. Accessed at https://www.wellsfargo.com/mobile-payments/mobile-wallet-basics/)

- **Beacon technology:** Allows mobile apps (running on both iOS and Android devices) to listen for signals from beacons (small pieces of programmed hardware) in the physical world and react accordingly. Beacons placed in various locations in a store can communicate with the mobile phones of the store visitors. (Accessed at http://www.ibeacon.com/what-is-ibeacon-a-guide-to-beacons/)

- **Artificial intelligence (AI):** Branch of computer science dealing with the simulation of intelligent behavior in computers. (Accessed at https://www.merriam-webster.com/dictionary/artificial%20intelligence)

- **Augmented reality (AR):** Technology that superimposes a computer-generated image on a user's view of the real world. (Accessed at https://en.oxforddictionaries.com/definition/us/augmented_reality)

- **Virtual reality (VR):** A realistic and immersive simulation of a three-dimensional environment, created using interactive software and hardware and experienced or controlled by movement of the body. (Accessed at http://www.dictionary.com/browse/virtual-reality)
- **Data analytics:** The analysis of qualitative and quantitative data from a business and its competition to drive continual improvement in business and marketing.

An Expert's Perspective

With all the different options for micro-targeting shoppers, gathering analytics to get a complete picture of the consumer is vital. Micro-targeting will improve conversion rate over a more generalized approach, but in addition, every Shopper Marketing effort must collect key and actionable data, and that data must be used to drive the messaging, offers and promotions that are presented to the buyer. The digitalization of Shopper Marketing has made it possible to do just that and measure success. With so many possibilities, again made possible by digital technology, being able to succeed as a shopping marketer is largely dependent on one's ability to create strategically sound campaigns that hit the target at multiple points in the shopping journey using a variety of digital and interactive formats.

- Chuck Gorder, CEO at Ready Set Promo!

Key Concepts

The emergence of shopper marketing is closely linked to the emergence of digital technology. Several key phenomena can explain this situation either because of the pressure that digital technology put on the sales promotion discipline to evolve or just because new digital applications open new opportunities that are perfectly aligned with the focus of shopper marketing.

Let's go through the main changes that the digital and the related mobile technologies have sparked and continue to spark for shopper marketing.

Increasing dominance of digital communications

The increasingly dominant role of digital communications and mobile capabilities is simply "forcing" the emergence of shopper marketing.

With the emergence of new digital communication formats and technologies such as live videos, geolocation and IP targeting, and mobile, traditional forms of communication such as TV, radio, and magazines, have taken a back seat. While these traditional forms of communication are more able to segment the viewing audience compared with years ago, they are nonetheless dwarfed by digital capabilities that can micro-target, micro-communicate, and forecast results with "digital" precision.

In fact, the digital and mobile technologies are so robust in terms of their ability to deliver practically bullseye content and promotional messages through computers, tablets, and mobile phones that the current role of traditional communications is now to supplement digital messages and drive customers to digital formats.

In fact, according to eMarketer, digital advertising spending will increase its dominance to reach $129 billion in the US in spending in 2021.

US Total Media Ad Spending, by Media, 2016-2021
billions

	2016	2017	2018	2019	2020	2021
Digital	**$71.60**	**$83.00**	**$93.75**	**$105.44**	**$117.53**	**$129.26**
—Mobile	$46.70	$58.38	$70.05	$82.31	$93.01	$102.31
—Desktop/laptop	$24.90	$24.63	$23.70	$23.13	$24.52	$26.95
TV*	**$71.29**	**$71.65**	**$71.93**	**$72.22**	**$74.03**	**$74.17**
Print	**$26.02**	**$24.30**	**$23.12**	**$22.61**	**$22.38**	**$22.26**
—Magazines**	$12.70	$12.44	$12.38	$12.30	$12.23	$12.16
—Newspapers**	$13.33	$11.86	$10.74	$10.31	$10.15	$10.10
Radio* **	**$14.33**	**$14.36**	**$14.41**	**$14.43**	**$14.46**	**$14.49**
Out-of-home	**$7.52**	**$7.67**	**$7.78**	**$7.86**	**$7.94**	**$8.02**
Directories**	**$4.25**	**$4.08**	**$3.95**	**$3.87**	**$3.80**	**$3.72**
Total	**$195.01**	**$205.06**	**$214.94**	**$226.44**	**$240.14**	**$251.92**

*Note: numbers may not add up to total due to rounding; *excludes digital; **print only, excludes digital; ***excludes off-air radio and digital*
Source: eMarketer, Sep 2017

230236 www.eMarketer.com

In this context, the amazing targeting and content creation/delivery abilities of digital technology through computers, tablets, and mobile phones clearly put pressure on the traditional sales promotion approach as it is now possible to communicate at any time in a far more sophisticated, targeted, pertinent, and impactful way. Importantly, this can be done throughout the shopping journey, in all shopping phases, and in all places—including the stores.

In its simplest terms, sales promotion can be associated with the "one-way, one-size-fits-all" approach that was the trademark of traditional communication methods and promotion formats.

Digital technology has "forced" sales promotion to morph into shopper marketing. Consequently, the goal of shopper marketing is to fully leverage digital technology to deliver the right offer to the right target in the right format and at the right time throughout the shopping journey.

Secondly, the multiplication and increased sophistication of the technologies and capabilities used for digital and mobile communications further promote the growth of shopper marketing. This is expected, in fact, to accelerate.

As mentioned before, the impact of digital technologies on the shopper marketing discipline is highly significant.

The arsenal of digital communication methods a marketer can use has become very large. This arsenal keeps changing and growing over time, with new formats and improvements being made to the existing formats. Whether it is the increased sophistication of mobile apps with virtual reality capabilities where consumers can virtually try products or new beacons that can interact with mobile phones with personalized communications, consumers are embracing these new technologies and the content-message personalization capabilities associated with them. What this means is that in order to drive sales, the marketer has to keep abreast of the ever-changing digital communications landscape and match its increasing sophistication by upgrading its promotional approach to a shopper marketing level where the choice of the technologies and applications to use for a promotional campaign will be driven by the target, objectives, and strategies as opposed to the "shiny object" logic as it might have been before.

This situation has clearly increased the complexity of the planning process and made it even more important to properly implement sound shopper marketing campaigns.

With constantly more sophistication in targeting, localization, messaging, and formats, thanks to new technologies and applications, digital technology offers robust opportunities to the shopper marketer to truly "market" to the shopper as opposed to just pushing offers and gifts.

Let's go through the impact some of the digital technologies have on the shopper marketing discipline. They are as follows:

IP-based geotargeting and behavioral targeting have provided the appropriate foundations for delivering the right message at the right time, including when the consumer is in a shopping mode. This is perfect for shopper marketing.

IP targeting and geotargeting are used together but they are different.

The simplest definition of IP targeting is the process of targeting Internet offers and advertising to *specific households* based on their Internet protocol address location (which is the string of numbers assigned to each computer with an internet connection by the Internet service provider).

Every visitor's computer has an IP address that indicates its specific location at a particular time. The first three digits of an IP address correspond to a country code, while the succeeding digits often refer to specific areas of that country.

What is called geotargeting is the process of targeting Internet offers and advertising to a *group of IP addresses* in a geographic area.

In a nutshell, geotargeting uses groups of IP addresses to target a geographic area (multiple IP addresses or computers) but IP targeting uses individual IP addresses to target specific households (an individual's computer). Think of it as sniper-like advertising reaching an exact target rather than advertising that blankets a local area.

The reason why IP and geotargeting are so important to marketers is that they improve the cost-effectiveness of marketing programs and have the ability to increase profitability for brands. On the simplest level, for example, if a product is an airline ticket from New York to Honolulu, then it will more likely sell to someone who is located in either of the two cities. If a person is in a different city, then a different set of offers, appropriate for where that person is located, would generate a stronger response.

According to Adobe, behavioral targeting refers to the "technique used by advertisers and publishers to utilize a web user's previous web browsing behavior to customize the types of ads the user receives." (Accessed at https://www.tubemogul.com/glossary/behavioral-targeting/). A program called a cookie needs to be loaded first onto the user's computer to allow the tracking of his or her web browsing.

For example, the tracked and observed behavior could be that the computer user is looking at car manufacturers' websites and focuses on family vans on those websites. Similarly, this same user looks at websites selling baby clothes. It could be safe to conclude the user will soon have an expanded family with children (maybe including a newborn) and is in the active shopping mode for a new car that will accommodate the expanded family. This is a solid opportunity for a car manufacturer to place an ad for their family vans on the websites that this user will visit, such as those featuring infant clothing.

Combined with geotargeting, behavioral targeting can have profound implications for shopper marketing programs.

Using the same example as before, the family vans ads could be shown with the name of the closest dealership and a shopper marketing offer to visit this dealership for a test drive.

Location-based marketing combined with mobile technology has brought geotargeting to the next level by allowing the marketer to send the right message at the right time . . . and now at the right precise location.

Location-based marketing is associated with the GPS and location detection capabilities of mobile phones.

A brand marketer is able to detect the location of a specific phone thanks to location-based technology. Through the use of this technology and mobile apps such as Facebook Places, Yelp, FourSquare, and specific brand apps (such as Victoria's Secret), shopper marketers can deliver pertinent messages via push notifications, text, or email to a specific user's phone.

This then enables a marketer to use their database information including customer profile, purchase, and behavioral data to deliver timely and personalized messages that are relevant to the user and delivered to the precise location of the user at a specific point in time.

For example, as part of a special campaign, the New York ice cream store Van Leeuwen provided users with mobile payment options and used this feature to track the location of the user via the PayPal app. As a part of this campaign, customers were required to install the PayPal app on their mobile device and link it to their PayPal account. Once that was done, the app used geolocation technology to detect when a consumer was near a Van Leeuwen store. (Accessed at https://blog.beaconstac.com/2016/04/4-brands-that-are-winning-at-location-based-marketing-and-how/)

At that specific moment, Van Leeuwen sent the consumer a custom message with an in-store deal to entice the consumer to go to that store and make a purchase. The consumer was also able to place an order and pay for it directly via the app, then pick it up in the store.

Another example is Whole Foods and their use of geo-fences (virtual geographic boundaries, defined by GPS or RFID technology). Geo-fence technology enables a company to trigger a specific message when a mobile device enters or leaves that particular "geo-fenced" area. Whole Foods used this technology around certain store locations and targeted ads and special offers to mobile users whose mobile phones came into the geo-fenced area. Whole Foods also employed geo-conquesting tools (by placing geo-fences near competitors' stores this time) to target ads at shoppers near competing grocery stores, thus incentivizing consumers to travel a bit further in exchange for better deals at Whole Foods. The campaign was successful and generated a 4.69 percent post-click conversion rate—more than three times the national average of 1.43 percent. (Accessed at https://en.oxforddictionaries.com/definition/geofence)

Omnipresence of mobile devices

The omnipresence of mobile devices has dramatically increased the shopper marketer's ability to leverage mobile to market effectively and more efficiently to the consumer.

As discussed in Chapter 2, mobile technology continues to outpace other formats and clearly leads the way for younger consumers.

The mobile interface is very powerful for the shopper marketer. It serves for two-way communication with the target customer at virtually all times. It allows the marketer the ability to ping customers at any and all touch points in the shopping journey—including in the store.

The opportunity is clearly amplified by a few key trends:

- The large and still growing number of mobile phone users in the world (planned to reach 4.78 billion users in 2020, according to eMarketer – September 2016)

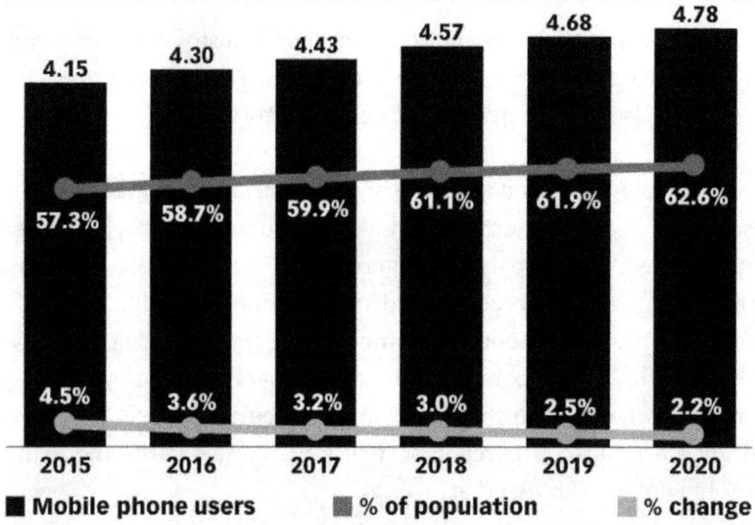

- An ever-increasing amount of time is being spent on mobile devices. (According to eMarketer, 28.5 percent of the average time spent with major media by US adults will be spent on a mobile device by 2019, second only to TV in the US) (eMarketer – April 2017).

Share of Average Time Spent per Day with Major Media by US Adults, 2014-2019
% of total

	2014	2015	2016	2017	2018	2019
Digital	**42.8%**	**45.1%**	**46.7%**	**48.2%**	**49.3%**	**50.2%**
—Mobile (nonvoice)	**21.5%**	**23.7%**	**25.3%**	**26.7%**	**27.7%**	**28.5%**
——Radio	6.0%	6.8%	7.1%	7.3%	7.4%	7.5%
——Social networks	3.1%	3.7%	4.1%	4.5%	4.8%	5.1%
——Video*	3.0%	3.6%	4.1%	4.5%	4.8%	5.1%
——Other	9.4%	9.6%	9.9%	10.4%	10.6%	10.8%
—Desktop/laptop**	**18.6%**	**18.2%**	**17.8%**	**17.6%**	**17.4%**	**17.2%**
——Video*	3.3%	3.4%	3.4%	3.4%	3.4%	3.4%
——Social networks	2.2%	2.0%	1.9%	1.8%	1.7%	1.7%
——Radio	1.0%	0.9%	0.9%	0.8%	0.8%	0.7%
——Other	12.2%	11.9%	11.7%	11.5%	11.5%	11.4%
—Other connected devices	**2.7%**	**3.2%**	**3.6%**	**3.9%**	**4.2%**	**4.4%**
TV***	**36.7%**	**35.3%**	**34.5%**	**33.6%**	**32.9%**	**32.4%**
Radio***	**12.4%**	**12.2%**	**11.9%**	**11.8%**	**11.7%**	**11.6%**
Print***	**4.4%**	**4.0%**	**3.7%**	**3.5%**	**3.3%**	**3.2%**
—Newspapers	2.6%	2.3%	2.1%	1.9%	1.8%	1.7%
—Magazines	1.9%	1.7%	1.6%	1.6%	1.5%	1.4%
Other***	**3.6%**	**3.4%**	**3.1%**	**2.9%**	**2.7%**	**2.6%**

*Note: ages 18+; time spent with each medium includes all time spent with that medium, regardless of multitasking; for example, 1 hour of multitasking on desktop/laptop while watching TV is counted as 1 hour for TV and 1 hour for desktop/laptop; numbers may not add up to 100% due to rounding; *excludes time spent with video via social networks; **includes all internet activities on desktop and laptop computers; ***excludes digital*
Source: eMarketer, April 2017

225416 www.eMarketer.com

- And for more and more activities, as illustrated by the following table from Pew Research Center

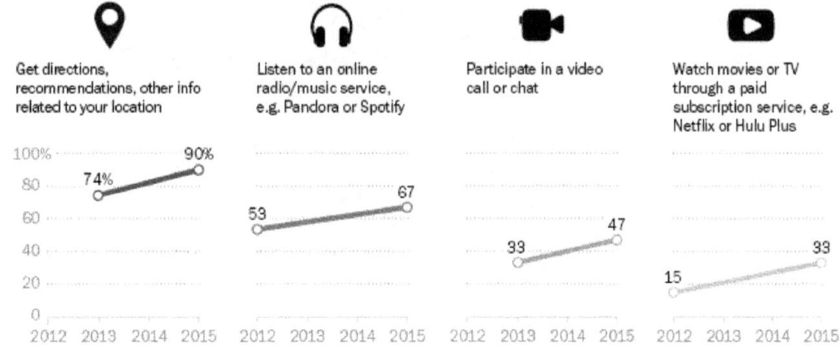

The omnipresence of mobile devices and their extensive usage for interaction, communication, and shopping offer a great number of opportunities to connect with the shopper across multiple touchpoints. Additionally, the accuracy of digital communications through mobile technologies theoretically increases the chances for a shopper marketer to succeed.

Mobile Applications are becoming "shopper-smart"

The new Mobile Wallet technologies are expanding the ability of shopper marketers to "make a sale" at the actual payment stage. This, in turn, can increase brand sales.

In essence, mobile wallet apps enable users to use their mobile phones to make payments at a store instead of paying with credit card or cash. Importantly, mobile wallet applications now also have the capability to deliver offers, send notifications, and place ads targeted to the consumer. This is powerful in that a company has the opportunity to influence the shopper at a crucial touchpoint: when he or she is actually ready to purchase and pay.

Marketers are using the mobile wallet advertising opportunities to drive sales to stores. For example, Honda has promoted one of its nationwide Honda Dream Garage Sales events through a mobile wallet ad campaign that invites consumers to tap a banner ad and save at the event. (Accessed at https://www.mobilemarketer.com/ex/mobilemarketer/cms/news/advertising/22294.html)

Another major player in the arsenal of mobile-related tools for the shopper marketing professional is mobile applications (apps).

The rapid growth and development of new apps have led to the predominance of apps in mobile phone use (90 percent of the time on mobile is spent on apps in the US market according to Flurry) (Flurry 2015)).

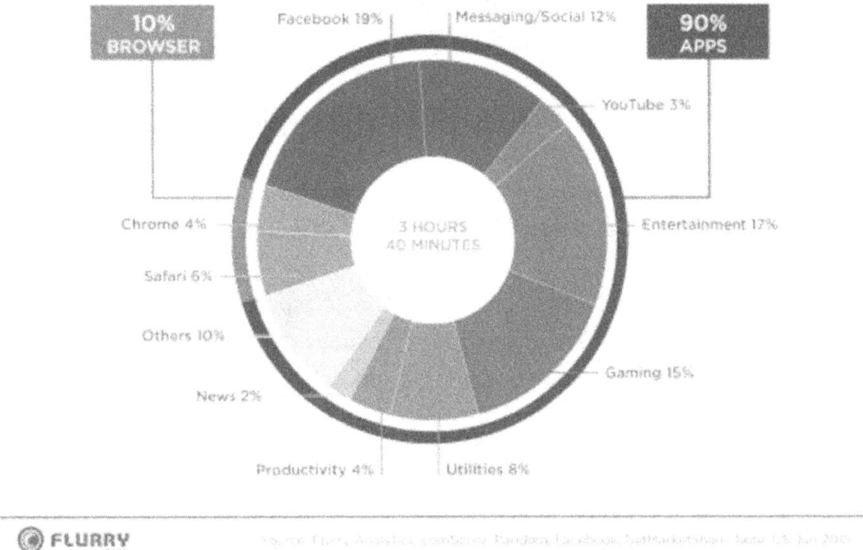

Apps are empowering to consumers because they connect the consumer to the brand and enable them to interact with the brand on multiple levels. Apps also provide instant results, e.g., information and the ability to purchase. Many retailers have an app that enables customers to order and pick up, search locations, etc.

For marketers, apps build brand strength and facilitate buying and advertising opportunities. According to AppAnnie, global in-app advertising spending is set to grow from $72 billion in 2016 to $201 billion in 2021 (AppAnnie 2017).

For brands, mobile apps offer a unique opportunity to help the consumers digitally experience the products in ways that were not possible before. For example, the 3D augmented reality mobile app "Get the Look" by Rimmel helps consumers "steal the cosmetic look" from friends and stars or models in magazines and apply that style on their own face. The "MyShade" mobile app by Clairol enables its users to virtually test any hair color shade on their own hair.

If you combine such mobile applications with specific offers or promotions that are targeted to each consumer based their profile, purchase habits, and behavior with the app, a marketer can create powerful shopper marketing messages and offers at relevant shopping touchpoints. Using the same example, if Clairol had data on a particular customer showing he or she purchased hair color at a specific time of day and also that this customer virtually tested another color via the app without purchasing on the spot, Clairol could send an offer to that customer for the hair color he or she virtually tested later on by email if the data demonstrate that this customer has a higher chance to purchase from emails than SMS, for example.

The increasing usage of shopper data

The store is the new "playing field" for digitalization and mobile technologies.

In addition to the mobile wallet technology already mentioned, there are systems (as outlined later) that further propel the sophistication of marketing and marketing communications in a store location, which is a good part of the shopper marketing discipline.

For example, **EPOS** (electronic point of sale) **systems** manage the check-out and cashier system of a store and store valuable purchase information that can be transferred to databases and used by shopper marketers to "push" offers to consumers (primarily via mobile) based on their purchases history. It also enables marketers to test offers to determine the most profitable ones.

Such systems can also be used to communicate to the salesperson in the store (through tablets or other mobile devices), what type of offers or messages to deliver to a store visitor as soon as it has been possible to identify this visitor through his or her name, his or her loyalty card, his or her mobile phone identification, etc.

One last example of the store digitalization with mobile applications is **beacon technology**.

According to ibeaconinsider (1995) (Accessible at http://www.ibeacon.com/what-is-ibeacon-a-guide-to-beacons/), "the term **iBeacon and Beacon** are often used interchangeably. iBeacon is the name for Apple's technology standard, which allows mobile apps (running on both iOS and Android devices) to listen for signals from beacons in the physical world and react accordingly." Beacons placed in various locations in a store communicate with the mobile phones of the store visitors through Bluetooth low energy technology. The store or business server behind the beacons responds to this trigger (when the beacon "recognizes" a mobile phone in its proximity) by sending back location-relevant information—such as sale information, a welcome message, or a coupon—to that precise mobile phone and with content that is tailored to that precise spot in that store.

For example, an American retailer, Burlington Coat Factory, ran a beacon-based promotion. When customers got close to the raincoats section in the store, a promotion that provided 20 percent off to specifically raincoats was sent to the mobile phones of those customers.

The department store Barneys New York has installed beacons to send personalized notifications and product recommendations to its customers when they are in the store. The notifications are based on the products that the customers have in their mobile shopping bag and wish lists.. (Accessed at https://blog.beaconstac.com/2016/04/top-8-tips-on-building-an-omnichannel-retail-strategy/)

CES, a popular consumer technology trade show, used beacons to run an interesting scavenger hunt at one of their recent trade shows. Beacons at various areas of the venue were used to trigger personalized notifications to attendees based on the various stages of the scavenger hunt, with great prizes at the end.

Meadowhall Shopping Centre in Sheffield, UK, uses iBeacon technology to gamify their Ladies' Night event with brands providing offers, discounts, freebies, and prize giveaways. (Accessed at https://www.linkedin.com/pulse/10-retailers-making-big-proximity-marketing-campaigns-shubhi-mittal)

QR Codes might come back

QR codes are two-dimensional barcodes that can be read by scanners on smartphones. They offer shopper marketers a wide range of opportunities to increase interaction with customers and prospects. This technology is used in offline media such as in print, in a magazine, or on a label on a product. Its purpose is to drive the offline view to an online view, for example, to a product website or product tutorial/video.

QR codes can help the shopper marketer gain exposure and deliver additional information to the consumer in such a way that the consumer does not have to execute a search him or herself. This is advantageous to assist the brand in moving the consumer from consideration of the brand to making the purchase decision in real time, i.e., at the moment he or she is ready to buy.

In this example, a wine marker is using bar codes in very creative way to lead the customers to its web site - where the customers can have more information on the wine making process and the grapes that are used as well as be exposed to more wine options from the same wine maker.

While very big outside the US, particularly China, QR codes did not really take off in the US. This might change if they were to be used more effectively like they are abroad.

For example, QR codes are at the heart of how users engage with the largest social media platform in China—WeChat.

Another example of QR codes application in China is with pop-up ecommerce stores that have posters featuring product images and a QR code for each item. People scan the items "on the go" and fill up a virtual shopping basket. Products are then delivered to their home. This strategy is already implemented in China by Yihaodian (the online division of Walmart).

Artificial intelligence (AI), augmented reality (AR), and virtual reality (VR)...The next frontier!

Artificial intelligence (AI) is a branch of computer science dealing with the simulation of intelligent behavior in computers. It is systems with the capability of a machine to imitate intelligent human behavior. And marketers are using these technologies. (Accessed at https://www.merriam-webster.com/dictionary/artificial%20intelligence)

According to eMarketer, marketers anticipate that technologies such as augmented reality (AR) and artificial intelligence (AI) will affect their business in the next year. That's according to a study by marketing and advertising services firm NewBase (formerly Publicitas International), which polled 1,019 marketers worldwide and asked them which types of technologies they plan to prioritize over the next twelve months (eMarketer June 2017).

In 2017, 30 percent of respondents planned to prioritize AI in the next twelve months as compared to a year ago when 13 percent said the same. Along the same lines, 24 percent of marketers worldwide said that AR will be a priority in 2017 as compared to 18 percent in 2016. (Accessed at https://www.emarketer.com/Article/Marketers-Thinking-Harder-About-Augmented-Reality-Artificial-Intelligence/1016058)

Technology Priorities According to Marketers Worldwide, 2016 & 2017
% of respondents

	2016	2017
Power of mobile devices	66%	63%
Big data	53%	53%
Mobile app development	56%	48%
Social media software	57%	46%
Security and data protection	35%	37%
Internet of things	51%	35%
Artificial intelligence	13%	30%
Cloud technology	31%	27%
Virtual reality	26%	26%
Mcommerce	60%	26%
Augmented reality	18%	24%
Voice assistants	-	22%
Wearable technology	21%	13%
3-D printing	7%	7%
Drones	-	6%
Blockchains	-	5%
Robotics	-	5%

Note: in the next 12 months; respondents chose their top 5
Source: NewBase, "Marketing Priorities 2017," June 14, 2017

228087 www.**eMarketer**.com

In terms of the way AI works, the AI system uses forecasting to project best scenarios. Traditionally, marketers use past purchases and profiles to find future customers who "look" like the previous purchasers. AI systems analyze real customer behavior to determine exactly what messages, media, and offers are most successful at generating sales. This technology has tremendous implications for the shopper marketing discipline in that it increases the efficiency and accuracy of offers and the channels being used.

Augmented reality (AR) is a technology that superimposes a computer-generated image on a user's view of the real world.

Virtual reality (VR) technology is a realistic and immersive simulation of a three-dimensional environment, created using interactive software and hardware, and experienced or controlled by movement of the body.

As reviewed before, many mobile applications such as "Get the Look" by Rimmel or "MyShade" by Clairol use augmented reality to help the consumer experience the product in a setting as real as possible.

Sephora went one step further by combining augmented reality and artificial intelligence with its Sephora virtual artist mobile app, which includes cheek try-on and color match for virtual try-on. Cheek try-on allows users to virtually try more than one thousand shades of cheek color.

Color match uses artificial intelligence to detect and estimate the shade in any photo and match it with lip, eye, or cheek products available at Sephora.

On a final note, digital technology supports the growth of shopper marketing with powerful capabilities including digital analytics and real-time reporting.

Increased Sophistication of Digital Analytics

Digital analytics allows for more precise shopper marketing campaigns that if strategically sound can deliver a stronger return on investment.

In the world of shopper marketing, data analytics is the idea of analyzing purchase patterns of the target customer in order to generate greater profits. When focused on analyzing patterns using digital technology, such as redemption of a coupon from a mobile phone as compared to redemption of a coupon from an in-store circular, this is called "digital analytics."

Part of the data analytics is, therefore, to understand and profile that best customer. Who is he or she exactly; where does he or she shop? What sites does he or she visit? What other products did he or she purchase? What is the shopping behavior of this person? What offers did he or she respond to? Who are his or her friends? Is he or she an influencer on social media?

More specifically, the ability to track purchases is driven by EPOS technology.

The ultimate goal of using data analytics is to impact shopping behavior for increased profitability. Greater revenue can be accomplished in a number of ways:

- The customer purchases more often (greater frequency)
- The customer purchases more (greater volume)
- The customer purchases more from your company (other products)

Real-time reporting—made possible thanks to digital technology—is a key condition for the success of shopper marketing.

Technology has enabled shopper marketing campaign results to be available to managers in real time. Real-time means as it is happening at any given moment, outside or inside a store. For example, a company is running a contest. Technology provides the marketer with the ability to find out, at any time during the contest entry period, how many entries there are. Managers can even see, for example, how many people are actively entering at any given moment.

Depending on the platform being used to host the promotion, the marketer may also be able to see demographics of the entrants as well as what device the entrant used, e.g., desktop, laptop, mobile device, etc. This holds true for many offer types, as long as there is a digital component to them.

What makes this powerful for shopping marketers is that they can access data as it is happening and make quick adjustments if need be. For example, in the previous case, if the contest entry level is poor, the marketer can take steps to promote the contest more heavily.

Impact(S) on Sales Promotion and Shopper Marketing

The traditional forms of communication to sell products and services, namely television, radio, direct mail, and promotional tactics such as coupons have been replaced by carefully crafted multi-channel personal messages designed to sell, using information gathered about the customer.

Shopper marketing is based on micro-targeting and increasing sales by using data analytics and an abundance of ways to communicate the sales message with digital formats leading the way.

The arsenal of digital technologies keeps changing over time with new formats and improvements being made to the existing formats. What this means for shopper marketing is that to drive sales, the marketer must keep abreast of the ever-changing digital communications landscape.

The reason digital formats are so powerful for shopper marketing and motivating customers is that these formats are highly interactive and they allow for quick personalization, and customization.

Feedback via the internet and distribution of data to shopping marketers enable them to not only deliver stronger offers, but project future marketing angles including trends, product developments, competitive activity and cost advantage analysis.

The mobile interface is powerful for the shopper marketer. It serves for two-way communication with the target customer. It allows the marketer to ping customers at all touchpoints in the shopping journey.

Data analytics are used to profile who the best customers are, identify new customers, optimize messages and offers, and retain and reward loyal customers to generate greater profitability.

Real-time reporting enables shopping markets to access data as it is happening to implement adjustments that can improve the impact of the marketing effort.

Here is an example from Quilted Northern illustrating the digitalization of Shopper Marketing is forcing brands to reconsider their traditional promotional approaches and embrace module technology.

Case Study:
Bringing Shopper Marketing To Life

CASE STUDY

2017 GOLD SHOPPER MARKETING EFFIE AWARD WINNER

"National Toilet Paper Day"

Quilted Northern® faced challenges growing in brick- and-mortar stores, with consumers less loyal and retailers favoring private label. Amazon needed to tackle low interest in buying toilet paper online. A partnership around a one-day promotion proved powerful: we combined Quilted Northern®'s promise of "Designed to be Forgotten®" and Amazon's Subscribe & Save feature (putting toilet paper shopping on autopilot) to create an activation around the year's most forgettable day: National Toilet Paper Day. The results were memorable: big sales, new audiences and a pipeline of loyal subscription customers.

COMPETITION:
Shopper Marketing Effie Awards

Ran in:
USA

CATEGORY:
Seasonal/Event

BRAND/CLIENT:
Quilted Northern
Georgia – Pacific

LEAD AGENCY:
Droga5

PRODUCT/SERVICE:
Bath Tissue

CLASSIFICATION:
National

DATES EFFORT RAN:
August 26, 2016 – August 26, 2016

PROGRAM ORIGIN:
Collaboration: Retailer + Brand Driven

CREDITS:
Johny Bauer
Richard Busby
Mara Buta
Ross Gillis
Jason Ippen
Byron Knight
Delphine McKinley
Brad Mumbrue
Evana Oli
Don Shelford

Version: Original

effie worldwide

Executive Summary

The Challenge

Quilted Northern® and Amazon's growth in the toilet paper category was challenged by entrenched shopper behaviors:

buying on deals and in brick-and-mortar stores.

The Idea

Together, Quilted Northern® and Amazon Subscribe & Save make buying and using toilet paper utterly forgettable—which is a good thing.

Bringing the Idea to Life

On National Toilet Paper Day, we launched a one-day promotion that encouraged Quilted Northern and Amazon shoppers to make buying and using toilet paper utterly forgettable.

The Results

A record-breaking amount of toilet paper was shipped, a substantial pipeline of online subscribers built and, for Amazon, a memorable step toward changing the way people shop for basic household staples was made.

State of the Marketplace & Brand's Business

A paper about a toilet paper promotion on Amazon may not sound very exciting, but we ask you to suspend judgement for just a bit.

What might look like a minor tactic is about more than shipping a few boxes of toilet paper. In a small but important way, it's about the future of how we shop for the stuff of our daily lives.

TWO COMPANIES, TWO SETS OF CHALLENGES

Toilet paper is a commoditized and fragmented market in which shoppers are increasingly less loyal to a single brand. Instead, they are buying on price within a limited set of brands, which cuts into margins. To make matters worse, Quilted Northern® was losing shelf space with brick-and-mortar retailers. To survive and thrive the brand would need to explore new channels for selling toilet paper and fostering loyalty.

We quickly recognized that Amazon, one of the largest online marketplaces in the world, had unlimited shelf-space but less than 3 percent of US households bought toilet paper online[1]. Toilet paper is still a so-called 'trip driver' in brick and mortar: running low triggers a major outing to the nearest big box store to fill up on household staples. To break this ingrained habit and make it easier for people to buy online Amazon offers the Subscribe & Save feature, which puts orders on autopilot, making regular purchases of basic household staples even easier.

COULD THIS BE A WIN-WIN?

Together, we decided to combine forces and challenge the status quo, but there were a few sizeable challenges:

- We needed to fundamentally change consumers' ingrained behavior in a low-interest category on a modest budget of $700K[2].
- We had to fuel Quilted Northern® sales on Amazon and get people signed up to buy Quilted Northern® via Amazon's Subscribe & Save.

What's more, this project was so important to both partners that Quilted Northern® made it the first-ever packaged goods

Deal of the Day on Amazon: a lot of expectations were riding on this - this was a project that could not fail.

1. Source: IRI Panel Data, 2016

2. Source: Quilted Northern

Shopper Segment

Our task was to find insights that could unify two disparate audiences:

1. **Premium toilet paper buyers** who buy in bulk at brick-and-mortar wholesalers (e.g. Sam's Club, Costco).
2. **Amazon customers** who are passionate about shopping on Amazon and loyal to the retailer, but have not bought toilet paper online in the last few years—or ever.

Qualitative research revealed that both groups lead busy lives and like to pack their schedules with as many activities as possible: volunteering, extracurricular activities for their kids, careers, travel and so forth. Which meant that for both audiences, toilet paper was truly the last thing on their mind.

Objectives & KPI's

We needed to reach our two audiences and change entrenched behaviors by encouraging them to buy Quilted Northern® toilet paper on Amazon and, ideally, subscribe to Quilted Northern® on Subscribe & Save. We'd measure success as follows:

GET ON OUR AUDIENCES' RADAR: Drive awareness of and buzz for the co-marketed partnership. Based on the results from prior promotions, we were hoping for 10 million earned impressions across social and PR channels

DRIVE SALES SHORT-TERM: For Quilted Northern, the goal for this partnership was outlandish, borderline impossible: "sell a month's worth of Quilted Northern® sales on Amazon—in a single day."

NURTURE ENDURING GROWTH: We know that a subscribed customer, while enticed with a small discount, is an extremely loyal one. Growing the number of subscriptions for Quilted Northern® on Amazon was critical. We wanted at least 30 percent of sales volume to come from customers signing up for Subscribe & Save.

Shopper Insight

Insight: Consumers want to completely forget about toilet paper - especially the process of buying it.

Quilted Northern® has devoted the last hundred years innovating to make the best toilet paper. Its ultimate purpose: to make the whole bathroom experience utterly forgettable. Because, let's face it, the only good bathroom experience is a forgettable one. In other words, Quilted Northern® is Designed to be Forgotten®. How could we take this brand insight and turn it into a shopper insight?

Ethnographic research[3] revealed the process of buying toilet paper in-store to be riddled with pain points:

1. Shoppers have to take time out of their packed day to go to the store.
2. There's the risk of running into someone you'd rather not see while clutching evidence of your bathroom needs.
3. Toilet paper is bulky and is annoying to cart around and bring home.

In other words, it's not high on the list of life's exciting experiences.

This is when the lightbulb went off: Amazon, and especially Amazon Subscribe & Save, could play a critical role in delivering the Quilted Northern® brand promise even more powerfully: having toilet paper delivered to their doorsteps every month meant consumers literally never had to think of toilet paper ever again.

The combination of Quilted Northern® and Amazon delivered not just a completely forgettable bathroom experience, but also a completely forgettable shopping experience.

3. Source: Ipsos, Quilted Northern Ethnographic Qualitative Research, March 2016

The Big Idea

Together, Quilted Northern® and Amazon Subscribe & Save make toilet paper, and the process of buying it, utterly forgettable.

Bringing the Idea to Life

THE IDEA: IF YOU BUY QUILTED NORTHERN® ON AMAZON ON THIS ONE DAY, YOU'LL NEVER HAVE TO THINK ABOUT TOILET PAPER EVER AGAIN.

To dramatize our shopper insight and reinforce the Quilted Northern® and Amazon promise, we picked the most forgettable day of the year—National Toilet Paper Day, Aug 26th—for a massive one-day promotion.

Like the product and the Amazon Subscribe & Save feature, the holiday itself is designed to be forgotten: there are no gifts, no parades and you don't even get the day off work. It's completely forgettable, and yet we're asking consumers to celebrate it. The least we could do is make an unforgettable promise:

On America's most forgettable day, we offered our audiences an incentive of up to 45 percent off Quilted Northern® on Amazon Subscribe & Save. Once subscribed, they'd receive Quilted Northern® on a recurring basis and would never have to think about buying and using toilet paper ever again. This was the essence of our one-day-only "Forgettable for All" campaign.

TAKING "FORGETTABLE" FURTHER

We brought the campaign to life through an integrated approach that reached and engaged our target across multiple touch points, online and offline:

- Our "Forgettable for All" co-marketing video introduced our idea and used a self-deprecating tone to acknowledge the ridiculous nature of this holiday. Targeted to reach our dual audiences, the video was promoted via the Quilted Northern® Facebook page, on YouTube and across Amazon.

Reminder: Entrants will copy their answers into the entry form in the online entry area for judging purposes – this document will not be uploaded for judging. Use this form to draft your responses and collaborate with team members.

- If we wanted to change an ingrained habit, we needed to attach it to an already established behavior—shopping for toilet paper at brick-and-mortar stores. So we built pop-up stores in New York City and Seattle with a major twist: they were miniature-sized, perfect for mobile engagement and purchases.
- To reach consumers who were not in New York or Seattle on National Toilet Paper Day, we created a 360-degree online tour of the pop-ups, where our target audiences could experience the stores in real-time on Facebook and find out more on our pop-up store microsite.
- We also leveraged the Amazon Advertising Platform to create a targeted display media campaign aimed at Amazon shoppers. This included a homepage takeover on mobile to appeal to the more than 40 percent of shoppers who only visit Amazon via mobile devices[4].
- Paid search targeted shoppers searching for toilet paper deals on Google, Bing and Amazon and drove them to the Amazon custom landing page where they could engage with the video and purchase toilet paper.
- Lastly, to reach Quilted Northern® customers, we created custom cover photos announcing the offer on all of the brand's social pages and refreshed the Quilted Northern® website to announce National Toilet Paper Day and showcase our video.

4. Source: Comscore, August 2016

Communication Touch Points - All

Branded Content

- During

Digital/Interactive

- During
- Developed Retailer Site Content
- Digital Videos
- Display Ads

Ecommerce

- During

Events

- During

Guerilla

- During
- Ambient Media
- Street Teams

Mobile/Tablet

- During
- Display Ad

PR

- During
- Post

Search Engine Marketing (SEM/SEO)

- During

Social Media

- During

Trade Communications/Promo

- During
- Post

Paid Media Expenditures

Current Year: September 2015 – August 2016

- $500-999 thousand

Year Prior: September 2014 – August 2015

- Not Applicable

Budget

- About the same as other competitors.
- More than the prior year's budget.

We increased the overall budget in 2016 to reflect our objective of increasing growth at Amazon, but that increase only brought us in line with our primary competitors. In 2015, we were spending less than our primary competitors.

Owned Media & Sponsorship

Owned Media: Social media platforms (Facebook, Twitter) and Branded Mini Pop-up Stores

Reminder: Entrants will copy their answers into the entry form in the online entry area for judging purposes – this document will not be uploaded for judging. Use this form to draft your responses and collaborate with team members.

Results

GET ON OUR AUDIENCES' RADAR: Drive awareness and buzz of the co-marketed partnership; goal: 10 million earned impressions, across social and PR channels.

Results:

- Our campaign garnered a total of 22 million earned impressions[5], across social and PR: 2 times higher than our projections.
    - 17.5 million impressions came from social media alone[6], and another two million impressions were generated from Quilted Northern®'s PR efforts[7].
- Our co-marketing video was viewed by 1.6 million people[8], pretty amazing for an online promotion for toilet paper, of all things.
- On National Toilet Paper Day, traffic for Quilted Northern® on Amazon was over 70 percent higher compared to the monthly averages[9], and it grew by over 200 percent vs. a year ago[10].
- On a single day, more than 32,000 people[11] interacted with our pop-up stores in New York and Seattle.

DRIVE SHORT TERM GROWTH: Sell a month's worth of Quilted Northern® sales on Amazon—in a single day.

Results:

- We sold two months of volume in a single day, representing a 6000 percent sales lift! This translates to half a million rolls of toilet paper, enough to span the width of the US, coast to coast, over 4 times[12].
- 46 percent of buyers had not purchased toilet paper on Amazon before, and 58 percent of buyers were new Quilted Northern® buyers[13]—we truly had changed entrenched behaviors!
- Moreover, Quilted Northern® Ultra Soft & Strong® 24 Supreme Roll's Best Seller rank in Health & Personal Care on Amazon shot from #96 to #1 within a few hours of the campaign's launch[14].

NURTURE ENDURING GROWTH: Drive subscriptions, with at least 30 percent of sales volume coming from customers signing up for Amazon Subscribe & Save

Results:

- Our subscribers increased 40-times versus the daily average and contributed 33 percent of total sales volume[15], translating to an incremental 20,000 units over time[16]—an enduring, profitable revenue stream beyond the day's sales.

Net, we sold a truckload of toilet paper, resulting in lots of high-fives at the Quilted Northern® and Amazon offices. But more importantly, we created a pipeline of loyal and valuable customers in a single day by bringing to life our brand promise like never before.

5. Source: Catalyst Media, August 26, 2016

6. Source: NetBase Social Listening, August 26, 2016

7. Source: Catalyst Media, August 26, 2016

8. Source: Facebook Insights as reported by Zenith, August 26, 2016

9. Source: Amazon Analytics, August 2016

10. Source: This includes custom paid traffic; Amazon analytics, August 2016

11. Source: Unit9 foot traffic reporting, August 26, 2016

12. Source: Amazon Analytics, August 2016

13. Source: Amazon Analytics, August 2016

15. Source: Amazon Analytics, August 2016

16. Source: Amazon Analytics, August 2016

Other Contributing Factors

Our two premium toilet-paper competitors each dropped a high-value coupon at the same time[17], and our promotion ran on a Friday, traditionally the day with the lowest volume of toilet paper sold on Amazon[18]. It stands to reason that without these adverse factors, sales would have been even higher.

17. Source: Amazon Analytics, August 2016

18. Source: Amazon Analytics, Jan.-June 2016

Reminder: Entrants will copy their answers into the entry form in the online entry area for judging purposes – this document will not be uploaded for judging. Use this form to draft your responses and collaborate with team members.

Application Workshop

Throughout this book, you will have formal application workshops and exercises with supportive tools to help you apply the information from each chapter to your case or assignment. You will also have access to lists of key decisions to be made or capabilities that you need to have in place at each step of the shopper marketing planning process.

For this chapter, the workshop will focus on building on the Chapter 2 workshop and the same brand or product that you have chosen, this time focusing on digital technology.

As you recall with the Chapter 2 workshop, you have identified the current touch points and new touch points requirements, along the identified customer journey.

Concentrate on digital technology and based on the content in this chapter, identify the following:

- The touchpoints where the selected brand or product leveraged appropriately any of the trends and concepts presented for the digitalization of shopper marketing, and, for each identified touch point, what trends or concepts did they leverage and how they did it.
- The touchpoints for which a stronger integration of digital should be considered; identify the concerned touch points as well the trends or concepts that the adjustments should be based on. What are your recommended adjustments and how you would suggest integrating them into the customer journey?

Conclusion

Data analytics and digital technology are vital components to the success of a shopper marketing campaign. A shopper marketer must have a keen sense of the customer and a firm handle on digital technologies available to reach that customer. Since selling is ongoing and digital technology is continuously evolving, success is predicated on the ability to leverage technology, integrate messages, and rely on data, both current and that which is forecasted.

Chapter 4: Shopper Marketing as an Integral Part of Marketing and Marketing Communications Planning

Learning Objectives

After completing this chapter, you will be able to do the following:

- Understand the overall shopper marketing planning process and the meaning of each step in that process
- Describe how it is linked to marketing and communications planning
- Identify the specific links between shopper marketing planning, marketing planning, and integrated marketing communications planning
- Define the actual planning steps to use to help ensure successful synchronization of the shopper marketing plan with the other components of the marketing and communication plans
- Understand how brands and businesses are properly planning for shopper marketing campaigns
- Start analyzing the effectiveness of the shopper marketing planning process employed by a given brand and business

Introduction

What Is the Chapter About?

This chapter introduces the planning process applied to develop effective shopper marketing campaigns. In addition to learning what the step-by-step discipline is and why it is required, this chapter also explains how shopper marketing planning is dependent on properly defined marketing and communication plans. These concepts are vital contributors to the marketing success of a product or service.

Why Is This Important?

Without a proper understanding of the shopper marketing process and its links to the marketing plan and integrated marketing communication plan processes, a marketer will likely generate tactical plans as opposed to ones based on strategy.

To be able to deliver the right offer to the right shopper target at the right touchpoints and the right time requires a highly disciplined planning approach that is based on key inputs that the marketing plan and integrated marketing communication plan provide. For example, in its simplest terms, a marketer needs to know the marketing target of a product, as this is from this target, that he or she will "extract" the shopper target. Similarly, a marketer needs to know the overall communication objectives associated with the brand to ensure that the shopper marketing campaign being developed will be delivering the correct messaging, messaging that is consistent with the communication objectives of the brand.

Key Terms

- **Planning:** The act or process of making or carrying out plans; specifically the establishment of objectives, strategies, and tactics for a business, marketing, marketing communications, or shopper marketing plan
- **SMART objectives:** The acronym SMART has several slightly different variations, but they all can be used to provide a more comprehensive definition of goal setting. The one used in this book is that a SMART objective needs to be **s**pecific, **m**easurable, **a**chievable, **r**elevant, and with a **t**imetable to be effective
- **Advertising response models:** Advertising response models are used to predict the individual customer behavior or response of a targeted consumer in response to various advertising efforts. They are used to help plan marketing communication campaigns
- **Hierarchy of Effects model:** The hierarchy of effects model is one of the response models used by marketing communications professionals. It tells advertisers to plan for various communications activities in a campaign in such a way that the customer goes through six pre-defined stages, namely awareness, knowledge, liking, preference, conviction, and purchase
- **Marketing value proposition:** A marketing value proposition is the unique combination of benefits and price that a brand or product offers to its target, as compared to its competitors. Benefits could be quantitative in nature (volume of product, number of features, etc.) or qualitative (e.g., brand image)
- **Marketing mix:** "The marketing mix refers to the set of actions, or tactics, that a company uses to promote its brand or product in the market. The 4Ps make up a typical marketing mix: price, product, promotion, and place." (Accessed at https://economictimes.indiatimes.com/definition/marketing-mix)

- **Promotional mix:** "A specific combination of promotional" (marketing communication) "methods used for one product or a family of products. Elements of a promotion mix may include advertising, direct marketing, personal selling," public relations, sales promotion/shopper marketing, and visual merchandising. (Accessed at http://www.businessdictionary.com/definition/promotion-mix.html)

- **Consumer promotion techniques**: Consumer sales promotion techniques are "used to entice customers to purchase a product" or for rewarding customers for making purchase(s). The promotions include a start and end date "and are used to achieve a specific purpose, such as increasing market share or unveiling a new product. A number of promotional techniques are commonly used by product manufacturers and" retailers. (Accessed at http://smallbusiness.chron.com/consumer-sales-promotion-techniques-1035.html)

- **Trade promotion techniques:** Trade sales promotion techniques are promotional incentives directed at retailers, wholesalers, or other business buyers to ultimately stimulate immediate sales

- **Product category:** A "product category" is "category of products to which a brand belongs. For example, if your brand is a shampoo brand, your product category is shampoo; if you sell a high-end car, your product category will be premium automobiles

An Expert's Perspective

In order to effectively communicate with the shopper in a retail environment, the marketer must understand the shopper mindset at the time and place of communication.

- Frank Oggeri, Group Creative Director at TracyLocke

Key Concepts

Overall Shopper Marketing Planning Process

As for any business or marketing-based project, proper planning is essential given the proliferation of new products and increase in competitive activity.

Effective planning requires a disciplined step-by-step approach in which

- key decisions are made at each step, and
- each subsequent decision is dependent upon the decision made for the previous step.

At the core, after the traditional analysis of the environments of a product or a brand (whatever is the "internal environment," such as the launch of a new product by your organization, or the "external environment," such as the emergence of a new competitor), effective planning requires the following decisions to be made, in the following order:

- What are the objectives?
- From the objectives, what are the strategies to use to achieve the objectives?
- What tactics will implement the defined strategies most effectively?

When applied to marketing planning, objectives refer to marketing objectives. Strategies refer to how the goals will be met as defined by the target market, the value proposition, and the positioning of the brand. The tactics refer to the marketing mix, that is, how the 4Ps (product, price, placement, and promotion) are manipulated to achieve the marketing objectives.

As another example, when applied to marketing communication planning, objectives refer to communication objectives (what specific response the brand is trying to obtain from the selected audience), and strategies refer to who is the audience to reach, the major selling idea, and the best media selection. Tactics refer to the promotional mix that will most effectively achieve the communication objectives, namely advertising, public relations, direct marketing, personal selling, sales promotion, and visual merchandising.

When applied to shopper marketing planning, objectives refer to shopper marketing objectives. Strategies refer, for example, to the target shopper and the shopper marketing campaign's big idea. Tactics refer to the actual promotion techniques that will be the most effective at implementing the strategies and achieving the objectives.

Here is an illustration of an effective shopper marketing campaign plan that will be covered in more detail in Chapter8.

As mentioned earlier and as illustrated in the flowchart, the marketing objectives, strategies, and tactics followed by the integrated marketing communication (IMC) objectives, strategies, and tactics must be defined prior to initiation and formation of the shopper marketing plan.

Importantly, there are situations in which, based on the marketing and/or integrated communication objectives, shopper marketing is warranted and in other cases is not. What's critical is that the shopper marketer is focused on the brand's objectives and uses them to guide whether funding should be applied to shopper marketing campaigns.

Key Marketing Plan Inputs for Shopper Marketing

Marketing as a discipline or function is, in fact, all about focusing on the "best" consumer, providing the "most attractive" value to this consumer in order to generate transactions and expanding on those transactions to build a lasting and profitable relationship.

So, when one defines marketing this way, it is easy to say that the value that a marketer proposes for his or her product is how to go about creating this relationship, starting with the first transaction or exchange.

Marketing Objectives

The end game of marketing is, in fact, to build profitable and lasting relationships with consumers.

Using that logic, there are four types of relationship-building that a marketer can consider, which are the core foundations of marketing objectives:

- **Acquisition:** When a marketer aims at new prospective customers to create new relationships

- **Loyalty:** When a marketer aims at current customers to grow the existing relationships
- **Retention:** When a marketer aims at current customers who are showing signs of "fatigue" by purchasing less or less often than they used to and the marketer tries to "retain" the relationships
- **Winback:** When a marketer aims at past customers (who broke the relationship by not purchasing the product for a significant amount of time) to recreate the relationships

Of course, marketing objectives are not strictly formulated in those terms, as they would be too generic, but these concepts are the core foundations of any marketing objective.

The objectives should incorporate the SMART principle as defined in the Key Terms section of this chapter, namely the objectives should be specific, measurable, achievable, relevant, and with a timetable.

For example, a SMART acquisition objective could be as follows: "Generate ten thousand new customers for your product A, from a thirty-five to forty-five-year-old women professionals target in New York City by December 2020."

As another example, a SMART loyalty objective might be to "increase by 20 percent the number of purchases per month of your cosmetic product from your loyal customers in the US market by August 2019."

The reason having SMART objectives is so important is so that all members of the marketing teams are clearly aligned and can assess results accurately.

Whatever marketing objectives you are given, you will need to develop a shopper marketing campaign that ultimately will help achieve those marketing objectives. Therefore, you need to know the marketing objectives to start with.

Marketing targets

As you receive the marketing objectives, you also need to obtain the marketing target as you will have to find your shopper marketing target(s) within that marketing target.

Without elaborating too much on how marketing targets should be formulated, it is obvious that the more specific and detailed the marketing target, the easier it is for the shopper marketing manager to find shopper marketing targets within it.

There is a caveat, though: If the marketing target is too specific and narrow, you might not find ways to break it into significant shopper groups as you might not have access to any information that will be specific enough and/or you might not have enough consumers to start with.

At the core, you have three generic marketing targets:

- Prospects (attractive consumers with which your brand has no relationship yet)

- Current customers
- Past customers

Once again, whatever marketing targets you are given, you will need to develop a shopper marketing campaign that ultimately will aim at this target or, more precisely, specific shopper types within this target. So, you also need to know the marketing targets to start with.

Marketing Value Proposition

Another key marketing component is the marketing value proposition that supports your product or service.

A marketing value proposition is the value that you provide (the benefits that your consumers receive with your product) in exchange for the money they pay for it.

In the end, purchase decisions are made in relative terms where the consumer makes a purchase decision by comparing the benefits for the price (value) of one product to the benefits for the price (value) for the competitive products.

Benefits can be the actual features and physical properties of the product but also can include intrinsic value, such as the quality brand image and customer service support. This can extend to promotional offers and psychological benefits such as social status associated with owning that product.

Part of the shopping process is to compare the value propositions of competitive products and to select the one that best matches preferences and purchase criteria.

That, in essence, is the link between the value proposition and the shopper marketing campaign, namely to enhance the value proposition in a way that most strongly influences the target shopper to purchase a brand. The idea for the shopper marketer is to alter the value proposition by providing more benefits and/or reducing the price (through the shopper marketing offers) to make this value proposition more attractive to the targeted shopper at the time of the promotion.

For example, when a gift is given with the purchase of a product, the benefits' side of the value equation is enhanced, making the overall value more attractive. When a price discount is offered with the purchase of a product, the price side of the value equation diminishes, making the overall value once again more attractive.

For example, if you were to ask the value proposition of Southwest, the discount airline, to its founder Herb Kelleher, the answer will be simply "less" benefits for a lot "less" price than its regular airline competitors.

You can also transform a core value proposition into a slogan that is reflecting its unique "benefits for price" relationship and its comparative terms.

Good examples of value proposition statements are the following:

- Uber—"The Smartest Way to Get Around"
- Digit—"Save Money without Thinking about It"
- MailChimp—"Send Better Emails"

Once again, whatever marketing value proposition you are given, you will need to develop a shopper marketing offer that will be built on the value proposition so you better know it to start with.

Key Marketing Communication Plan Inputs for Shopper Marketing

Just like marketing planning, IMC planning and shopper marketing planning are highly connected as the latter also depends on the former to start its planning process as well. In fact, shopper marketing is one of the marketing communications methods or disciplines that can be used as part of an integrated marketing communications (IMC) campaign.

As a reminder, aside from shopper marketing (so far, more traditionally called sales promotion), other well-known marketing communication methods are used as part of IMC to make the targeted consumer move along his or her journey:

- **Advertising:** TV commercials, radio ads, search engine marketing ads, social media ads, etc.
- **Public relations:** Press releases, events, social media posts, etc.
- **Direct marketing:** Direct mail, telemarketing, email, etc.
- **Personal selling:** Store sales staff, online pop-up windows sales staff on ecommerce sites, etc.
- **Visual merchandising:** Displays, assortments, posters, etc.

Each of those methods has a particular purpose, and the methods with a purpose that is aligned with what the campaign tries to achieve will be selected for that campaign.

Let's do a quick review of the key purpose of each marketing communication method:

- Advertising's main purpose is to *generate awareness big and fast*
- Public relations' main purpose is to *generate goodwill*
- Direct marketing's main purpose is to *generate an immediate response*
- Personal selling and visual merchandising's main purposes are to *generate purchase conversion in the store*
- Sales promotion or shopper marketing's main purpose is to *generate a temporary boost of sales*

Communication objectives

What a brand or product IMC campaign tries to achieve is ultimately defined by the communication objectives that are set for the campaign.

Communication objectives are formulated through the responses that are expected from the targeted consumer at each step of a brand or product campaign. To formulate these responses, marketers use models that set the types of responses that are expected—in sequence—from the targeted consumer for a campaign to work properly.

One of the most famous and widely used models is the Hierarchy of Effects model, which was created in 1961 by Robert J. Lavidge and Gary A. Steiner (Lavidge and Steiner 1961). This marketing communication model suggests there are six steps from viewing a product advertisement to product purchase. The job of the advertiser is to encourage the customer to go through the six steps with various campaign communications activities and purchase the product in the end.

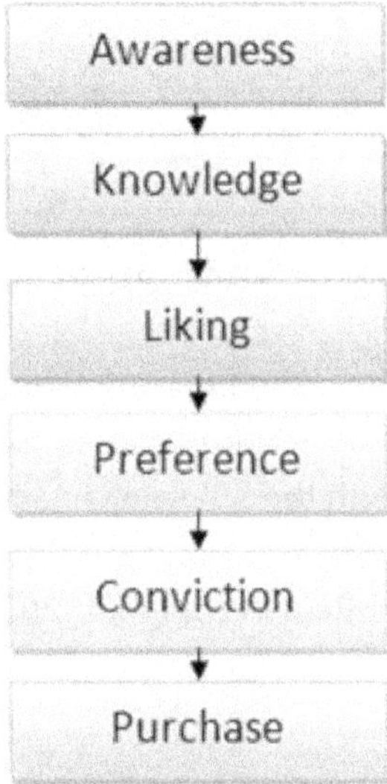

The logic is that each step needs to be "achieved" before the next one can be addressed in any particular campaign. Each of these steps, in fact, describes the type of response that consumers need to "give back" to the brand for the communication activities to be considered effective. It can happen that one communication activity in a campaign might be aimed at achieving several steps at once. For example, a TV commercial might help to achieve awareness about the brand, knowledge about the product benefits, and liking for the product at the same time. Or, it could be decided that a TV commercial will just take care the awareness step, and public relations will take care of the knowledge and liking steps.

In all cases, the achievement of the expected responses from the targeted audience needs to be verified through surveys and other means.

Another way to look at this model is to decide that each step corresponds to a core communication objective for a campaign.

Of course, these response steps as currently named are not specific enough to provide you with enough information to build an IMC campaign. That is why, as for the marketing objectives, they have to be "smartized" with specific, measurable, achievable, relevant, and timed (SMART) characteristics that will be driven by the unique product, situation, consumers, marketing objectives, marketing targets, etc. for your brand.

For example, a "smartized" *awareness* communication objective for a new brand could be as follows: "Achieve 70 percent spontaneous awareness of the brand (mentioned in the top three brands for your product category) with thirty-five- to forty-year-old women professionals living in five-plus million people cities in the US market by June 2019."

A "smartized" *conviction* communication objective for that same new brand could be as follows: "Have 50 percent of our targeted exposed audience checking our customers' reviews and product ratings for the selected product on our website between July and August 2019."

A "smartized" *purchase* communication objective, for once again the same new brand, could be as follows: "Have 25 percent of our targeted exposed audience (who checked our customers' reviews and product ratings for the selected product on our website) purchase the product between July and August 2019."

What is important is that the objectives are clear and specific.

At that stage, it is obvious that the marketing communication methods that will be selected for a brand or product IMC campaign are the ones for which the purposes fully align with the set communication objectives for that campaign—as illustrated with the following image.

Marketing Communications Mix

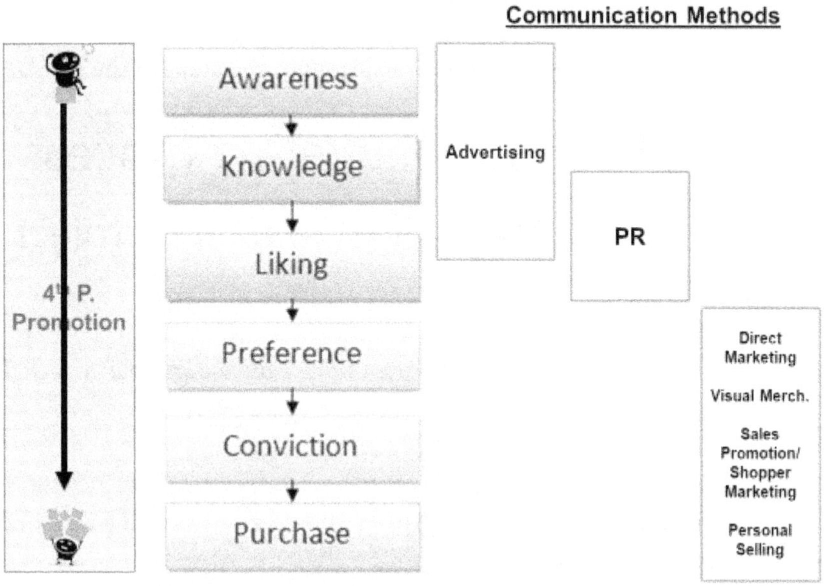

Communication Methods

4th P.
Promotion

Awareness
Knowledge
Liking
Preference
Conviction
Purchase

Advertising

PR

Direct Marketing
Visual Merch.
Sales Promotion/ Shopper Marketing
Personal Selling

In other words, if the IMC campaign for your brand is all about awareness, then advertising with "generating awareness big and fast" will make perfect sense. If the focus is awareness, knowledge, and liking, then advertising and public relations will make sense.

Shopper marketing becomes an interesting marketing communication method to add to the mix when the campaign has clear preference, conviction, and of course purchase communication objectives, as those communication objectives focus on the shopper and the formal shopping stages.

Therefore, it is very important for the shopper marketing manager to know the communication objectives of an IMC campaign as this information will help detect if shopper marketing is needed and, if so, what specific communication objectives he or she can align with for the formulation of the shopper marketing objectives.

Remember that properly-formulated communication objectives are "smartized," so they should provide very clear directions about what needs to be achieved from a communication standpoint.

It is important to note that your IMC manager might be using different response models to build his or her communication objectives, and this is just fine. What is important is that the objectives have been well formulated. Using a response model help in that regard, but your IMC manager might not do so. No matter what, you are now equipped to detect when a communication objective is indeed a well-formulated communication objective, and this will help you manage your working relations with your IMC colleagues more effectively.

By combining your understanding of the marketing and the brand IMC campaign behind a product, the shopper marketing manager will be in the best position to develop the most effective and pertinent shopper marketing campaign.

Without this alignment, shopper marketing will work on its own with all the misalignment issues that will come with it: misaligned messages, budget waste, wasted resources, etc.

Based on this understanding, we can now introduce the steps of the shopper marketing process.

Steps of the Shopper Marketing process

Step 1: The Shopper Marketing Campaign Project Brief

The brand manager distributes a brief to the shopper marketing manager.

This brief includes detailed information on the product for the campaign, including, for example, the following:

- The core rationale behind the need for a campaign, the associated marketing objectives, marketing targets, and communications objectives (so that the shopper marketing campaign is aligned with them)
- The marketing value proposition of the product or service
- Details on the product, such as how and when it is used; seasonality, if any; price point; competitive information; target customer (with as much detail as possible)
- The shopper marketing campaign strategy statement (a brief statement on how the campaign should be achieving the objective)
- The brand experience and values that the shopper marketing campaign must respect or, even better, support
- The budget and desired timing for the shopper marketing campaign
- The retailer, etc.

Step 2: Defining the Shopper Marketing Objectives

Using the brief, the shopper marketer sets the objectives of the campaign. As for marketing objectives, shopper marketing should incorporate the SMART principle.

When setting the shopper marketing objectives, they should be linked to the shopper and therefore defined in shopping terms. This is because shopper marketing is designed to ultimately drive sales, so the objectives should be stated as such to generate more sales at the time the promotion is executed.

A few examples of common shopper marketing objectives used by businesses include the following:

- Increase purchase frequency

- Generate product trial
- Increase transaction size
- Increase usage occasions
- Increase the number of distribution outlets
- Increase the shelf space
- Increase the in-store presence
- Expand the selling season

This list is not exhaustive; importantly, it relates to increasing sales for a particular product or service and implies a change in or a shift of shopping behavior at the time of the promotion.

As mentioned before, your shopper marketing objectives have to be aligned with your marketing objectives. Let's go through a few examples.

If your generic marketing objective is acquisition against prospects, there are obvious shopper marketing objectives that cannot be selected, such as "increasing transaction size or purchase frequency" as this can only be done with current customers.

If you launch a new upgraded product for your current customers (like iPhone does with its successive versions), this will relate to a loyalty marketing objective. In that case, a "generating trial" for your new product or "increasing in-store presence" of your new product at the time of the launch might work as shopper marketing objectives.

If you have an existing product and you want to expand its sales to another season, this might be loyalty for current customers. In that case, "expanding selling season" and "increasing in-store presence" of this product during the new season might work as shopper marketing objectives.

If your marketing objective is retention against current customers who are shopping less with you and assuming that they purchase less from you because they purchase more and more in your product category at a retailer where your brand was not yet sold but will be soon, "increasing the shelf space" or "increasing the in-store presence" at the new retailer when the product is launched might be good shopper marketing objective candidates for the time of the promotion.

Similarly, your shopper marketing objectives should be aligned with the communication objectives that are applicable to shopper marketing.

Going back to one of the communication objective examples mentioned earlier ("Have 50 percent of our targeted exposed audience checking our customers' reviews and product ratings for the selected product on our website between July and August 2019"), a great shopper marketing objective might be to "generate trial" for the new product and as part of that trial generation, to give incentives to the targeted shopper for visiting the site and checking the customers' reviews and product ratings.

As another example, if the communication objective is, this time, "have 25 percent of our targeted exposed audience (who checked our customers' reviews and product ratings for the selected product on our website) purchase the product in our store between July and August 2019," the shopper marketing objective could also be "generating trial" and "increasing in-store presence" for the product for the time of the launch.

You get the point.

Step 3: Understanding the Target Purchase Behavior and Reviewing Past Sales Promotion and/or Shopper Marketing Campaigns

Effective shopper marketing planning requires a thorough analysis of the following:

- The target customer and his or her behavior
- The competition
- The environment surrounding the product or service

For shopper marketing, this research and analysis relate to the purchase and shopping behavior of the target customer that has been provided by the marketing manager in the project brief.

It is imperative and directly impacts the success of the campaign to fully understand the purchase behaviors (and their evolutions) of this target customer for both the product category your product belongs to and your particular product. This provides a fundamental understanding of the context and feasibility to achieve the stated shopper marketing objectives.

In fact, the shopper marketing objectives that you have established imply a certain purchase behavior to occur for those objectives to be achieved. For example, if your shopper marketing objective is to "increase purchase frequency," that means your marketing target, when he or she has reached the shopping stage to buy, must come more often to the store during the promotion.

In this scenario, it would be important to start with a shopper target whose current purchase behavior will be the easiest to increase the purchase frequency with. Objectively, consumers who purchase your product regularly could be a very good shopper marketing target as they might be more easily convinced to increase their purchase frequency during the time of the promotion.

Analysis of shopping behavior enables the shopper marketer to detect what type of shopper within the marketing target is best to focus on for the campaign.

Another important aspect of this step in the planning process is to analyze past sales promotion or shopper marketing campaigns to learn from their results. To the extent possible, this analysis should include results for your brand as well as for its competitors. By doing this, the shopper marketer can be certain of what worked and what did not. This, in turn, will help direct what elements should be kept for the new campaign and what should be avoided. For example, if certain retailers proved to be great partners, this is good to know so that you can focus on involving them again. If particular consumer promotion techniques, such as a coupon, had poor results, it would be beneficial to avoid a promotion offering money off.

This analysis can also identify how popular trends have impacted promotional activity, thereby pointing you, as the shopper marketer, in a direction that could prove successful. It can also make you aware of new promotional techniques and twists that can be incorporated into the new campaign. It is also important to review past promotion results for your brand so that you have a point of comparison for the new campaign. Setting SMART goals involves being able to measure your success and without a point of reference (such as a previous promotion); any measurement is in a vacuum and less actionable.

Step 4: Selecting Your Shopper Marketing Target(s)

Once you have completed step 3, you are in a position to select, from the shopper types within your marketing target, which are the best to focus on to achieve your shopper marketing objectives.

According to Don Shultz, a recognized sales promotion author and expert, the five types of shopper marketing targets, defined by their shopping behaviors, are as follows (Shultz 1998):

- **Loyal users:** Shoppers in your product category, who purchase your product or service more or less regularly
- **Competitive loyals:** Shoppers in your product category, who purchase a competitive product or service more or less regularly
- **Switchers:** Shoppers in your product category, who switch between various brands or products or services within your category. They might be switching to your product from time to time or they might be switching between competitive brands all the time.
- **Price buyers:** Shoppers in your product category, who make purchase decisions exclusively based on the price. The logic is simple: Whatever product has the lowest price at the time of purchase will be purchased.
- **Non-users:** Individuals who do not purchase any products in your product category. It could be because they have no need for it or because these products in the category are too expensive, or for any other reason.

Several key considerations to keep in mind as you select your Shopper Marketing target

Your Shopper Marketing targets selection is "directed" by the marketing target that you have been given.

If your marketing target is prospects, you can not select loyal users as your shopper marketing target, but you could select all other shopper marketing targets options as long as they are not your customers. The choice will depend on your competitive situation, your marketing objective, the assumes changed of purchase behavior that is expected, the size of the shopper segments, etc.

If your marketing target is current customers, you could pick loyal users, of course, but also switchers (if switchers switch to your brand from time to time) or even price buyers (if this is the type of consumer for which you aim), as shopper marketing targets.

If your marketing target is past customers, again you cannot select loyal users as your shopper marketing target, but you could select all other shopper marketing target options, as long as they are not your customers anymore. In fact, your past customers might have become competitive loyals, non-users (as your past customers might have decided to stop shopping in your product category), switchers (but not to your brand) or even price buyers (if this is not the type of consumer which you normally aim).

Shopper Marketing Typologies

While we will be using the shopper typology from Don Schultz, this is not the only one available.

Many shopper marketing agencies or related businesses create their own typology or sometimes, the uniqueness of the challenge might force a brand or product to create their own typology.

For example, Rakuten, the major Japanese eCommerce platform, offers this shopper typology to their business clients trying to promote their products on Rakuten:

- Discount dependent
- Luxury loyalists
- Impulse led
- Couch converters

As another example, Euromonitor, the market research organization, classifies shoppers as follows:

- Conspicuous consumers
- Spontaneous socializers
- Savvy quality seekers
- Cautious loyalists
- No-frills savers

No matter what the shopper typology your use or create, you need to have one to select the right shopper marketing targets.

Shopper types selection scope

It is possible that you could find multiple shopper types to focus on or that you find only one. It depends on the scope of your marketing target, the type of shoppers that your product category attracts, and the type of shoppers that your particular product or brand attracts.

Shopper types selection logic

In this stage, the key is to select the shopper types that will be the easiest to influence toward the purchase behavior changes that you have established as the objective *and* with enough consumers in the groups to prove fruitful.

Going back to the example described in Step 2 where the objective was to "increase purchase frequency," let's say the consumers who purchase your product regularly might not be numerous enough to help you achieve your purchase frequency increase objective. In that case, you would need to add another shopper type that could be second best for your promotion to change their purchase behavior and increase purchase frequency. Maybe, for example, you could add a switcher shopper marketing target. While not as good as loyal users, the "switcher shopper" might switch to your product from time to time, so they are still quite well predisposed to help you achieve your shopper marketing objective of increased purchase frequency, i.e., they might respond to your promotion and buy more often.

Step 5: Defining the Specific Expected Changes of Purchase Behavior

This step is the formalization of the specific changes in purchase behavior that you want to obtain from your shopper marketing targets during the campaign.

If once again, your shopper marketing objective is to increase the purchase frequency of your shoppers, depending upon the outcomes of your analysis in Step 2, you might have loyal users and switchers within your marketing target. Therefore, it could make sense to select both as your shopper marketing targets.

For loyal users, we now know that they purchase your product or service more or less regularly. They might purchase your product one time per week and you will need to move them to two times per week. In that case, the change of purchase behavior that you expect is for them to shop twice per week for your product (as opposed to once a week).

For switchers, it could be that they switch to your product 10 percent of the time. So, for them, the change that you would like to see is that every time they are in a shopping mode for your product category, they switch to your product more often—maybe 20 percent of the time.

It is important to define the specific changes in purchase behavior to be sure you are aligned with the shopper marketing objectives and also to help select the most effective promotion techniques for your campaign (that will be discussed later in this book). By way of a quick example, some promotion techniques, such as "Buy One Get One Free," are excellent ways to increase transaction size, while coupons with a price discount offer on the next purchase are an excellent way to increase purchase frequency.

Step 6: Engaging the Shopper Marketing Creative Process

Once you have established your shopper marketing objectives, targets, and the expected changes of purchase behavior, the actual campaign creative process is the next step.

The Campaign Big Idea

Definition

The definition of a "big idea" is an interactive process that involves multiple rounds of brainstorming and discussions. The key challenges and/or opportunities for the brand serve as the foundation of the process. Part of this process also includes product category and consumer research to highlight key purchase behavior and marketplace changes.

Based on these insights, a core solution is developed to address the identified challenge or leverage the identified opportunity. From that solution, a shopper marketing campaign big idea is developed and will serve as the creative gravity center of the campaign.

This gravity center will then drive the creative development of the actual campaign communications assets.

Consumer Promotion Techniques Selection

Part of the big idea development is to consider the consumer promotion techniques that would be most impactful to bring the shopper marketing idea to life.

The consumer promotion techniques are aimed at the consumers and are here to stimulate the change of purchase behavior that has been previously outlined in Step 5.

That is the reason why it is important to know which change of purchase behavior you expect to achieve before you select the promotion techniques and tactics.

It is also important to properly align the consumer promotion tactic with the brand experience on which the marketing manager briefed you in Step 1 Some techniques might work well to achieve the change in purchase behavior but at the expense of what the shopper target thinks of the brand. For example, a coupon offer can help increase purchase frequency, but if the selected shopper marketing target is loyal users, a coupon offer may diminish the brand image because while loyal users might respond to a coupon offer, they believe it "cheapens" the brand.

A shopper marketer must be very careful with the selection of the consumer techniques (e.g., coupons, bonus packs, gifts with purchase, sweepstakes) to use as part of the campaign.

Consumer promotion techniques will be covered in more detail later in this book.

Trade Promotion Techniques Selection

Once the consumer promotion techniques have been selected, the trade promotion techniques need to be selected as well.

Trade promotion is used in multiple ways to achieve multiple objectives. They refer to the promotion techniques used by a manufacturer to "influence" a selected retailer to do what is necessary for the consumer promotion to succeed in the store.

Using the same example, if your shopper marketing objective is to increase purchase frequency, that might mean you need to have your product more visible to consumers, which in turn might mean that you need more displays of your product in the store. The trade promotion technique to use, in that case, will be an advertising allowance where you give a set amount of cash or credit to the retailer if they prove that your posters and displays are indeed set up in the store.

The important point is that the retailer has to be motivated to cooperate to help you achieve your goals. That is the reason for trade promotion, to incentivize retailers.

Upon completion of this step, the shopper marketing campaign recommendation is complete.

Step 7: Developing Your Shopper Marketing Campaign Communication Plan

With the campaign developed, including how it will work in terms of offers and the promotion techniques, the next step is to define how you will communicate the shopper marketing idea and offer to your shopper marketing targets.

As you plan the shopper marketing communication activities, thoughts must be given to communication activities both inside and outside the store. Activities outside the store would be designed to make your target aware of the promotion and come to the store. Communications inside the store (from the entrance of the store to the product shelf) would be designed to be sure that once your target is in the store, he or she is reminded about your offer and directed to the product on the shelf to make the purchase once at the shelf.

The selection of the media and channels best suited to communicate the campaign will be driven by the media habits of your shopper marketing target(s). These channels can be online, offline, and/or a combination of both. This will be covered in detail later in this book.

Step 8: Financial Projections

While this is presented in Step 8, the financial analysis of a shopper marketing campaign plan starts sooner but is finalized once all aspects of the campaign have been set.

Just like any other marketing investment, a shopper marketing campaign is subject to financial return expectations. Again, and importantly, the fundamental job of a shopper marketing campaign is ultimately to increase profits. Accordingly, financial projections are an integral step in the planning process. Company management must be made aware of the financial projections of the campaign in order to provide approval to go ahead with it.

The notion of return could be absolute (such as a specific amount of profit to be achieved) or relative (such as when you try to avoid bigger losses that would occur if the campaign were not to be launched).

The most desirable financial outcome is to generate more sales such that the additional sales surpass the total cost of the campaign, thereby resulting in a net profit gain.

The financial analysis of shopper marketing campaigns will be further explained in Chapters 7 & 8.

Step 9: Campaign Launch, Control, and Evaluation

This first part of this step is the actual campaign launch.

In this step, it is critical that everyone in the company and in the product's distribution chain is made aware of the campaign. This would include the details of the campaign, such as when it starts and ends, as well as the details of how it works. This information should be distributed to campaign partners and company employees including customer service departments and sales teams.

The second part of this step is the ongoing control of the campaign implementation and results. Paying close attention via real-time reporting, social media, and retail partners to campaign progress is part of this step and highly important. To the extent possible, any problems and/or complaints should be addressed quickly. This includes making adjustments to the campaign.

Post-campaign evaluation through a thorough analysis of all aspects should be implemented, including the following:

- Shopper marketing results
- Sales and financial results
- Implementation effectiveness
- Potential areas of improvement

This step of the Shopper Marketing process will be also explained in further details in Chapter 8.

Here is an example from Flonase illustrating the power behind proper marketing planning in regards to clearly defining the target market, and marketing communications integration for an effective Shopper Marketing campaign.

Case Study:
Bringing Shopper Marketing To Life

CASE STUDY

2016 GOLD SHOPPER MARKETING EFFIE AWARD WINNER

"FLONASE ALLERGY RELIEF OVER-THE-COUNTER LAUNCH"

Launching prescription-strength FLONASE over-the-counter meant introducing the brand into a category where people traditionally shop on autopilot. In order to grab their attention, we created the biggest launch in GSK history, using an omnichannel approach to educate allergy sufferers about the more complete allergy relief of FLONASE, and drew their attention to the allergy aisle at top retailers nationwide. Within the first six months of the launch, we exceeded our target brand share and in the process, grew the category for all of our retail partners.

COMPETITION:
Shopper Marketing Effies

Ran in:
USA

CATEGORY:
New Product of Service

BRAND/CLIENT:
FLONASE Allergy Relief/
GlaxoSmithKline

LEAD AGENCY:
Epsilon

CONTRIBUTING COMPANIES:
Geometry Global Brand Union

PRODUCT/SERVICE:
OTC Allergy Nasal Spray

CLASSIFICATION:
National

DATES EFFORT RAN:
01/01/2015–Ongoing

CREDITS:
Amardeep Kahlon
Chris Noe
Jason Andree
Cara Kahaly
Janet Barker-Evans
Tim Moore
Phil Bruno
Karen Gebhart
Lori Murphy
Meredith Daca

Version: Edited

Executive Summary

There are over 50 million allergy sufferers in the U.S., and over half of them aren't happy with their current treatment. For those millions looking for relief beyond simple antihistamines, the over-the-counter launch of FLONASE Allergy Relief was a game-changer. We leveraged a fresh brand identity for FLONASE, including a comprehensive range of digital and in-store communications, retailer co-creation initiatives, and a national activation event. As a result, FLONASE achieved its two most ambitious goals - achieving a strong share of the allergy category, as well as an aggressive sales goal.

Category

In February 2015, FLONASE Allergy Relief Nasal Spray became available without a prescription. While the medicine itself has been a trusted source of allergy relief for years, the arrival of the product over-the-counter meant introducing the FLONASE brand into the shopper marketing landscape.

State of the Marketplace & Brand's Business

Allergy is a highly competitive, crowded, and growing category with $2.2 billion in sales annually, with 50MM allergy sufferers in the U.S.* The main players in the category are the antihistamine pills Claritin, Zyrtec and Allegra, as well as the intranasal steroid spray Nasacort (launched in Feb 2014). Claritin lead the antihistamine category with 19% of the total allergy category share, followed by Zyrtec (17%) and Allegra (14%) as of May 4, 2013.** These allergy brands invest heavily in above-the-line and below-the-line brand support per the below chart†

Total Media Spend (000's)	**2012**	**2013**	**2014**
Claritin	$75,704.2	$77,498.7	$73,673.4
Zyrtec	$41,029.0	$45,401.6	$84,219.0
Allegra	$75,608.3	$54,770.0	$62,686.7
Nasacort	$0	$0	$68,474.0

Private label has a very strong presence in the allergy category, with retailers promoting PL equivalents for the top three antihistamine competitors.

To provide allergy relief to millions of allergy sufferers, the decision was made by the makers of FLONASE, the #1 prescribed allergy medicine in the U.S. for over 20 years,†† to make it available over-the-counter without a prescription. Successful conversion of the prescription users to the OTC product was a component of the launch. However, the nasal spray form was new in OTC allergy, with the only other intranasal spray competitor being Nasacort. The majority of consumers were not yet used to the new form of a spray allergy medicine.

**Source: http://acaai.org/news/facts-statistics/allergies, * * Source: IRI Advantage, †Source: Nielson AdViews, ††Source: Vector One™ from Verispan*

Strategic Marketing Challenge

The world is filled with allergy sufferers; 54% of the population in the U.S. is affected by 1 or more allergens or allergy producing substances.* And the number of people afflicted is only growing due to increasing levels of carbon dioxide and higher temperatures in our environment.**

Suffering from allergies has real consequences on peoples' lives. Allergies can leave you irritable, breathless, sleepless, fatigued and confused. They can make you struggle with daily activities such as work or school, and miss out on the things you enjoy doing because your symptoms leave you feeling compromised and sluggish. To treat allergies, most shoppers turn to what they know: antihistamines. But what they don't know is that these pills only block one of the allergic substances - histamine - produced by the body in reaction to allergens. They don't know there is something better out there. Something that provides more complete relief of their symptoms and allows them to feel better, conquer their allergies and get back to the things they love the most.

With the OTC launch of FLONASE, we set out to bring game-changing relief to millions of people who suffer needlessly from allergies. Because FLONASE works differently than antihistamines to help block six of the chemical responses of the body, it provides incomparable relief to dramatically improve quality of life.

Reminder: Entrants will copy their answers into the entry form in the online entry area for judging purposes – this document will not be uploaded for judging. Use this form to draft your responses and collaborate with team members.

FLONASE redefines how allergy medicines work and what allergy relief looks like to millions of people who haven't had access to the prescription product by going over-the-counter and providing more complete relief to symptoms that works right at the source.

By going over-the-counter we will provide easier access to this life-changing allergy medication for those existing and lapsed FLONASE Rx users, as it will no longer require a prescription.
*Source: http://www.nih.gov/news/pr/aug2005/niehs-04.htm, **Source: Beggs PJ. Impacts of climate change on aeroallergens: past and future. Clin Exp Allergy. 2004;34:1507-1513.

Objectives & KPIs

Objectives:

1. Introduce the FLONASE OTC brand and achieve FLONASE brand share of [REDACTED] in year 1
2. The sales goal for year 1 was [REDACTED] in gross sales with a consumption goal of [REDACTED]

Shopper Segment

The target is "Empowered Controller" shopper segment, who is highly engaged in maintaining his/her health and is always looking for something new that will improve his/her quality of life. Aged between 29 and 59, they are moderate to severe allergy sufferers and they treat their allergies frequently and early, actively managing their allergies 80% of the time. They take their health very seriously with active prevention strategies, and are willing to pay more for quality products. The shopper is generally female and buying for herself (92%) but also for other family members (spouse 36%, kids 15%).*

*Source: GSK Shopper Insights Studies (Ipsos) Allergy/2012

Shopper Insight

Leveraging GSK's research into the allergy shopper's purchase journey and his/her behaviors and attitudes while shopping, we identified a key insight that allergy sufferers feel like they are doing everything they can, but their allergies are still getting in their way. They are looking for a total answer to triumph over their allergies so that they can enjoy the things that matter every day. They currently use antihistamine pills and have achieved moderate relief, however don't understand that better relief is achievable. The shopper barrier is that they are simply not aware that OTC FLONASE offers more effective relief than their current allergy product.

Since our target demographic relies heavily on their own research, pre-shop educational tactics will be important. They are usually shopping on auto-pilot, so in-store communication must be disruptive and eyecatching enough to differentiate FLONASE from its competitors, and convey the new news that FLONASE is available for more complete relief.

The Big Idea

Let allergy sufferers across the U.S. know a new level of more complete allergy relief is available over-the-counter with FLONASE, so that they can be greater than their allergies.

Bringing the Idea to Life

We knew we needed to:

- get on the shopping list before shoppers get to the store
- stand out in a crowded category with disruptive and engaging in-store activation and simple, solution-focused messaging and;
- convince shoppers that FLONASE is new and better by communicating our product superiority.

Reminder: Entrants will copy their answers into the entry form in the online entry area for judging purposes – this document will not be uploaded for judging. Use this form to draft your responses and collaborate with team members.

First and foremost, we needed to inform our target demographic pre-shop that FLONASE was available OTC and get on their shopping list. Because 94% of allergy shoppers have made their brand decision BEFORE they get to the store,* we had to have a strong presence online where our Empowered Controller was doing research.

Next, we needed to make FLONASE stand out in-store by leveraging disruptive tactics to break through the clutter of a crowded category. We continued to convince shoppers that FLONASE is new and better through our use of simple visuals, distinct shapes and a bold spectrum of colors. Simple, impactful messaging let consumers know FLONASE was now available OTC, and is superior to the other OTC allergy products on the market.

*Source: Ipsos Shopper Insights Study 2012

In addition to creating a national launch plan for shoppers across the country, we partnered with retailers to ensure our launch was successful, leveraging each retailer's unique equities and shopper insights and creating custom retailer plans for GSK's top 8 customers: Walmart, CVS, Walgreens, Costco, Target, Sam's Club, Rite Aid and Kroger.

Informative pre-shop messaging within banner ads, retailer websites, and FSIs, as well as targeted direct mail and emails, created awareness and educated our target about FLONASE. We generated excitement about the launch with "Coming Soon" messaging for two months prior to launch, accompanied by a pre-order campaign at the top 8 customers. During launch we continued to drive awareness with shoppers before going in store to purchase.

For the Walmart shopper who often doesn't purchase from the OTC category at Walmart, we needed to capture them in trip planning mode by providing relevant allergy content within a dedicated brand experience page on Walmart.com, including articles and illustrated guides. We also reached Walmart shoppers pre-shop via a segment within the Dr. Oz show, one of the Walmart's shoppers' favorite programs for Health & Wellness information. When they got to store, we disrupted them with a custom half pallet, aisle violators and crosscategory signage in other parts of the store, as well as endcap displays featuring video screens loaded with short FLONASE brand videos.

CVS shoppers are highly connected digitally, with 87% of them using smartphones.** To reach them with our life-changing message about FLONASE Allergy Relief, we placed beacons in the top 1,000 CVS stores and through a partnership with Shopkick, we sent push notifications to shoppers entering the store, in addition to running a Shopkick lookbook pre-shop. When they went to their local CVS, shoppers noticed we had 'painted the store' with custom a lama display, dump bin, basket liners, window clings and other tactics.

With Walgreens, one of the nation's largest health & wellness destinations, we hosted a 2-day activation at their flagship New York store and beyond, driving traffic to stores across the U.S. We gave allergy shoppers the chance to celebrate how they are greater than their allergies on the massive Walgreens Times Square digital billboard. In Walgreens across the country, a custom tower display, circular rack signage and a high aisle violator disrupted shoppers and convinced them to buy, once inside the store.

At Costco, where tens of thousands of Rx users refill their script, we had the unique opportunity to partner with the pharmacy department to reach prescription fluticasone users with announcement letters and a rebate upon refill of their fluticasone prescription. We also placed FLONASE brochures in the pharmacy and included messaging on pharmacy bags. Not to mention the custom pallet skirt and trays placed inside the OTC area of the club to disrupt shoppers on their shopping trip.

Kroger is an everyday shopping destination for many, and the #1 floral retailer in the U.S. but only 25% of their food consumers convert to the health and beauty care department. The FLONASE launch provided a perfect cross-promotional opportunity to drive the multitude of floral shoppers into the health and beauty care department, as well as drawing in shoppers from the pet and cleaning aisles.

Additionally, we delivered a multi-channel experience at Target with their Digital Spotlight, Cartwheel Social Savings program and in-store, we delivered our message with disruptive endcap placement and inline displays. The Sam's Club FLONASE launch activation included a brand page and an impressive media presence on samsclub.com with a strong in-club presence of pallets with skirts, at-shelf PDQ trays, optical and pharmacy trays and in-club digital signage. At Rite Aid a custom targeted direct mail got us on the list pre-shop, and in-store tactics like pharmacy counter signs, dedicated endcaps and Wellness Ambassador events disrupted shoppers in-store.

**Source: comScore, Plan Metrix, August 2015, †Source: Dunnhumby

Path to Purchase Communications & Marketing Components

Pre	During	Post
Retail Experience	**Retail Experience**	**Ecommerce**
-Pop	-Pop	
-In-Store Video/Kiosk	-In-Store Video/Kiosk	
-In-Store Merchandising	-In-Store Merchandising	
-Sales Promotion	-Sales Promotion	
Direct	**Direct**	
-Mail	-Mail	
-Email	-Email	
-Retailer Specific	-Retailer Specific	
Print	**Print**	
-Retailer Specific Publication	-Retailer Specific Publication	
Digital/Interactive	**Digital/Interactive**	
-MFR/Retailer Website	-MFR/Retailer Website	
-Developed Retailer Site	-Developed Retailer Site	
Content	**Content**	
-Display Ads	-Display Ads	
-Digital Video	-Digital Video	
Pricing	**Pricing**	
-Trade	-Trade	
-Couponing	-Couponing	
Mobile/Tablet	**Mobile/Tablet**	
-Messaging/Editorial/Content	-Messaging/Editorial/Content	
-Display Ad	-Display Ad	
-Location-based Communications/Real Time Marketing	-Location-based Communications/Real Time Marketing	
-Other	-Other	
Ecommerce	**Events**	
Branded Content	**Radio**	
Search Engine Marketing (SEM/SEO)	-Spots	
Social Media	**Ecommerce**	
	Trade Shows	
	Branded Content	
	Search Engine Marketing (SEM/SEO)	
	Social Media	
	Other	
	-FSI, Product Integration into Dr. OZ Television Segment	

Paid Media Expenditures

September 2014 - August 2015

- $5-10 million

September 2013 - August 2014

- Not Applicable

Budget

- More than other competitors.
- Prior year's budget not applicable.

Owned Media & Sponsorship

None.

Reminder: Entrants will copy their answers into the entry form in the online entry area for judging purposes – this document will not be uploaded for judging. Use this form to draft your responses and collaborate with team members.

Results

Overall, launch results are strong and we have exceeded key KPIs:

1. Introduce the FLONASE OTC brand and achieve FLONASE brand share of [REDACTED] in year 1
    a. Flonase exceeded the primary goal by achieving [REDACTED] share* as of 8/30/15, with six months of the year, including fall allergy season remaining in year 1
    b. Additionally, FLONASE grew the size of the overall category overall by [REDACTED] (1/l/15-8/30/15)*
    c. Request by several customers to "rewrite the Rx to OTC switch playbook"
    d. Retailer feedback:
        - "Love the Growth - World Class Activation," - Walmart
        - "Our Best Rx to OTC Switch Results, Ever" - CVS
        - "FLONASE is 2015 #1 priority in Healthcare" - CVS
        - "Keep doing what you did for launch year in 2016 - it's working!" - Kroger
2. The sales goal for year 1 was [REDACTED] in gross sales with a consumption goal of [REDACTED]
    a. Within the first six months of launch, we achieved [REDACTED] in gross sales*. With four months remaining in the first year of launch, we will exceed our sales goal by year-end.
    b. Consumption at a 142 index versus budget (as of 8/30/15) *
    c. Pre-order sales generated more sales than any other OTC switch in each account*
    d. Best-Selling SKU within the category, including HBC*

*Source: IRI Advantage 8/30/15

Other Contributing Factors

At the same time our shopper elements were in the market, there was also national brand support for the launch, including TV spots, digital program, annual media plan, PR and social media efforts.

Reminder: Entrants will copy their answers into the entry form in the online entry area for judging purposes – this document will not be uploaded for judging. Use this form to draft your responses and collaborate with team members.

Application Workshop

Throughout this book, you will have formal application workshops, and exercises with supportive tools to help you apply the information from each chapter to your particular case or assignment. You will also have access to lists of key decisions to be made or capabilities that you need to have in place at each step of the shopper marketing planning process.

For this chapter, the workshop will focus on analyzing shopper marketing campaign or activities and assess, based on additional research, what could have been the marketing objectives, the marketing targets, and the communication objectives at the origin of the shopper marketing offers.

Based on this initial analysis, you will be asked to try identifying the shopper marketing objectives, shopper marketing targets, and consumer promotion techniques that were used for this promotion and the communication activities to promote this offer.

To make things more simple, we will ask you to pick one of your recent sales promotion or shopper marketing activities or, by default (and if you are a student), to go to a grocery store and find an example of sales promotion or shopper marketing.

This promotion can include any consumer promotion techniques and can refer to any shopper marketing objectives that we have seen so far.

To facilitate the linkage with the application workshops from Chapters 1 and 2, we suggest that you use the same brand or product, but this is your choice and this might not be necessarily possible.

It is important, though, that you pick a brand or product on which you can obtain business and marketing information through searches or databases. If it is your own product, it is easy.

If it is not, then you need to pick a sales promotion example for a brand for which you can easily obtain business and marketing information.

As you have the sales promotion or shopper marketing offer example, to the best of your abilities do the following:

- Identify what product is the subject of the promotion
- Find out about **the business situation** that the product or the business behind that product is currently facing
    - Is the business new? Established?
    - Is the business growing, stagnating, or declining?
- Find out about the marketing behind that product
    - What are the marketing objectives of this product? Are they clear?

  - What are the marketing targets? Are they clear?
  - Do they have a clear value proposition? Which one?
- Find out about **any IMC campaign** going on or that happened recently (no more than two years old) for this product
  - What are the communication methods used for this campaign?
  - What are the communication objectives attached to this campaign?
- Now look back at the sales promotion or shopper marketing offer example
  - What is the actual offer ("Buy One Get One Free" + a sweepstake or just a price discount or a coupon with a refund offer for the next purchase, etc.)?
  - What are the shopper marketing objectives that are behind this offer? Are they obvious?
  - What are the shopper marketing targets that have been selected to achieve the shopper marketing objectives? Are they obvious?
  - What are the communication activities used to promote this shopper marketing campaign?
  - Using your observations, **complete this first shopper marketing example analysis scorecard** (https://drive.google.com/open?id=0B80ePSvryN3acjBKWXA1elJHOW8).
  - How would you rate the performance of this shopper marketing offer example?
- Based on this analysis, **what would you recommend** they do differently?

Conclusion

Shopper marketing depends on well-formulated marketing and integrated marketing communication plans. With key quality inputs from those plans, like marketing objectives, marketing targets, value proposition, and communication objectives (amongst others), a shopper marketer will be able to develop an effective shopper marketing plan and resulting campaign.

On that basis and as for all effective planning, shopper marketing planning follows a precise developmental process that will lead to successful plans. The steps are as follows:

- Step 1 The shopper marketing campaign project brief
- Step 2: Defining the shopper marketing objectives
- Step 3: Understanding the target purchase behavior and reviewing past campaigns
- Step 4: Selecting your shopper marketing target(s)

- Step 5: Defining the specific expected change of purchase behavior for the selected shopper marketing target
- Step 6: Engaging the shopper marketing creative process
- Step 7: Developing your shopper marketing campaign communication plan
- Step 8: Financial projections
- Step 9: Campaign Launch, Control, and Evaluation

It is essential to use this process in a thorough and disciplined way to strategically align with the business, marketing, and marketing communications priorities of the brand and accomplish the SMART objectives set for the campaign.

Chapter 5: Consumer Promotion Tactics

Learning Objectives

After completing this chapter, you will be able to do the following:

- Learn about the specific consumer promotion tactics available and what shopper purchase behavior changes each can achieve for each shopper type/shopper marketing target
- Understand the importance of selecting the optimal consumer promotion tactics driven by the marketing and shopper marketing objectives and targets as well as the shopper marketing campaign concept statement
- Fully comprehend why strategic thinking, when it comes to selecting the appropriate consumer promotion tactics, is essential to the success of a shopper marketing campaign
- Start analyzing the effectiveness of the consumer promotions by a given brand and business as part of a shopper marketing campaign

Introduction

What Is the Chapter About?

This chapter is about the specific consumer promotion tactics that manufacturers and retailers use to engage and motivate consumers on their shopping journey from need recognition to actually making the purchase. The specific tactics are explained in detail, including the types of objectives that each can potentially accomplish.

Importantly, how strategic thinking and planning drives the development of the consumer promotional elements of a given shopper marketing campaign is described.

Why Is This Important?

Having a thorough understanding of the available consumer promotion tactics will enable a shopper marketing practitioner to make the proper decisions in regards to what consumer promotion tactics are the most applicable and appropriate for each given shopper marketing campaign with its unique set of shopper marketing objectives, shopper marketing targets, and purchase behavior change expectations.

Knowing which one(s) to use and when to accomplish which objectives are critical to building customer loyalty and resulting in revenue.

Given the proliferation of products and intense competition, the choice of which tactics to use in what sequence and at what point in the shopping journey is an on-going, significant challenge for shopper marketers. Therefore, gaining this knowledge and developing the ability to navigate the options increase chances for success.

Key Terms

- **Price promotion:** Promotion where the incentive given to the consumer is monetary, such as a coupon or temporary price reduction
- **Coupon redemption:** The action by the recipient of the coupon to use it and receive money off the purchase
- **Coupon slippage**: Coupons distributed but not redeemed
- **Product promotion:** Promotion where the incentive given to the consumer is a product in addition to the product already being purchased, such as an additional product for free
- **Sampling**: Promotion where the incentive given to the consumer is a sample of a product (either a small size or the full product)
- **Prize promotion:** Promotion where the incentive given to the consumer is to win a prize(s) either by chance or based on skills
- **Social media promotion:** Sales or shopper marketing offers communicated and promoted through social networks
- **Cause-related promotion:** Promotion where the incentive given to the consumer is a donation made by the sponsoring company when the consumer makes a purchase of the sponsored product
- **Reward and continuity promotion**: Promotion where the incentive given to the consumer is goods and services tied to purchases made

An Expert's Perspective

Sales Promotion for the last several years has been very effective in reaching our clients targets through pricing discounts as well as volume pricing incentives.

– Loretta Volpe, Partner GMLV, Integrated Marketing Agency

Key Concepts

Consumer promotion tactics must be carefully planned

A shopper marketing practitioner is best served to consider an array of factors before selecting the consumer tactic to use. These factors, discussed earlier in this book, are listed to emphasize their importance. As will be shown on the subsequent pages, there are a vast array of options for consumer tactics, thereby increasing the importance of thoroughly answering these questions in order to optimize the tactical solution.

1. What are the marketing objectives and marketing targets for the product that is the subject of the shopper marketing campaign?
2. What are the internal and external factors that may impact the shopper marketing campaign? This means, for example, what is the corporate philosophy, what is the economic climate at the time the promotion is supposed to be executed?
3. What are the primary shopper marketing objectives for the shopper marketing campaign?
4. Who exactly are the shopper marketing targets and the associated shopper types?
5. What is the change(s) of purchase behaviors expected from the shopper targets through the promotion?
6. What is the key shopper marketing big idea or sales promotion concept as introduced in Chapter 4?
7. What are the budgetary constraints?

Different promotion tactics are generally used to achieve different objectives

It is important to identify all the elements previously mentioned before we can identify the consumer promotion tactics that will make sense:

- **Marketing objective(s):** Is the Shopper Marketing campaign requested to help the following:
    - Acquire new customers
    - Build further loyalty with the current customers
    - Retain current customers who are on their way out
    - Win back past customers
- **Marketing target(s):** In relation, should the shopper marketing campaign focus on the following:
    - Prospects

  - Current customers
  - Past customers

- **Shopper marketing objective(s):** In the context, what specific shopper marketing objectives should the planned shopper marketing campaign focus on?

  Examples include the following:

  - Increase purchase frequency
  - Generate product trial
  - Increase transaction size
  - Increase usage occasions
  - Increase the number of distribution outlets
  - Increase the shelf space
  - Increase the in-store presence
  - Expand the selling season

- **Shopper Marketing target(s):** What are the specific shopper types that the shopper marketing campaign should focus on to help achieve the shopper marketing objectives? What are the characteristics (demographics, psychographics, etc.) of such targets?

  - Loyal users
  - Competitive loyals
  - Price buyers
  - Switchers
  - Non-users

Consumer Promotion Tactics Need Specific Parameters

Consumer sales promotion tactics are used to entice shoppers to purchase a product.

All shopper marketing campaigns with consumer promotion tactics need specific components to be addressed, including the following:

- Start and end date
- Inducement

- Required action: Typically, there is an action or behavior required by the target customer
- Impact on purchase: Sales promotions are meant to drive purchase; it may require a series of promotions to result in the purchase
- Clearly defined objective(s), two to three maximum
- Measurability: Promotions should be measurable

The consumer promotion tactics can be categorized as follows:

- Price promotions
- Product promotions
- Gifts and premiums
- Sampling
- Prize promotions
- Cause-related promotions
- Continuity programs

Price Promotion Tactics

Definition and Description

These promotions provide the strongest incentive to the consumer to make a purchase: *money*!

Potential Applications

Price promotions are used because they can generate immediate sales. When used properly, price promotion can motivate consumers as follows:

- To switch from one brand to another
- To purchase on impulse
- To try a new product
- To purchase a larger quantity or greater volume
- To stimulate (i.e., push) the next purchase
- To push for the purchase of multiple units

Price promotion types

Coupons

A voucher entitling the holder to a discount off a particular product.

By showing a picture of two (2) Ortega products in this image, the sponsor is using a visualization to attract customers to redeem the coupon and buy 2, not one product. The products are large also reinforcing the idea of buying two. In addition, the red font for "Save $1.00" makes the message of the coupon stand out.

Refunds and rebates

Partial money back after purchase.

In this image, the creative design for this offer is designed to quickly communicate what the offer is and create a point of differentiation for the product over its competition. More specifically, the size of the design elements allow the consumer to quickly see what is being offered, i.e. $10 (very large font) rebate (next largest font), mail in (3rd largest font) and what has to be done in the smallest font. In addition, the text in the largest font is in white letters, whereas the details of the offer are in black.

Price discounts

Cents off/reduced price offers

Product package indicates the price is lower than the regular price.

The creative design is very strong in this image to communicate the message and motivate consumers to redeem the coupon. More specifically, the design focuses the reader on the main points very quickly, namely, how much the coupon is worth (40 cents per gallon), what it is for (a picture of gasoline) and how to redeem (click for coupon).

Buy One Get One (BOGO)

With money off the second item (buy one item and get money off the second of the same item).

In this image, use of a bright color such as pink adds emphasis to the message. In addition, the reader will immediately see the 50% off, because of the very large font size and be prompted to read the rest of the message. The offer of buying one and receiving 50% off the second one will induce the consumer to buy the additional pair of shoes, thereby bringing incremental sales to the sponsor.

In the above image, a buy one, get one free offer is a strong offer in and of itself, however, the impact of this creative execution is powerful and likely instrumental to spark consumer participation. Importantly, the creative approach ties in well with a holiday feeling, i.e. "share joy." The creative design, layout and copy all work to engage the consumer and motivate him/her to take advantage of the promotional offer. More specifically, the font choice for "share joy" is festive, the colors are holiday oriented and the copy points reinforce sharing good times with friends and family.

Even though a strict BOGO offer might be perceived as a gift with purchase, this is, in fact, a price discount offer. Now, this is not presented as such, as the manufacturer or the retailer behind the offer does not want the brand to be associated with a discount per say, but they know their customers are price sensitive. Therefore, they still aim at the price sensitivity mindset of their target shopper and use a BOGO offer because it is softer and less likely to negatively impact the brand's image.

These promotions can be executed on the package or off the package. For example, you can obtain a coupon that has been affixed to the product (an instantly redeemable coupon (IRC)), inside the product packaging, or in a store circular, newspaper, online, or via your mobile device.

Advantages and Disadvantages

All in all, price promotions have multiple advantages and disadvantages as listed:

Advantages

- Immediate sales!
- Easy and fast to distribute to the manufacturer or retailer in the case of coupons
- Return on investment calculation is relatively easy
- Easy for the consumer to redeem the coupon. Redemption means using the coupon for a purchases
- In the case of coupons, they are versatile and can be used for many purposes, as previously indicated

Those advantages explain why marketers are investing as much in price promotions as coupons. As shown in the chart from Valassis, US consumers were offered $550 billion in coupons savings in 2015.

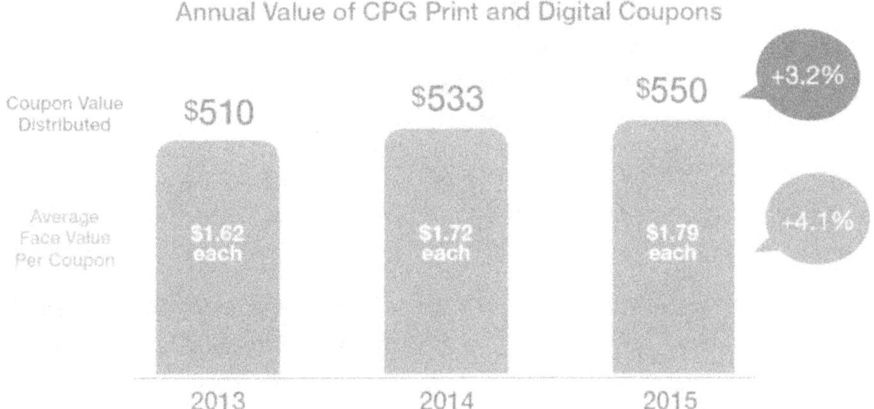

Disadvantages

- Creates price sensitivity among consumers. By this we mean if there are continuous price offers, consumers pay attention to pricing. This is not advantageous to companies because consumers will take notice of any price changes they make
- Creates "stockpiling" by consumers. By this, we mean that consumers buy more than they normally would or need when the product is discounted. This is not advantageous to companies because the consumer purchased the product ahead of time and then buys nothing later because they have enough of the product on hand
- Can be wasteful in that the loyal customer of the brand would have purchased the brand without the price promotion

- There is potential to erode and dilute the brand image because too many prices offers have negative connotations to consumers

- Blurring in the minds of consumers—too many prices offers cause confusion for consumers

The key to a price promotion is the decision regarding how much money to give (i.e., what is the amount of the reduction or how much is the coupon value?). The following are factors that come into play for making this decision:

- What, if anything is the competition doing? For example, if your competitor is offering $2.00 off a purchase, you would need to do the same or more to persuade the consumer to purchase your product over the competition.

- What is the past redemption rates for your product based on the amount of the price promotion? If in the past the redemption rate for a $2.00 coupon generated the greatest return on investment, it would make sense to offer the same coupon amount.

- It has been proven that any discounts representing less than 15 percent of the initial price will have virtually no effect on additional purchases, so is it always worth doing?

- What exactly is the purpose of the price offer? If your goal is to obtain a trial of the product, you might consider offering a higher value coupon to motivate a new buyer. If, on the other hand, your objective is to motivate a consumer to switch to your brand from the competition where there is no coupon offer, you may not need a high-value coupon because a price reduction may motivate the switch regardless of the amount.

There are advantages for manufacturers to use coupons as opposed to the other forms of price promotions

- A manufacturer can control who to send the coupon to and when exactly to send it. Compare this to a rebate that is on the package stating money will be sent back to you when you write it for a rebate. In this case, the manufacturer could not control who sees the offer.

- The concept of "coupon slippage" is an advantage for manufacturers. This means that the manufacturer distributed the coupon *but* a certain percentage of those who received or saw the coupon purchased the product but did not use the coupon. Hence, the coupon succeeded in generating the sale at no cost to the manufacturer. Actually, according to NCHMarketing, for the first half of 2017, only 0.6 percent of the distributed coupons are indeed used by consumers (NCHMarketing 2017). (Accessed at https://www.nchmarketing.com/CouponIndustryTrends.aspx)

- Only those who have the coupon can save, enabling the manufacturer to obtain sales from some people at the regular price (because they did not receive the coupon).

- Coupons are very easy to track as to who redeemed them and where they were redeemed. That translates to being able to measure and more easily adjust the coupon amount and method of distribution.

Price promotion tactic appropriateness varies greatly by shopper type. So, a shopper marketing manager has to be very careful about which tactics to use.

Appropriateness of Each Tactic

The tables that follow describe the appropriateness of each price promotion tactic for each possible shopper target type and under what circumstances each should be used.

Coupons

Coupons are particularly appropriate for switchers and price buyers as they work on the price side of the value proposition.

Shopper targets	POSSIBLE PURCHASE BEHAVIOR CHANGE(S)	APPROPRIATENESS OF A COUPON AS A CONSUMER PROMOTION TACTIC
Loyal users	• ***Reinforce behavior*** • ***Increase consumption*** • ***Change purchase timing***	• ***Might encourage users to buy more than they normally would buy*** • ***May potentially negatively impact brand image***
Competitive loyals	• ***Break loyalty to another brand to switch to your product***	• ***Users are loyal to other brands so price is not the issue by itself*** • ***If coupons are used, they must be of high value***
Switchers	• ***Persuade to "switch" to your product more often***	• ***Excellent for coupons*** • ***Good for variety seekers*** • *Good to push new or low selling items*
Price buyers	• ***Match their value requirements to make them stay with your product***	• ***Might be appropriate if coupon value is high enough***

Refunds and Rebates

Refunds and rebates are also particularly appropriate for switchers and price buyers as they work on the price side of the value proposition.

The appropriateness of refunds and rebates is questionable for loyal users because a loyal user may buy the brand no matter what the offer is.

SHOPPER TARGETS	POSSIBLE PURCHASE BEHAVIOR CHANGE(S)	APPROPRIATENESS OF REFUNDS AND REBATES AS A CONSUMER PROMOTION TACTIC
Loyal users	• **Reinforce behavior** • **Increase consumption** • **Change purchase timing**	• **Most likely to take advantage of refunds, with questionable impact on sales increase** • **Might be appropriate for the following:** – **Infrequent impulse purchases** – **Purchase timing change** – **Gaining new products trials** – **Multiple purchases**
Competitive loyals	• **Break loyalty to another brand to switch to your product**	• **Unlikely to be influenced**
Switchers	• **Persuade to "switch" to your product more often**	• **Might be successful when** – **purchase reasons are linked to variety or value** – **there is a high-value product that is still profitable after refund**

Price buyers	• **Match their value requirements to make them stay with your product**	• **Most likely to be attracted by big refund** • **Questionable long-term value for the brand**

Price Discounts

Price discounts are, of course, particularly appropriate for price buyers as they work on the price side of the value proposition. They might also work for certain categories of switchers.

Price discounts are often used to fight competitive activity. As described earlier, it is preferable to soften the brand cheapening perception associated with price discounts by using, for example, a BOGO offer.

SHOPPER TARGETS	POSSIBLE PURCHASE BEHAVIOR CHANGE(S)	APPROPRIATENESS OF PRICE DISCOUNT AS A CONSUMER PROMOTION TACTIC
Loyal users	• **Reinforce behavior** • **Increase consumption** • **Change purchase timing**	• **Good tactic if used to motivate the shoppers to stay with your brand –and ONLY to counter competitive moves** • **If used for immediate consumption, offer will have to be presented as a BOGO offer to lessen negative impact of a price discount on the brand image**
Competitive loyals	• **Break loyalty to another brand to switch to your product**	• **Often used by businesses BUT require large discount to attract a loyal user** • **Questionable profitability**
Switchers	• **Persuade to "switch" to your product more often**	• **Good for value buyers and variety seekers** • **But very short-term focus**

Price buyers	• **Match their value requirements to make them stay with your product**	• **Price-offs are a very good match for this shopper type** • **But very short-term focus**

Example of price promotion: coupon

The example that follows illustrates a scenario in terms of shopper marketing objectives, targets, and expected purchase behavior changes. When reviewing the example, it is important to take note of the strategic thinking regarding the selected offer for the likely target customer as well as the creative execution.

Jet.com "Start the semester with savings—get $10 off your first 3 orders"

The Shopper Marketing Offer and Its Communication

The offer was presented as a coupon included in the package targeting college students when they ordered a textbook from Chegg.com, an online textbook shop. The offer was for $10 off the first three orders from Jet.com, on a minimum purchase of $35.

The Shopper Marketing Technique

Coupon

Background Information

Jet.com is an American e-commerce site.

Marketing Strategy

The marketing strategy seems to be focused on acquisition with a prospective target being new users since they are reaching out to people who haven't ordered from them before with an offer to try Jet.com and to "stay" with Jet.com for at least three orders.

Shopper Marketing Objectives

To first generate a trial and, by doing so, increase purchase frequency of purchase.

Shopper Marketing Targets

Shoppers who are competitive loyals (e.g., Amazon customers) and switchers (who are switching between various e-commerce platforms)

Purchase Behavior Change – Desired Results

- **Competitive loyals:** To break their loyalty away from their current e-commerce platform and then to stay with Jet.com
- **Switchers:** To switch to Jet.com as often as possible when needing to make an online purchase

Product Promotion Tactics

Definition and Description

Free product(s) is the offer; the free product is the incentive to make a purchase. The free product can be the same brand *or* another free product that has a related appeal to the target audience. More details on the types of product promotions can be found under the section "Product Promotion Types."

If the gift is another product, then this will also relate to the sampling consumer promotion tactic that is covered later in this chapter.

These promotions are executed in store, typically on the shelf where the product is found and/or on a special point of sale display. The product offer is advertised right on the package.

Potential Applications

Such tactics are used to do the following:

- Encourage a consumer to purchase a larger volume
- Motivate a consumer to switch to the brand on promotion
- Reward existing customers and build brand loyalty
- Encourage a consumer to trade up in size

Product promotion types

Bonus packs are products packaged together with a "bonus." The "bonus" can be extra for the promoted product or another related product.

Potential Applications

- Encourage a consumer to purchase a larger volume
- Motivate a consumer to switch to the brand on promotion
- Combat competitive activity
- Cross-sell other brands, thereby gaining exposure and increasing cost efficiency

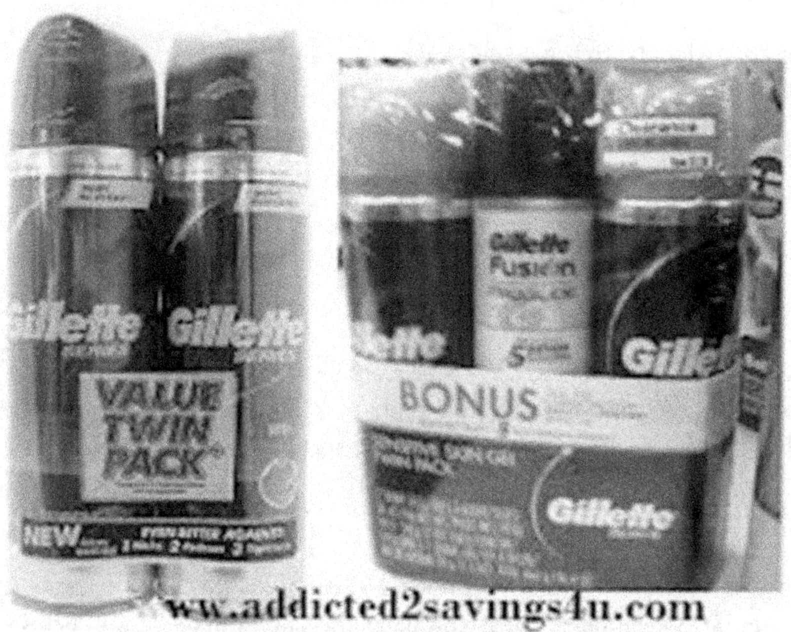

In the above image, the communication of the offer is the first element of the package that a consumer can see because of the colors and fonts used in the package design. More specifically, the size of each label "Value Twin Pack" and "Bonus" is relatively large as the color red helps the message stand out. The URL is also a strong creative element focused on savings.

In this image, the use of a blue background, makes the offer of a free cup of Reese's stand out. That blue appears as a flag on the left side of the package to let consumers know that this is a bonus pack. Also, the yellow font for the word "free" also makes that word pop out to emphasize what consumers like to see, i.e. something for free!

Bonus packs have a variety of ways to be executed as follows:

Extra fill, extra product free

Here, the consumer gets a larger size or greater quantity but the price remains the same as the "normal" pack.

The illustration above makes it very clear to the consumer that the offer has a bonus and via the contrasting color of blue on the yellow, the offer stands out on the shelf. This in turn will help the sponsor twart competition and sell additional product.

The offer in the above image is communicated strongly as a visualization to help consumers see just how much the bonus would be. More specifically, the creative design of the package is such that the 20% bonus label is roughly 20% of the package thereby reinforcing what a great offer it is and motivating purchase.

Banded packs of the same product

The label in the above image is highly creative in that it circles the two products in such a way to form a loop indicating continuity. The label is also largely yellow to indicate sunshine which is what this product relates to. These elements in addition to the words "twin pack" quickly and creatively communicate the offer of 2 of the same product for a lower cost than if two (2) were purchased individually.

Banding together the same product is easier to execute than the "extra product free" because it is easier from an operations standpoint to simply "band together" multiple items than it is to manufacture a new package (as shown in the Charmin example).

Banded packs of assorted products

Can be multiple products from the same manufacturer or multiple products from different manufacturers.

In the image above, use of green with rays of light coupled with a great looking car creates an alluring visual designed to attract consumers. Once looking at the pack, the font, size and white typeface for the words of the offer "Gift Pack" communicate to consumers that there is something special about this product, designed to motivate the purchase. In addition, the visuals of the products in the gift pack provide consumers with a clear understanding of what is included which is a creative way to strengthen the offer.

In the previous example where two or more brands are packed together to offer multiple products, there are potential benefits for all brands involved, namely the following:

- New exposure for each brand if there are multiple manufacturers
- Executing the promotion and exposing it to different consumers
- Enhanced brand value based on the association with the other participating brands

Specialty container

Specialty containers are limited edition packages or product containers that can be reused or that add value to the product. Examples of specialty containers are frequent in the soda category as illustrated.

In the two (2) images above, Diet Coke has used creative appeal to sell more soda. More specifically, by varying the shape (in the first image) and the images (in the 2nd image) the can becomes more attractive and hence stands out on the shelf. In addition, the creative choice of graphic representations of people on the cans are highly compelling and consistent with the "Diet Coke" brand image. Lastly, it is because of the strength of the creative application of the offer that consumers would want to purchase the specialty container and this in turn, drives product sales.

Advantages and Disadvantages

Advantages

- Immediate sales!
- Return on investment calculation is relatively easy
- High perceived value to the consumer
- Appealing to manufacturers because the cost of the free product is less than the amount of the discount, thereby increasing the revenue for the manufacturer

Disadvantages

- Creates "stockpiling" by consumers. By this, we mean that consumers buy more than they normally would or need when the product is discounted. This is not advantageous to companies because the consumer purchased the product ahead of time and then buys nothing later because they have enough of the product on hand
- Can be wasteful in that loyal customers of the brand would have purchased the brand without the free product

The appropriateness of this consumer promotion tactic varies greatly by shopper type. So, a shopper marketing manager has to be very careful of when and how to use it.

Appropriateness of each tactic

The table that follows describes the appropriateness of product promotions tactics for each possible shopper target type and under what circumstances each should be used.

Product promotions are also particularly appropriate for loyal users and certain categories of switchers as they work on the benefits side of the value proposition.

For switchers, the attractiveness of such offers is reinforced if the switchers are already customers of the brand; they value the brand proposition enough to buy the product from time to time.

SHOPPER TARGETS	POSSIBLE PURCHASE BEHAVIOR CHANGE(S)	APPROPRIATENESS OF PRODUCT PROMOTIONS AS CONSUMER PROMOTION TACTICS

Loyal users	• **Reinforce behavior** • **Increase consumption** • **Change purchase timing**	• **Most likely target group to be affected by such "value-added" promotions** • **Will help increase consumption through cross-selling and/or upselling offers**
Competitive loyals	• **Break loyalty to another brand to switch to your product**	• **Will not be influenced**
Switchers	• **Persuade to "switch" to your product more often**	• **Can be very strong incentives for switchers, especially if they are current customers of your brand**
Price buyers	• **Match their value requirements to make them stay with your product**	• **Not appropriate as they only care about the "lowest price on the shelf"**

Example of product promotion: Bonus Pack

The example that follows illustrates a scenario in terms of shopper marketing objectives, targets, and expected purchase behavior changes. When reviewing the example, it is important to take note of the strategic thinking regarding the selected offer for the likely target customer as well as the creative execution.

The Shopper Marketing Offer and Its Communication

This bonus pack offer for Charmin offered 20 percent more product for the same price at Costco—a major retailer with its own private brand of toilet paper.

The Shopper Marketing Technique

Bonus pack

Background Information

Procter & Gamble (P&G) acquired Charmin Paper Company in 1957. This is a very competitive market with a border-line commodity perception by consumers and many private brands available at lower prices.

Marketing Strategy

The marketing target for this promotion seems to be primarily aimed at current customers (with a loyalty marketing objective) because you would be more likely to overstock this product if you are a current customer. The objective might also be retention driven, i.e., to keep their current customers because Charmin may be under assault by the cheaper Costco private label bathroom tissue brand.

Shopper Marketing Objectives

- Increase transaction size (with the 20 percent more product)
- Maintain or increase purchase frequency (as with this offer, Charmin might try to keep their customers purchasing their product when they are in an actual shopping mode for bathroom tissue)

Shopper Marketing Targets

- **Loyal users** of Charmin
- Current customers who are switchers between Charmin and other brands

Purchase Behavior Change – Desired Results

- **Loyal users:** Reinforce their purchase behavior
- **Switchers:** Make them switch to Charmin

Free Gifts and Premiums Tactics

Definition and Description

Free gift offers (also known as premiums) are gifts in the form of merchandise or a service given away in exchange for a purchase.

Potential Applications

- Gain trial among new users
- Target a specific segment of users
- Reward existing customers
- Attract new customers to the brand
- Stimulate repeat purchase
- Introduce a new product
- Overcome seasonal variations in sales
- Push for switching of brands
- Build brand equity
- Respond to competitive activity

Free gifts and premiums promotion types

Special Packs

Special packs are simply product packaging (packs), and they are called "special" because the gift that is given with the purchase is either inside the pack (called in-pack), attached to the pack (called on-pack), or given separately to the pack (due to the size of the gift for example) (called near-pack).

Important Considerations

Just as careful consideration has to be given to finding the right promotion "partner," so too does consideration need to be given to finding the right free gift. This can be tricky because the consumer, as we have already established, is savvy. If the free gift does not fit the brand properly and/or the free gift is not valued properly in relation to the cost of the product, this can potentially damage the brand image.

In addition, free gifts and premiums are costly to the manufacturer, so it is important to calculate how many units of the product must be sold to "pay back" the cost of the premium. If a company gives away a premium that is too expensive, it may be unlikely to recover the cost of that premium, which would obviously be problematic.

Lastly, as a general rule, the more of the product the consumer has to buy in order to get the premium, the more likely the consumer has a negative impression of the promotion. On the other hand, the less of the product the consumer has to buy in order to get the premium, the more receptive the consumer is to the promotion and the less likely the consumer views the promotion as manipulative.

The appropriateness of this consumer promotion tactic varies greatly by shopper type. So, a shopper marketing manager has to be very careful of when and how to use it.

Appropriateness of each tactic

The table that follows describes the appropriateness of the Special Packs tactic for each possible shopper target type and under what circumstances each should be used.

Special packs are very appropriate for loyal users and certain categories of switchers as they work on the benefits side of the value proposition.

For switchers, the attractiveness of such offers is reinforced if the switchers are already customers of the brand as, while they are not loyal per say, they value the brand proposition enough to buy the product from time to time.

SHOPPER TARGETS	POSSIBLE PURCHASE BEHAVIOR CHANGE(S)	APPROPRIATENESS OF SPECIAL PACKS AS CONSUMER PROMOTION TACTIC
Loyal users	• **Reinforce behavior** • **Increase consumption** • **Change purchase timing**	• **Most likely to be affected by "value-added" promotions**

Competitive loyals	• **Break loyalty to another brand to switch to your product**	• **May be influenced** • **BUT loyalty to another brand could make them ignore the promotion**
Switchers	• **Persuade to "switch" to your product more often**	• **Can be very strong incentives for switchers, especially if they are current customers of your brand**
Price buyers	• **Match their value requirements to make them stay with your product**	• **Might be appropriate if premium is of exceptional interest for them and if the price of the brand is also low**

Example of free gift promotion: Special Pack

The example that follows illustrates a scenario in terms of shopper marketing objectives, targets, and expected purchase behavior changes. When reviewing the example, it is important to take note of the strategic thinking regarding the selected offer for the likely target customer as well as the creative execution.

Verizon Wireless-- Get the Galaxy S7 on America's best network

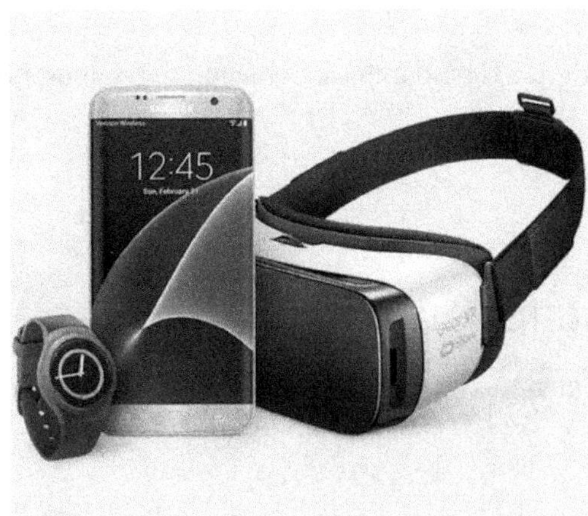

The Shopper Marketing Offer and its communication

"Get a free Gear S2 or Gear VR with purchase of the Galaxy S7 edge. An online exclusive offer."

The offer was on the verizonwireless.com homepage.

Background information

Verizon Wireless is an American broadband telecommunications company and the largest wireless communications service in the US. Verizon's main competitors are AT&T, Sprint, and T-mobile. Verizon is an established company with high brand recognition.

Marketing Strategy

The marketing strategy might be acquisition and/or retention. Verizon might be aiming at prospects to motivate them to switch to Verizon and/or they may be focused on stealing customers away from the competition. Also, the strategy might be aimed at current customers (with a loyalty marketing objective) to push them to upgrade to a new version of the phone.

Shopper Marketing Objectives

- Generate trial of Verizon (for new customers)
- Maintain (and maybe increase) mobile services transaction size (for current customers)

Shopper Marketing Targets

- **Competitive loyals** who may have a phone with AT&T or T-Mobile but are looking for a better offer (acquisition)
- **Loyal users:** Verizon customers looking for a new, upgraded phone (loyalty)

Purchase Behavior Change - Desired Results

- **Competitive loyals:** To make them break their loyalty with the competitive brand and move to Verizon.
- **Loyal users:** To reinforce their purchase behavior and maybe even increase their consumption with Verizon

Sampling

Definition and Description

Sampling is giving the consumer a quantity of the product (typically a trial/smaller size) at no cost to encourage trial.

Sampling is typically done face to face and near the point of sale, e.g., in a store, near a store, or on crowded street corners. The main objective of sampling is to get new users, that is, stimulate trial of the product.

The sample could be also the product given as a gift for a product promotion offer, as mentioned earlier in the product promotions section.

Samples can also be distributed

- by mail,
- packed in with the product,
- in mobile vehicles, and
- at events and street fairs.

While sampling is effective to gain trial, it is very expensive because of the cost associated with the production of the trial size and distributing it.

According to a VSS Communications Industry Forecast, $2.21 billion was spent on samples in 2009—(https://www.vss.com/ 2009.) According to the "Product Sampling Study" by Arbitron and Edison Media Research, 70 million customers received some type of samples every quarter (Arbitron and Edison Media Research 2008, https://www.marketingcharts.com/industries/retail-and-e-commerce-6211.) So, this is expensive.

Now, according to the same study, one-third of those trying the sample buy the product during the same shopping trip. So, this is very effective.

Potential Applications

As we know, sampling is very expensive but this is one of the sales promotion techniques that can have the most impact on the most shopper targets.

For loyal users, this could be a great way to introduce an improved version of the product that the user already consumes; sampling convinces the loyal user to upgrade.

For competitive loyals, this might be the only way for them to experience your product without any real resistance to do so (if the price is an obstacle) and maybe convince the consumer to change his or her mind. This is especially true if a "new and improved" version of your product is available and by getting a sample, the competitive loyal user might be convinced the reason he or she did not choose your brand previously is no longer valid.

Sampling is also very appropriate for switchers to be sure that they remember to purchase your product from time to time.

Finally, sampling is the only sales promotion technique that could make a non-user decide to purchase into your product category and to start doing it, of course with your product. In general, marketing dollars are not spent trying to attract non-users since they are the least likely segment to make a purchase of a product category they don't already use. However, in the case of sampling, this is one tactic that is used to gain a non-user.

Appropriateness of the sampling tactic

The table that follows describes the appropriateness of the sampling tactic for each possible shopper target type and under what circumstances each should be used.

SHOPPER TARGETS	POSSIBLE PURCHASE BEHAVIOR CHANGE(S)	APPROPRIATENESS OF SAMPLING AS A CONSUMER PROMOTION TACTIC
Loyal users	• **Reinforce behavior** • **Increase consumption** • **Change purchase timing**	• **Very appropriate for new "additional" or "linked" products to the "original" product the consumer is already loyal to**
Competitive loyals	• **Break loyalty to another brand to switch to your product**	• **May be the only way to make them "really" change**

Switchers	• **Persuade to "switch" to your product more often**	• **Good for infrequent users**
Price buyers	• **Match their value requirements to make them stay with your product**	• **Unlikely to be affected**
Non-users	• **People who don't use any product in the category**	• **Only SP tactic that is really applicable to non-users**

Example of sample promotion

The examples that follow illustrate a variety of scenarios in terms of shopper marketing objectives, targets, and expected purchase behavior changes. When reviewing the examples, it is important to take note of the strategic thinking regarding the selected offer for the likely target customer as well as the creative execution.

Abeille Royale Replenishing Eye Cream from Guerlain - Samples

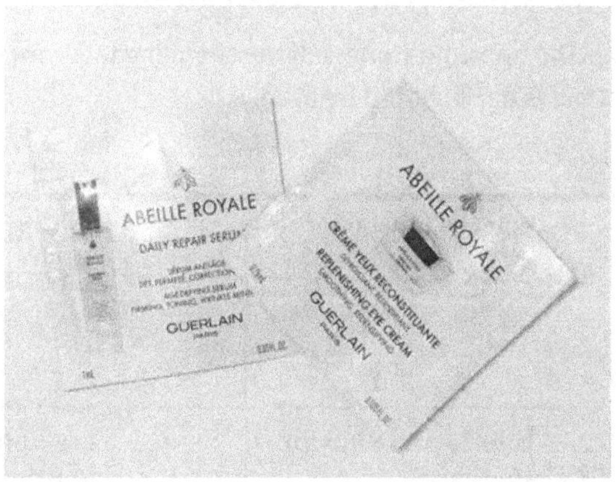

The Shopper Marketing Offer and its communication

Two samples for the Abeille Royale Daily Repair Serum and the Abeille Royale Replenishing Eye Cream from Guerlain given at the time of purchase of another product at the store.

Background Information

Guerlain is an established French brand founded in 1828 that started as a perfumery but has branched out to cosmetics and skincare as well. It is a subsidiary of LVMH Moët Hennessy, a French global luxury conglomerate that is still growing.

Marketing Strategy

By giving customers free samples at the point of purchase, Guerlain is trying to inspire increased *loyalty* from their *current customers*.

Shopper Marketing Objectives

- Generate a trial of new products and ultimately increase the transaction size by having current customers purchase more than one product per transaction.

Shopper Marketing Targets

- **Loyal users:** Guerlain is aiming at their loyal users in order to increase loyalty.
- **Switchers:** Guerlain is also aiming to motivate current customers to switch to their products and therefore purchase their products more often.

Purchase Behavior Change - Desired Results

- **Loyal users:** Reinforce purchase behavior leading to bigger transaction sizes through multi-product purchases
- **Switchers:** Switch to Guerlain more frequently for more products

Prize Promotion Tactics

Definition and Description

Prize promotions are promotions where there is a prize given away. It's about winning! Prize promotions consist of the following:

- Sweepstakes
- Contests
- Games

Prize promotions are promotions unlike price or product promotions. Although they generate immediate action (to enter or play), they are designed for longer-term impacts of building a database for future marketing, brand enhancement and engagement, and reinforcement of specific brand messages. In addition, they provide a platform for major synergistic marketing efforts (advertising and public relations) to support the promotion.

This is indeed the only consumer promotion tactic that can have some awareness objectives attached to it.

There are three main components for a prize promotion:

- Prize (giving away free goods and services)
- Chance (random selection of winners)
- Consideration (purchase or a significant amount of time)

The key is that only two of these three components can exist in the same promotion for the promotion to be legal. If all three of these components are in the same promotion, it is considered illegal.

Potential Applications

- Generate trial
- Increase in sharing/collaboration/referrals
- Boost website traffic
- Build database/lead generation for one to one communications
- Enhance brand image
- Obtain survey information from the target customer
- Obtain product reviews
- Communicate product news and education about product benefits
- Interact with the target customer in a pleasurable, fun, entertaining way
- Differentiate brand from the competition at the point of purchase to cause brand switching
- Increase requests for a quote or submission of product warranty information
- Generate in-store traffic

Prize promotions fall into two main buckets as follows:

- A promotion that requires a consumer to buy the product and skill determines winners (a contest)
- A promotion that can *only* ask the consumer to buy the product (no purchase required), and random selection determines winners (a sweepstakes or game)

Prize promotions can be distributed in a multitude of ways, both on and off-pack, including, for example, on the outside of a cereal box, inside a frozen food entrée, or an email or text alert with a link to a website to enter and play the game.

Contest

A contest of skill is a prize promotion in which no element of chance exists because the entries to the contest are judged, not selected at random.

A contest of skill requires the following:

- Real skill to complete the contest challenge (such as creating a video)
- Judge(s) that are qualified to judge the submissions (e.g., a recipe contest must be judged by people who know about cooking)
- A larger budget because each entry must be judged
- A purchase of the product (required in certain states)
- Permission to use content if that content has a copyright. For example, the company would like to do a lip sync video contest using a specific song. The company would need written permission from the songwriter to use the song

Sweepstakes or Game

A sweepstakes or game is a prize promotion in which the winner is chosen at random, not judged as with a contest. A sweepstakes or game requires that no purchase be necessary to enter.

Games that are set up so that the player becomes aware at the time of gameplay if he or she did or not win is called an Instant Win Game. Games that require a participant to scratch a designated area are "scratch-and-win" games and those that require a participant to match the same objects or letters are "match-and-win" games.

Important Considerations

It is important to carefully think through the following points when planning a prize promotion:

- The prize for winning should be "dreamlike" or "aspirational." In other words, consumers are looking to win the dream, not mundane, everyday items.
- The prize(s) should be highly appealing to the target customer and substantial; if the budget does not permit the sponsor to do so, consideration should be given to not using this tactic.
- The subject matter should warrant a contest of skill. For example, if the company is a spice manufacturer, it would make sense to execute a recipe contest so that consumers use the spice in cooking and the "best recipe" wins. The best recipe would require skill. This not only

educates consumers on the use of the spice, it also creates a platform to advertise those ideas. If, on the other hand, the company is a headphone manufacturer, it makes little sense to execute a contest because there is no skill required to listen to music.

- Since a sweepstakes or game does not require effort on the part of the consumer (other than to enter with contact information or answer a few questions), there are typically many more entries in a sweepstakes or game as compared to a contest of skill. This is an important consideration because if, for example, one of the focuses of the promotion is to build a database of names for future marketing purposes, then sweepstakes would make more sense because more entries would likely be received. If, on the other hand, the objective is to use the promotion to create a press event or for future advertising purposes, then a contest of skill would make more sense because a contest generates the "best" entry that would be worthy of advertising, as opposed to a sweepstakes entry that would be obtained strictly by chance, thereby potentially producing an entry not worthy of advertising.

- The choice of the prizes provides a unique opportunity to properly target the selected marketing target and shopper target within it as the nature of the prize will have to be closely linked to the demographic, psychographic, etc. characteristics of the target. For example, for a target that is minded of protecting the Earth, a top prize as a participation in an expedition in the Amazon forest with an illustrious environmentalist would be a great choice.

- Prizes pyramid structure: To be really attractive to consumers, the contest, sweepstakes, or game must have several levels of prizes with a large prize at the top (that will be the one on which communication will be built), a series of smaller prizes of intermediate value in the middle, and a large number of small value prizes at the bottom. That way, shoppers will feel excited to participate because of the big prize and will feel that it is worth it because of the higher number of prizes and therefore the higher chance to win something.

- It is important when planning to execute a prize promotion to comply with "prize promotion law." More specifically, prize promotions are regulated and there are specific laws that must be followed be in compliance. The ramifications of not complying can include, for example, being fined, being ordered to stop the promotion (even if it has not ended), and even a class action lawsuit.

The Official Rules

One of the main components of a prize promotion is the "official rules" that govern the promotion, and these official rules can be complex and often times require legal counsel to assist and/or draft. In fact, there are law firms that specialize in prize promotion law and these attorneys not only draft the rules, they are also hired to review the creative materials (such as the promotion advertising) to be sure it is compliant with the law as well as consistent with the official rules.

A fundamental legal requirement in prize promotions is that a sponsor cannot force a consumer to make a purchase as a condition to enter, that is, make a purchase for a chance to win.

Here are three main components of a prize promotion:

- Prize (giving away free goods and/or services)
- Chance (random selection of winners, such as pulling the name of the winner(s) from a hat)
- Consideration (making a purchase or spending a significant amount of time entering, such as filling out a long survey before being able to enter)

All Three of the Above Cannot Be Present at The Same Time in the Same Promotion. By Doing That, the Sponsor is Breaking the Law.

Said another way, this means that one promotion cannot tell a consumer he or she has to buy the product for a chance to win and have the winner of the promotion selected at random.

Let's examine sweepstakes versus contests to illustrate how two of the three components exist, but not all three.

- In a sweepstakes:
    - there is a prize and
    - the winner(s) are selected at random, *but*
    - there is no purchase required to enter.
- In a contest of skill:
    - there is a prize,
    - the winner(s) are not selected at random but rather they are judged by experts based on skill, and
    - there can be a purchase required.

In addition, from a legal perspective, prize promotions must comply with the following:

- Specific requirements imposed by any platforms being used as a place where consumers can enter, such as Facebook or Twitter
- Data collection requirements in general and more specifically for children under the age of thirteen
- Registration requirements in various states, for example in New York and Florida
- CAN-SPAM (cannot send emails to people that have not opted in)
- Direct mail (there are specific disclosures that must appear in direct mail materials)

Advantages and Disadvantages

While prize promotions have advantages in that they can accomplish many objectives, the following disadvantages are equated with prize promotions:

- Prize promotions are criticized largely for the difficulty in equating their contribution to sales
- Sweepstakes have a relatively poor image in the minds of some consumers and professionals, making their use obsolete in those cases
- The phenomenon of "sweepstakes junkies" detracts, at times, from the sweepstakes ability to accomplish the objectives. A sweepstakes junkie is a person who enters sweepstakes with no interest in the brand and whose goal is to win by entering as many such promotions as possible

Appropriateness of this consumer promotion tactic varies greatly by shopper type. So, a shopper marketing manager has to be very careful of when and how to use it.

Appropriateness of Each Tactic

The table that follows describes the appropriateness of the prize promotions tactics for each possible shopper target type and under what circumstances each should be used.

Contests, sweepstakes, and games might be good sales promotion techniques for loyal users as they reinforce the attractiveness of the brand and serve as an excellent platform for upselling and cross-selling.

They are also appropriate for switchers as this might be the "final" argument to persuade them to purchase your product when they are in an actual shopping mode at the store.

SHOPPER TARGETS	POSSIBLE PURCHASE BEHAVIOR CHANGE(S)	APPROPRIATENESS OF CONTESTS, SWEEPSTAKES, AND GAMES AS CONSUMER PROMOTION TACTICS
Loyal users	• **Reinforce behavior** • **Increase consumption** • **Change purchase timing**	• **Good for the following:** – **Immediate consumption or for stockpiling** • **When entry tied to product usage** – **Cross-selling** • **Two products tied in the sweepstakes**

Competitive loyals	• **Break loyalty to another brand to switch to your product**	• Unlikely to be tempted • Only for consumers not so loyal to competitors, due to inertia
Switchers	• **Persuade to "switch" to your product more often**	• **Highly likely to be influenced by such programs** – **Lasting effect on sales is questionable** – **Requires that entry is easy and quick** – **Good for value seekers and variety seekers**
Price buyers	• **Match their value requirements to make them stay with your product**	• **Unlikely to be tempted**

Examples of contests, sweepstakes and games promotions

The examples that follow illustrate a variety of scenarios in terms of shopper marketing objectives, targets, and expected purchase behavior changes. When reviewing the examples, it is important to take note of the strategic thinking regarding the selected offer for the likely target customer as well as the creative execution.

Office Depot (sweepstakes)

- Potential application(s): Drive sales and in-store traffic

In this image, Office Depot used the allure of a large sum of money ($10,000 in the form of an office makeover) to attract customers. In addition, the idea of a "messy" office would resonate among busy executives thereby motivating purchase at Office Depot. It was advertised on Facebook because the sponsor believed their audience was on Facebook and would, therefore, see the promotion.

Kelloggs (instant-win game)

- Potential application(s): Drive sales and increase awareness of other Kellogg cereal brands

This image featuring a woman excited to start the day (with Kelloggs) provides a powerful message to the target customer that eating Kelloggs cereal will help ensure a great day. That message, along with the sweepstakes to win 1000's of prize, in turn, helps promote future sales and builds the customer database.

Jimmy Dean (sweepstakes)

- Potential application(s): Drive sales and obtain qualified consumer leads for future marketing

Since Jimmy Dean is known as a breakfast food, in this image the use of "yellow" to indicate sunshine is a way to motivate potential customers to respond, thereby building the database. In addition, the short survey, allure of winning $1500 cash, and use of a photograph of a woman sipping a refreshing drink are jointly being used to attract customers.

Princess Cruises (match-and-win game)

- Potential application(s):
    - Educate customers about onboard experiences and partnership with Discovery Communications
    - Obtain agreement from consumers for future marketing efforts
    - Create brand engagement and excitement among consumers

PRINCESS CRUISES
PRESENTS
Discovery at SEA
MATCH & WIN SWEEPSTAKES
Play for a chance to
WIN a FREE cruise for two!
Choose from a variety of destinations around the world, including the Caribbean, Alaska, Europe, Mexico and the Panama Canal.
To celebrate 50 years of cruising and the launch of our partnership with Discovery Communications, you could win a cruise to five destinations around the world. Play our match and win game to learn more about our new Discovery themed onboard experiences and the chance to win daily instant win prizes from your favorite Discovery shows!
View Prizes.
Enter Your Email To Get Started
SUBMIT

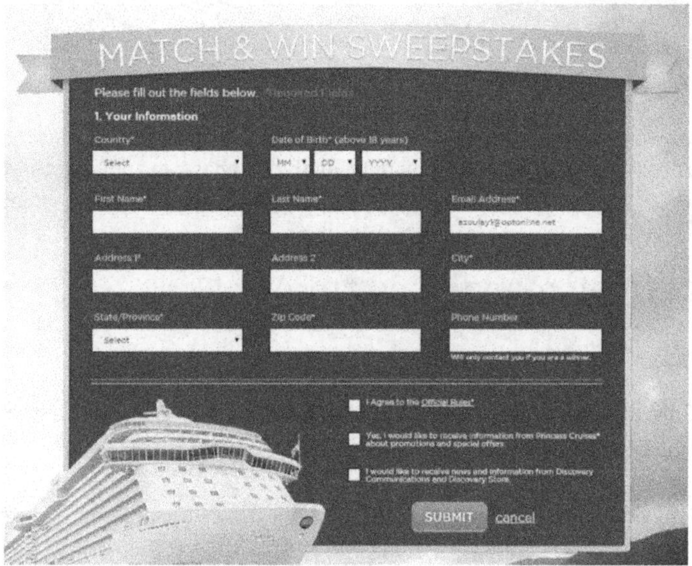
MATCH & WIN SWEEPSTAKES
Please fill out the fields below.
1. Your Information
Country*
Select
Date of Birth* (above 18 years)
MM
DD
YYYY
First Name*
Last Name*
Email Address*
Address 1*
Address 2
City*
State/Province*
Select
Zip Code*
Phone Number
Will only contact you if you are a winner.
I Agree to the Official Rules*
Yes, I would like to receive information from Princess Cruises* about promotions and special offers.
I would like to receive news and information from Discovery Communications and Discovery Store.
SUBMIT
cancel

The three (3) images above use a crisp creative approach to make the "game" easier to play. More specifically, the yellow and medium brown text pops out more to the reader when surrounded by dark colors of black and dark blue. Using a match and win technique whereby potential customers are asked to match images under the yellow area reinforces main benefits of the sponsors' products. Also, the images of a cruise ship and family help potential customers "visualize" him/herself enjoying a vacation!

MilkPEP Sweepstakes Program—2013 Effie Silver Award

(Source: Effie Awards)

The Shopper Marketing Offer

Enter your name on Facebook.com/milkmustache and win a Latte Lovers Essentials Kit (one winner every hour)

Background Information

Women's milk consumption in the US decreased and sales of milk as a category was declining

Marketing Strategy

The marketing strategy was clearly to win back women consumers of milk and increase consumption.

Shopper Insights

Women consume a significant amount of milk but through coffee products (in particular, coffee latte) bought at coffee shops and similar retailers, not as a stand-alone product at grocery stores.

Shopper Marketing Objectives

To expand the usage occasions of milk consumption at home by "convincing" women to prepare their own coffee latte at home.

The Idea

Provide a fun and rewarding experience to women to assist preparation of Caffe Latte at home by providing an online preparation guide and a chance to win a Latte Lovers Essentials Kit

Shopper Marketing Targets

- **Competitive loyals:** Consumers are loyal to another drink category (coffee)
- **Switchers:** Consumers who switch between milk and coffee as their preferred stand-alone product category
- **Non-users:** Consumers who are no longer a user of milk at home as a stand-alone product

Purchase Behavior Change—Desired Result

- **Competitive loyals:** Persuade women to use milk at home to prepare their preferred coffee latte drink as opposed to buying coffee at coffee shops
- **Switchers:** Convince them to use milk at home for coffee occasions as often as possible
- **Non-users:** Convince them to start using milk again at home

Cause-Related Promotions

Definition and Description

Cause marketing or cause-related marketing refers to a type of marketing involving the cooperative efforts of a for-profit business and a non-profit organization for mutual benefit. (Accessed at https://formomentum.com/cause-marketing-terminology-clarified/)

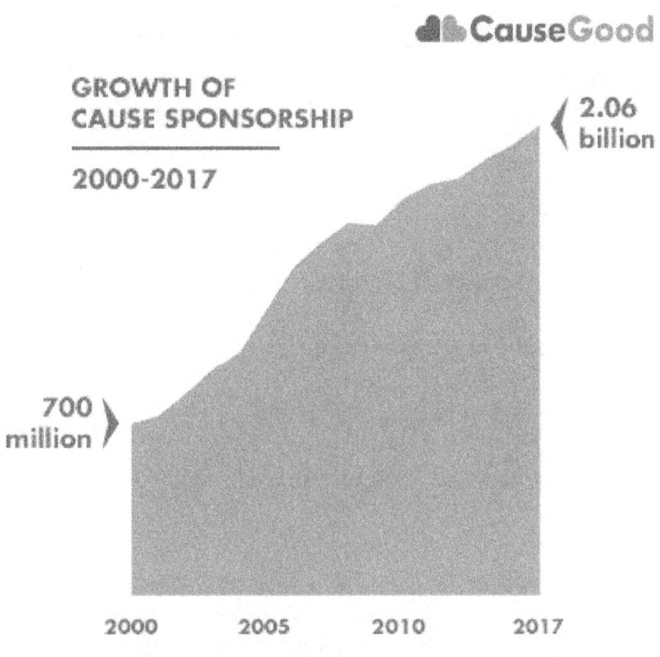

Cause marketing or cause-related marketing is aggressively growing and there are a number of reasons for this increase, as follows:

- Corporate attitudes about the strategic corporate partnership with non-profit causes have moved from the "nice to have" category to the "must have" imperative. This is because companies embrace their responsibility to go beyond profitability to help society. Participating in cause-related marketing activities is considered as providing societal benefits as well as serving to build positive brand perceptions. Forbes research reports that 93 percent of the global executives surveyed believe their company can "create economic value by creating societal value."

- Pressure to raise funds has pushed non-profit organizations to look to strategic partnerships to help achieve fundraising goals.

- Consumers are highly aware of and receptive to cause-related initiatives. In fact, consumers view the sponsoring companies as trustworthy.

Now, in itself, cause-related marketing is not part of shopper marketing but of public relations, as the focus of PR is to create and maintain goodwill toward the product, brand, and business from all stakeholders, starting with the consumers, which is what being "permanently" associated with a cause will do.

Now, shopper marketing has leveraged this cause-related marketing trend by piggybacking on it through temporary offers called cause-related promotions.

For example, if a brand or product has a regular cause that they are associated with where, for example, they normally give $1 for that cause for every purchase made but for a limited time, they give $2, that will be a cause-related promotion. If, as another example, the brand has no relation to any cause but, for a limited time, will give $1 to a selected cause for every purchase, this is once again cause-related promotion.

Potential Applications

- Stimulate sales of the sponsoring product
- Increase donations to the non-profit organization
- Increase in levels of brand advocacy over time
- Build database/lead generation for future fundraising efforts
- Enhance brand image

The appropriateness of this consumer promotion tactic varies greatly by shopper type. So, a shopper marketing manager has to be very careful of when and how to use it.

Appropriateness of Cause-Related Promotion Tactic

The table that describes the appropriateness of the cause-related promotion tactic for each possible shopper target type and under what circumstances should be used.

Cause-related promotions are highly appropriate for loyal users as the feel-good factor that they provide to the consumers reinforces their loyalty to the brand and may push loyal users to make additional purchases.

The same is true for switchers for very similar reasons, i.e., the feel-good factor might lead them to more frequent purchases as well.

SHOPPER TARGETS	POSSIBLE PURCHASE BEHAVIOR CHANGE(S)	APPROPRIATENESS OF CAUSE-RELATED PROMOTION AS A CONSUMER PROMOTION TACTICS

Loyal users	• **Reinforce behavior** • **Increase consumption** • **Change purchase timing**	• **Very appropriate** – **Feel good factor** – **Bolsters brand against competition** – **May persuade for additional purchases**
Competitive loyals	• **Break loyalty to another brand to switch to your product**	• **Not the best target for cause-related promotions** • **Only effective when the cause is really of concern for the target**
Switchers	• **Persuade to "switch" to your product more often**	• **Excellent incentive for switchers** – **Might lead to continuous purchases**
Price buyers	• **Match their value requirements to make them stay with your product**	• **Unlikely to be affected**

Example of cause-related promotion

The example that follows illustrates a scenario in terms of shopper marketing objectives, targets, and expected purchase behavior changes. When reviewing the example, it is important to take note of the strategic thinking regarding the selected offer for the likely target customer as well as the creative execution.

(Source: Effie Awards)

The Shopper Marketing Offer and its communication

"Get an A+ in Eye Care" by Alcon (a leader in eye care solutions with category leaders such as HEeyeSOLUTION™ brands—Zaditor, Opti-free, Clear Care, Systane, and I-Caps).

When a consumer likes the "TheEyeSolution" Facebook page, Alcon donates $1 to Kids Vision for Life charity.

The cause-related promotion was complemented with coupons in the store and was communicated on the promotion Facebook page and in stores through special displays.

Marketing Strategy

The marketing strategy might be to stimulate brand loyalty in a strictly "need-based" product category (i.e., People purchase eye relief products based on what they "always buy" or what is on sale).

Shopper Marketing Objectives

- Maintain/increase purchase frequency for Alcon products
- Maintain/increase transaction size for Alcon products

Shopper Marketing Targets

- **Loyal users:** Consumers who always purchase Alcon products
- **Switchers:** Consumers who switch between Alcon and other brands—depending on the sale offer

Purchase Behavior Change – Desired Results

- **Loyal users:** Reinforce their current purchase behavior and maybe obtain additional purchases
- **Switchers:** Persuade switchers to purchase Alcon products rather than the competition when they are in an actual shopping mode for eye care products

Reward and Continuity Programs

Definition and Description

Promotion programs designed to attract and reward customers. It's about building brand loyalty!

Multiple studies have shown that brand loyalty or keeping a customer (customer retention) has a direct impact on profitability. That is why the tactic is being used by many companies and across a multitude of categories.

Across studies, it is consistently shown that acquiring a new customer is more expensive than retaining an existing one—anywhere from five to twenty-five times more.

Furthermore, according to Frederick Reichheld of Bain & Company (the inventor of the net promoter score), increasing customer retention rates by 5 percent increases profits by 25 percent to 95 percent (Reichheld 2000).

And current customers spend more. According to Marketing Metrics, the probability of selling to an existing customer is 60 to 70 percent, while the probability of selling to a new prospect is only 5 to 20 percent.

From a digital perspective, the concept of brand loyalty has extended to encompass the development of brand advocacy, which is a focus of corporate leaders worldwide. As Joe Tripodi, former Chief Marketing Officer at Coca-Cola said: "Awareness is fine, but advocacy will take your business to the next level." (Accessed at http://www.merlotmarketing.com/how-we-are-influenced-brand-advocates-are-key-to-business-success/.)

This is why corporations are investing in brand advocacy programs.

Reward and continuity programs promotion types

- **Loyalty programs**, such as airline point systems; points can be redeemed at any time or accrued
- **Reward programs** including escalating rewards and digital rewards:
  - Escalating rewards: Promotions such that the more the customer purchases the greater the reward
  - Digital rewards: Promotions handled electronically such that the rewards (a magazine subscription, music download, movie ticket) are requested, selected, and provided to the customer electronically. These types of rewards are popular because they are easy to execute and relatively inexpensive since the reward is handled electronically and does not require shipping and handling.

Now, it is very important to distinguish a loyalty program as a product benefit and a reward program as a shopper marketing tactic.

If it is a product benefit, this falls under the product management function in the marketing mix. If it is a shopper marketing tactic, this falls under shopper marketing, of course.

Loyalty programs such as airlines or credit cards' points system are part of the product management mix, with (for most of them) no time limit as long as you are a customer of such brands. They are *not* shopper marketing offers.

Rewards programs where time-limited offers are generated are shopper marketing tactics, as it is the case with the following:

- **Grocery retailing—continuity programs** with trading stamps, free turkey, free items from series, over time

or

- **Frequent-shoppers programs** with time-limited discounts on current purchases or discounts for purchases over time

The use of bright colors for reward cards in the image above has several benefits for customers. First of all, a bold color makes the card easier to find a wallet, secondly it reinforces the brand name and lastly, it reminds the customer to use it! In general, the creative look and feel of the card is simple and not busy, again, in hopes of communicating one (1) main point, that of encouraging use of it!

The most ancestral form of a shopper marketing rewards program is the punch card that a customer has to have punched every time he or she makes a purchase, and, after a set of a number of purchases, the consumer receives a gift. The process then starts again; such offers are often with a timeline attached.

Potential Applications

Shopper Marketing Rewards Programs could be used for the following applications:

- Influence purchase behavior, by motivating customers to do the following:
    - Buy more often
    - Buy for more occasions
    - Buy more from the same company

- Stimulate trial
- Enhance brand image

Important Considerations

- Loyalty programs are labor intensive to set up and require longer-term management and a serious financial commitment
- The proliferation of reward and loyalty programs has created a "blur" in the minds of consumers, so careful planning is vital in order to capture the commitment of the consumer
- Measuring return on investment is difficult, so again, careful planning is essential so that costs are controlled and thought through
- The strong appeal of the reward/higher perceived value is a plus
- Offer a range of reward options
- There need to be some aspirational rewards
- The perceived likelihood of achieving the rewards needs to be great enough
- Easy redemption is key to success
- Really strive for best value; consumers can see through a "scheme"

Appropriateness of Rewards Program Tactic

The table that follows describes the appropriateness of the rewards program tactic for each possible shopper target type and under what circumstances each should be used.

Rewards programs are highly appropriate for loyal users as they help to hook the consumers to your brand by rewarding them. The goal is to lead the customer to purchase more, more often, and more products from you.

Rewards might also be the only way to prevent or limit a switcher from switching to competitive brands.

SHOPPER TARGETS	POSSIBLE PURCHASE BEHAVIOR CHANGE(S)	APPROPRIATENESS OF REWARDS PROGRAMS AS CONSUMER PROMOTION TACTICS

Loyals users	• **Reinforce behavior** • **Increase consumption** • **Change purchase timing**	• **Once enrolled, even less likely to switch to another brand** • ***Tempted to buy more***
Competitive loyals	• **Break loyalty to another brand to switch to your product**	• **Less effective** • **Only applicable to consumers not highly loyal to a competitor**
Switchers	• **Persuade to "switch" to your product more often**	• **Highly likely to be influenced by such programs** • **Lasting effect on sales is questionable** • **Less appropriate for variety seekers**
Price buyers	• **Match their value requirements to make them stay with your product**	• **Unlikely to be tempted, unless the rewards are highly desirable**

Examples of rewards programs

Rewards Programs Examples Targeting the Consumers

The use of the Panera logo and colors for the reward card in the above image is a great way to reinforce the brand. Having uniformity of messaging across multiple platforms, as discussed earlier in this book, is critical to success. When it comes to a rewards program, simple and consistent colors and messages is helpful to keep the brand top of mind.

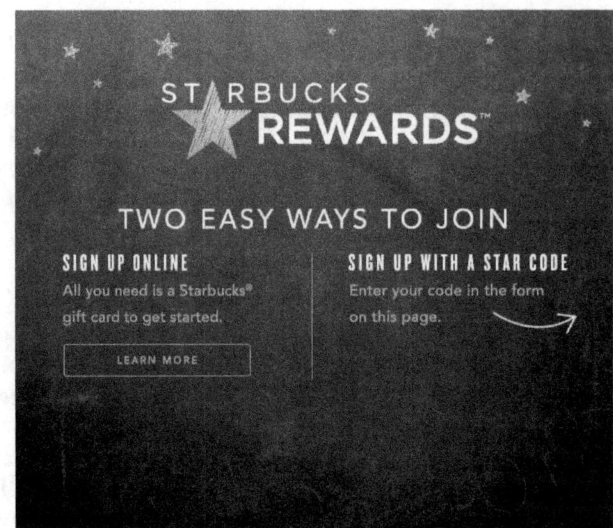

In this image, a black background with white typeface is a creative look that represents boldness, definitiveness and power. While this is true in this image, the font used softens the look so that overall, the image is designed to target a frequent user of Starbucks that is a particular type of person, one who would be attracted to the look and feel of this image. The gold stars are also a way to reach this audience who are the type of people that want to succeed and would appreciate receiving a "gold star" for excellent work. The simplistic nature of the copy points is also designed to make the point quickly and easily, again, benefits the type of customer that frequents Starbucks would want, i.e. quick service.

Case Study by Makenzi Adams

Dunkin' Donuts Rewards Program

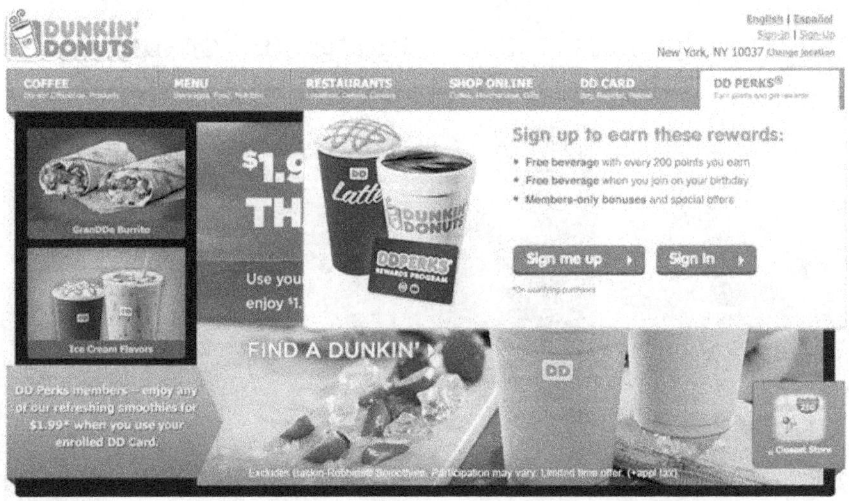

The Shopper Marketing Offer and Its Communication

"Sign up to earn these rewards: Free beverage with every 200 points you earn, free beverage when you join on your birthday, members-only bonuses and special offers." The offer was communicated on the Dunkin' Donuts website under the DD Perks tab. The offer could also be seen on the homepage of Dunkin' Donuts.

Background Info

Dunkin' Donuts, founded in 1950, is one of the top coffee and bakery companies, with more than 11,500 locations open around the world

Marketing Strategy

With this offer, Dunkin' Donuts clearly is targeting current customers to stimulate brand loyalty

Sales Marketing Objectives

- To increase purchase frequency and transaction size among current customers with an upsell and cross selling strategy

Sales Promotion Target

- **Loyal users:** Loyal users are the primary target
- **Switchers:** Among its customer base, the promotion is also targeting switchers to motivate them to choose Dunkin' Donuts more often

Purchase Behavior Change - Desired Results

- **Loyal users:** Reinforce their existing behavior and increase consumption
- **Switchers:** Persuade them to switch and then stay with Dunkin' Donuts

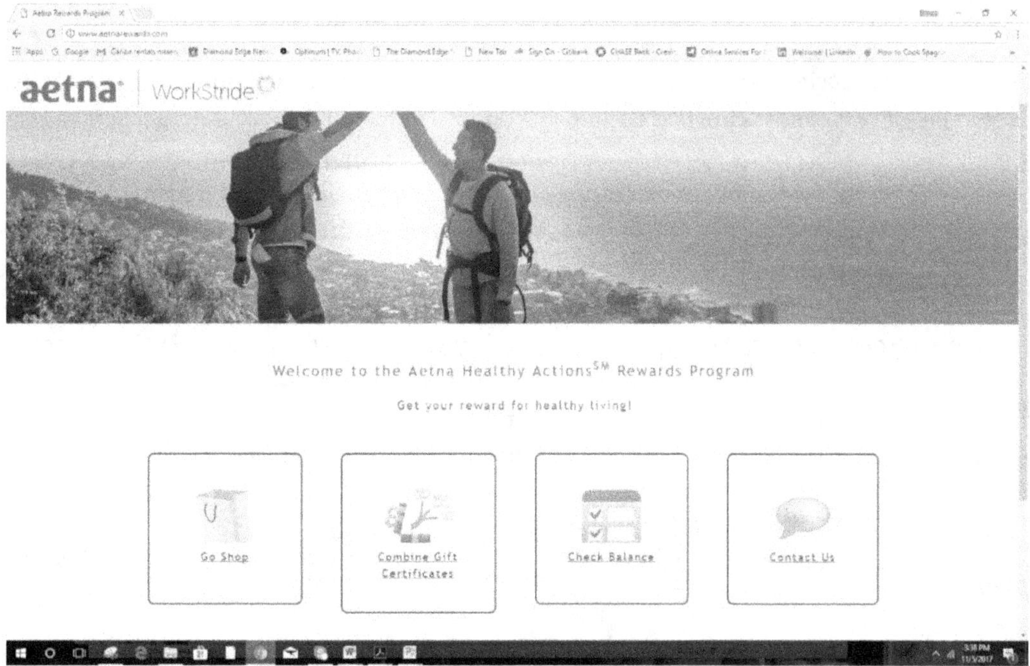

Shopper Marketing and Social Media Promotions

Definition and Description

Social media promotions are promotions executed via social media channels such as Facebook, Twitter, Instagram, Pinterest, and YouTube. Sales promotions via social media typically involve some form of interactivity with the goal of creating meaningful contact with customers. These include the following:

- Sharing
- Liking
- Submitting a review
- Competing

Social media promotions can be executed just on social media or on social media *and* traditional media. In other words, as discussed earlier in this book, traditional media, such as television can be used to drive viewers to social media to take part in a social media promotion. This is especially important because the social media promotional environment is highly cluttered, which makes it difficult to gain consumer participation. Having a solid strategy regarding how to drive participation is critical to the success of a social media promotion.

Potential Applications

A primary application of social media for sales promotion is to provide new channels to communicate the various tactics, including price and product promotions, gifts, sampling, prize promotions, and cause-related or rewards promotions.

The choice to use social media as a channel is driven by media consumption of the target customer. In fact, social media is the most effective channel to connect with a millennial's shopper target.

Other than the traditional shopper marketing objectives, with social media acting as the channel, new forms of social media promotion are emerging where the intention is to drive customer engagement and foster brand advocacy and brand loyalty. In other words, companies have shifted in how they engage with customers. As discussed earlier in this book, creating on-going, meaningful, and relevant communication with customers throughout the shopping journey is a key way to build stronger CLV (customer lifetime value) and increase revenue. One way to create the interaction is through social media promotions. As such, social media promotions can be used throughout the brand purchase continuum, from consideration to researching options, to making the purchase and, finally, providing feedback.

Advantages and Disadvantages

Advantages

- These promotions have a powerful advantage to be executed in a viral way, thereby capturing new viewers. In other words, by virtue of the simple fact that social media is inherently a "sharing" platform, it is easy and desirable for companies to add a component to the promotion, motivating consumers to share the promotion with friends. This increases participation and fosters organic growth

- There is typically a high degree of interactivity between the customer and the brand, thereby increasing consumer interest in the brand. Done correctly, the social media promotion can reinforce and enhance brand imagery
- These promotions can build a community and foster brand advocacy through on-going executions

Disadvantages

- It is difficult to measure their impact on sales
- Corporations are not totally up to speed on the value of social media and its ability to generate positive ROI (See also https://mashable.com/2009/10/27/social-media-roi/#mKX75EQSbqqt).
- Results can be marginal because exposure was insufficient and the cluttered social media channels cause diffusion of messages and lack of participation
- There is a misconception that social media promotions are a new breed of promotion and you just "do them." As discussed previously, success in this arena requires planning

Examples of social media-based shopper marketing offers

Burlington Coat Factory (Sweepstakes)

- Potential application(s):
    - Create brand engagement and excitement among consumers
    - Create "testimonials" about their products

The layout of the image is setting up an easy way to engage viewers to read the testimonials. More specifically, the photograph of each person who is bragging about what was purchased is bringing the testimonial to life and drawing in readers to motivate them to read the testimonial. The font used for the word “Brag” about it makes it very clear what the promotion is about and the orange font for the words “Win a $100” instantly communicates the benefit of bragging to the potential customer.

TD Ameritrade (Game)

- Potential application(s):
    - Generate awareness and interest in their trading platform
    - Foster brand interaction

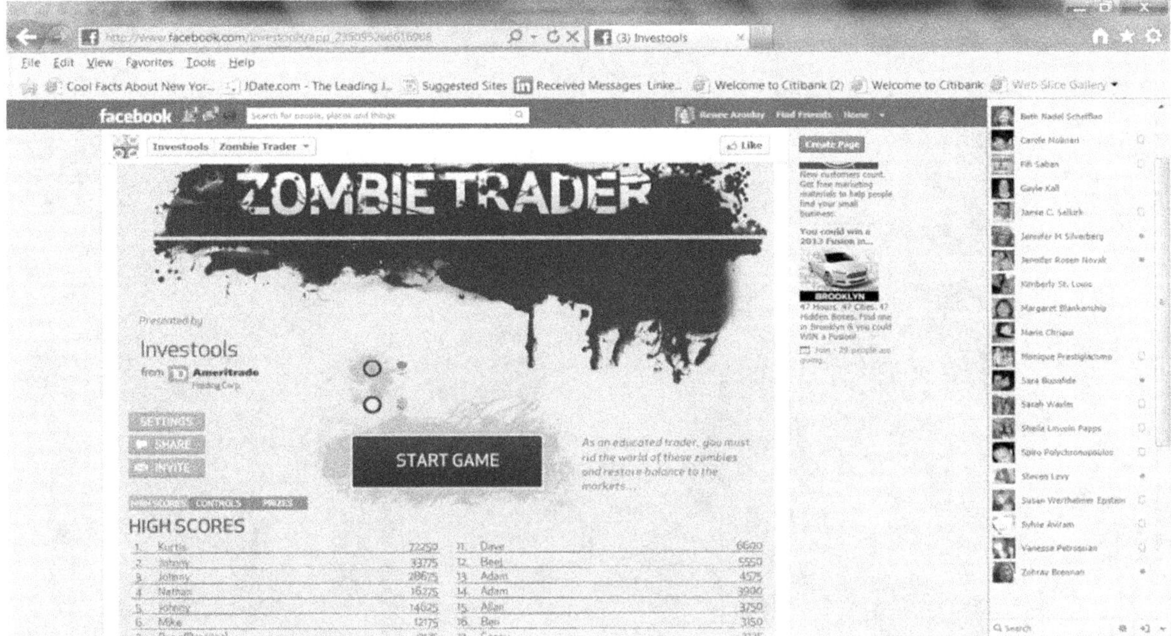

Having an understanding of the potential target audience, in this image, the sponsor has creatively applied what the target customer is interested in, namely zombies. Furthermore, the font used and the graphics potentially connoting "dripping blood" associated with zombies strongly communicates the idea and hopefully engages the target customer to play the game and learn about the sponsor's products.

Nutella (Sweepstakes)

- Potential application(s):
    - Generate awareness of a new "usage" application for Nutella spread
    - Stimulate purchase of Nutella

By using a picture of pancakes with Nutella in the image above, the consumer is being prompted to consider using Nutella in a way he/she may not have thought about before seeing the picture, hence potentially driving additional sales as this would be a new usage occasion. Furthermore, the picture of a stack of pancakes is a strong visualization of the idea.

Application Workshop

Throughout this book, you will have formal application workshops and exercises with supportive tools to help you apply the information from each chapter to your particular case or assignment. You will also have access to lists of key decisions to be made or capabilities that you need to have in place at each step of the shopper marketing planning process.

For this chapter, the workshop will expand on the analysis in which you have already engaged for your workshop in Chapter 4.

As for Chapter 4, this workshop will focus on analyzing shopper marketing campaigns or activities examples, assessing what could have been the shopper marketing objectives, shopper marketing targets behind this promotion, the changes of purchase behaviors expected from this target with this promotion, and determining the consumer promotion techniques that were used.

Now, for this workshop and based on what you have learned in this chapter, you will also need to determine if the consumer promotion techniques choices were the most appropriate for the chosen shopper marketing objectives, shopper marketing targets, and the expected changes of purchase behaviors through this campaign.

To make things more insightful, we will ask you to pick a different sales promotion example than the one that you selected for the Chapter 4 workshop. So, pick a new example from one of your recent sales promotion or shopper marketing activities or by default (and if you are a student) by going to a grocery store and finding another example of sales promotion or shopper marketing.

This promotion can include any consumer promotion techniques and can refer to any shopper marketing objectives and targets that we have seen so far.

As you have the sales promotion or shopper marketing offer example, to the best of your abilities, do the following:

- Identify what product is the subject of the promotion
- Look at the sales promotion or shopper marketing offer example:
    - What is the actual offer ("Buy One Get One Free" + a sweepstakes or just a price discount or a coupon with a refund offer for the next purchase, etc.)?
    - What are the shopper marketing objectives that are behind this offer? Are they obvious?
    - What are the shopper marketing targets that have been selected to achieve the shopper marketing objectives? Are they obvious?
    - What changes in purchase behavior do they try to obtain from the targeted shopper marketing targets? Are they obvious?
    - What specific consumer promotion techniques do they use for this promotion?
- Using your observations, **would you conclude that the brand behind the promotion selected the "correct" consumer promotion techniques** for achieving the expected changes of purchase behavior for the selected shopper marketing target(s)? If yes, how? If no, what could have been some more appropriate consumer promotion techniques for such promotion? Why?

  You might want to use the "How appropriate is each consumer price promotion tactic for each shopper marketing target (or shopper type)" tables presented in this chapter for each consumer promotion technique, to help you develop your analysis and conclusions.
- Based on this analysis, **what would you recommend** they do differently?

Conclusion

Given the proliferation of products and intense competition, coupled with the sophistication of the consumer as a buyer, the choice of what tactics to use to convince consumers to purchase has become challenging for shopper marketers.

On top of that, digital technology has added significant opportunities for companies to communicate and promote to consumers. This, in turn, has made the job of shopper marketers even harder because they have the daunting task of navigating the multitude of options and potential touchpoints along the shopping journey to "win" the customer and keep them loyal.

That is precisely why strategic thinking and planning are at the forefront of shopper marketing. In addition, success relates directly to having a thorough understanding of what consumer tactics are available as well as what each one can accomplish. Knowing how and when to use a particular tactic is of vital importance because there are an abundant number of tactics, and they are not all equal in what they can accomplish and how pertinent they are across the different shopper marketing targets and the different changes of purchase behaviors that a shopper marketing professional expects to accomplish with his or her campaign.

Planning is everything!

Chapter 6: Trade Promotion

Learning Objectives

After completing this chapter, you will be able to do the following:

- Understand the specific trade promotions tactics and why each one is used
- Understand the importance of selecting the optimal trade promotion tactics as driven by consumer promotion tactics decisions and, ultimately, by the marketing and shopper marketing objectives and targets as well as the shopper marketing campaign concept statement
- Learn how consumer and trade promotion are synchronized to create a fully integrated shopper marketing campaign.
- Learn how manufacturers and retailers form partnerships to provide mutual benefit to their respective businesses and to consumers
- Fully comprehend why strategic thinking, when it comes to the specific trade tactics, is essential to the success of a shopper marketing campaign
- Start analyzing the types and effectiveness of the trade promotion tactics used by a given brand and business as part of a shopper marketing campaign

Introduction

What Is the Chapter About?

This chapter is about the specific trade promotion tactics that manufacturers use with their retailers to ensure that such retailers support the manufacturer's consumer promotions.

When it is strategically planned, trade promotion is all about motivating the trade (the retailer) to engage in activities that are needed to support the implementation (and ultimately the success) of a consumer promotion at that same retailer.

While it is not strategically driven, per say, this is a way for the manufacturer to "tactically" boost the sales of a product to meet some sales volume objectives at specific times of the year.

In all cases, the specific tactics are explained in detail, including the types of objectives that each can potentially accomplish.

Of course, this is very important as, just like for consumer promotions, proper strategic thinking and planning drive the development of the trade promotional elements of a given shopper marketing campaign.

Why Is This Important?

Having a thorough understanding of the available trade promotion techniques will enable a shopper marketing practitioner to make the proper decisions in regards to what trade promotion tactics are the most applicable and appropriate to support the implementation of a successful consumer promotion and will generate the specific support needed from the retailer to make this happen.

Trade promotion is linked to the same unique set of shopper marketing objectives, shopper marketing targets, and purchase behavior change expectations, than the consumer promotion part of the campaign.

Key Terms

- **Joint promotion:** A promotion where two companies partner to promote their brands together for mutual benefit
- **Co-op advertising and promotion:** Manufacturers provide incentives to retailers, typically in the form of cash, in exchange for the retailer advertising the manufacturer's brand to the consumer
- **Trade promotion:** An incentive given by the manufacturer to other business stakeholders such as retailers, wholesalers, distributors, store employees, or members of a salesforce
- **Buying allowance:** Discount given by the manufacturer to the retailer on the purchase of a brand at a certain time
- **Free goods:** Additional "free" amount of the product given to the retailer with the purchase of a minimum quantity
- **Slotting allowance:** Payment made by the manufacturer to retailers for the introduction of new products at retail
- **Failure fees:** Compensation fees paid by the manufacturer to the retailer if the new product does not succeed
- **Off-invoice:** A price reduction given to the retailer by the manufacturer for a certain period of time
- **Spiff promotion:** Commissions paid by the manufacturer to sales personnel at retail, based on specific pre-determined sales goals.
- **Cash rebate:** Cash discount is given by the manufacturer to the retailer if the retailer completes the agreed-upon tasks

- **Advertising or display allowance:** A credit given by the manufacturer to the retailer for proven support of a promotion
- **Mystery shopper promotion:** A method used by companies to verify and analyze if employees selling their product or service are performing properly
- **Point of sale (POS):** Point of sale represents in-store printed materials such as window clings and displays.

An Expert's Perspective

Shopper Marketing programs take a very long time as they require a lot of planning, partnership, and coordination. Retailers can truly only support a few Shopper Marketing programs a year as they take a ton of coordination and investment from both parties. 'I want the program to get sold into the retailer'. .'If the program doesn't get sold or doesn't get put up in store, then there was no point and it was a loss.'

- Christy Pugh, Retail Activation Director at TracyLocke (1).

Key Concepts

A major focus for manufacturers

For shopper marketing, trade promotion tactics are promotional incentives directed at retailers, wholesalers, or other business buyers to ultimately stimulate immediate sales. This includes employees at the store level and/or sales personnel.

Importantly, trade promotion spending has been steadily increasing. It represents the number one controllable overhead for most businesses and is the largest share of the marketing budget.

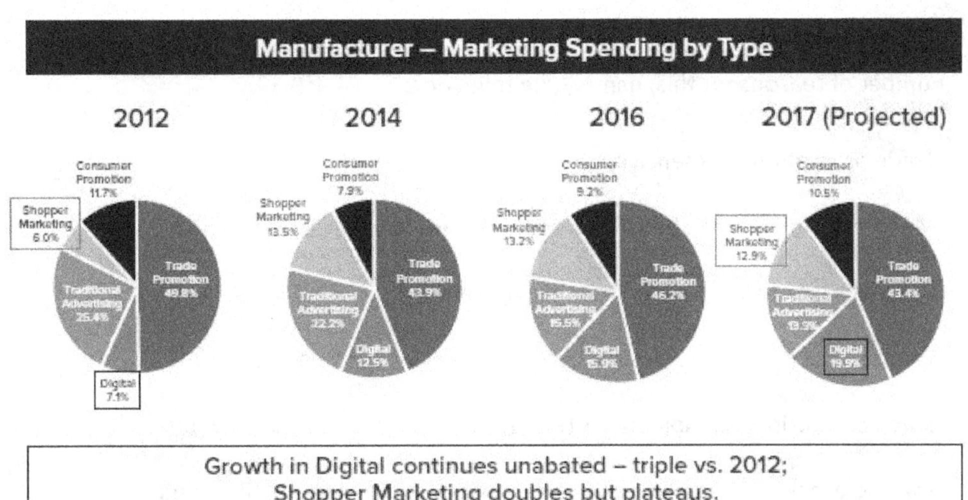

Source: Cadent Consulting Group 2017

The reasons that manufacturers must focus on the trade and why trade spending has been increasing are as follows:

- Retailers have increased power by virtue of their ability to use EPOS (electronic point of sale) systems to track sales (as discussed in previous chapters), which puts pressure on manufacturers to step up their game
- The influx and success of private label brands have taken shelf space from brand name products, thereby increasing competition for that space
- The net result for manufacturers, in order to keep selling their products, is as follows:
    - Compete for retail shelf space and promotional support
    - Keep up their level of trade promotion to remain relevant
    - Conform to the demand of retailer in terms of their particular preferences regarding the types of promotions executed and promotional material placed in their stores
    - Work to form solid productive relationships with retailers

Unfortunately ... not always profitable!

While trade promotion is a major focus for manufacturers, only a limited percent of the trade promotions ends up being profitable

According to Infosys, in 2004, consumer product goods firms in the US spent $100 billion on trade promotion, but less than 30 percent of the programs were profitable. The average return per dollar spent on promotions was about $0.65. (Accessed at https://issuu.com/manisha229249/docs/trade-promotions-management-pov).

There are a number of reasons for this, namely the following:

- Trade promotion is expensive
- Manufacturers rely too heavily on trade promotion to move merchandise
- There is a lack of accurate and timely information
- There is a lack of standardized metrics to measure performance
- Trade promotion decisions are often rushed and based on sub-par data
- There is a lack of integration both internally and with external partners
- There is a lack of cross-functional department collaboration and collaborative processes

This boils down to the fact that if a company does not plan trade promotions strategically and does not utilize processes and systems that measure its performance, trade promotion executions will remain poorly effective. (Accessed at https://en.wikipedia.org/wiki/Trade_promotion_management.)

Trade Promotion Tactics

Prevalence of price-based trade promotions

Price-based trade promotions are used to drive new product introductions, maintain or reduce inventories, maintain shelf space, and obtain promotional support and additional product facings.

They are as follows:

- **Buying allowance:** Discount on purchase of a brand at a certain time (often tied to a number of purchased units)
- **Off-invoice allowance:** Price reduction for a certain period of time
- **Free goods:** Additional "free" amount of the product with the purchase of a minimum quantity (e.g., the retailer pays regular price for a case of product and receives six free bottles).
- **Slotting allowances:** Payment made by the manufacturer to retailers for the introduction of new products at retail. These fees are charged by the retailer to "cover" the costs to integrate the product into their system and sell it
- **Failure fees:** Compensation fees (for all the pain) paid by the manufacturer to the retailer if the new product does not succeed
- **Direct price reductions:** Provided in the invoice price given by the manufacturer to the retailer. These price reductions are typically linked to a pre-set sales level
- **Returns**: Whereby the manufacturer agrees to take back unsold quantities
- **Temporary price reductions (TPR)**: Either directly or indirectly lowering the cost per unit of a product. Also called "cents off," which means the manufacturer temporarily reduces the price of a product (with the hope the discount is passed onto the consumer)
- **Dating:** Retailer obtains the merchandise and pays for it at a later date
- **Scan down/Scan backs:** A discount given to the retailer, based on effective sales during a specific period of time, as evidenced by the retailer's EPOS (electronic point of sale) scanning system

- **Cash rebate:** Cash discount if retailer completes the agreed-upon tasks such as increasing shelf space for the product or putting up a display or buying more of the product than typically purchased (stockpiling)
- **Advertising or display allowance:** Similar to a cash discount, but in the form of a credit, for proven product support by retailers for putting up a display, providing consumers with markdown/special pricing as advertised.

Also used to motivate retailers and stores' employees

Manufacturers use a variety of trade promotion tactics to increase sales by targeting store employees. The target for these promotions includes retail salespeople as well as store managers.

The goal of the promotion varies and can include the following:

- Increased sales
- Education compliance, such as viewing a training video
- Suggestive selling (suggesting a product to a customer who did not ask for it per say)

These types of promotion tactics are as follows:

- **Spiffs,** which are commissions paid to sales personnel based on specific pre-determined sales goals.
- **Mystery shopper programs** in which the manufacturer pays for people posing as shoppers to visit a retail outlet and monitor what the sales staff in the store does. If the salesperson does what he or she was required to do by the store manager, then he or she is rewarded. The action required by the salesperson can be to recommend a particular product or make suggestive sell (as previously described). The reward is a gift or cash.
- **Sales contests,** which can be executed in a variety of ways and involve rewarding "best" salespeople. The rewards can be small, such as movie tickets or large such as a trip.

Success requirements

The likelihood of trade promotions to be effective is increased when trade promotions are aligned and focused on the core marketing objectives

The manufacturer's core sales objective is to sell more products to consumers. To achieve this, the manufacturer will set specific marketing objectives against specific marketing targets. If the trade promotion focuses on helping achieve such objectives, there will a better-more aligned use of resources.

This concept is illustrated in the following table.

IF THE MANUFACTURER'S CORE OBJECTIVE(S) IS TO...	TRADE OBJECTIVES MIGHT BE TO...
Acquire new customers	Obtain more shelf space or have the store showcase the promotion in a big way, such as setting up a display or putting up posters
Acquire new customers specifically through the introduction of a new product	Establish a retail inventory, that is, get the product stocked at the store, and get the product put on the shelf.
Keep the customer loyal and/or obtain more purchases from the customer	Get the retailer to support a promotion by setting up a display or getting the product put in another area of the store, or in a prime location in the store. It might also be to get the retailer to build retail inventory, that is, buy more of the product than they typically buy
Either have existing customers purchase a new product or keep the same customers buying an existing product	Motivate, educate and/or train employees to sell more and/or learn about the product
Win customers back or combat competition or a brand decline	Maintain (as opposed to losing) shelf space or encourage the trade to maintain their level of product inventory (as opposed to buying less)
Sell through the remainder of a product to their current customers, to make room for the introduction of a new one	Reduce their inventory by selling more to the stores

The likelihood of shopper marketing campaign success is further increased when consumer and trade promotions are formally aligned and focused on the same shopper marketing objectives

As a manufacturer plans for specific consumer promotion with several consumer promotion tactics in it, it will very often—if not systematically—require specific support from the retailer.

It makes sense for the manufacturer to calibrate its trade promotion tactics to the retailer support requirements as described in the table that follows.

IF FOR YOUR CONSUMER PROMOTION, YOU NEED...	THEN...

A new slot on the shelf	A slotting allowance or a failure fee will be applicable
An intense product presence in the store	-Buying allowance -Off-invoice allowance -Free goods -Price reductions -Temporary price reductions (TPR) -Dating -Scan down/ Scan backs …will be applicable
A stockpiling, shelf-space increase, or a full product line display	A cash rebate will be appropriate
Special displays, a markdown offer advertised in the retailer's circular or a price-off shelf feature	An advertising or display allowance will be appropriate
An active support by the store staff	A spiff or mystery shopper program is applicable

These are just examples of what is needed for a retailer to make a consumer promotion successful. The bottom line is that trade promotion must be aligned with consumer promotion to make a shopper marketing campaign successful.

Maximizing use of in-store tactics

Retailers and manufacturers activate consumer promotion at the store level as ways to stimulate greater sales. Typically, the manufacturer covers a sizeable portion of the cost and the retailer provides the space in the store to conduct the activity.

These tactics are as follows:

- In-store events are activities in the store to showcase products. Specifics include the following:
    - Product sampling
    - Taste demonstrations
    - Video placement
    - Interactive experiences
    - Games and giveaways
- POS materials are placed in prominent places in the store and are called points of sale (POS). Importantly, retailers have their own policies regarding what type of POS they will permit in their stores. It is important for a shopper marketer to know what is permissible before creating the promotion materials.
    - Prominent position in the store includes the end of an aisle ("end cap" display), by the cash register and other locations that consumers pass as they shop
    - There are many forms and sizes of POS materials:

- Banners
- Window and door clings
- Mobiles
- Posters
- Displays
- Tabletop
- Moving displays
- Interactive displays
- End-aisle displays
- Signs

Manufacturer and retailer collaborations

To fuel success and based on necessity, manufacturers and retailers work together to sell products

As discussed in Chapter 1, the consumer has gained significant power along the shopping journey.

With the emergence of the Internet and digital capabilities, consumers have the power to learn about brands, make educated choices, and consequently influence manufacturers via two-way communication.

Not only can they better understand and formulate their needs through online research, guides, peer advice, and videos, but they can also compare options and prices in real time. This has added pressure to both manufacturers and retailers to provide consumers with the brands they want, with appealing offers in the places they choose to make the purchase, at the exact time they want to make the purchase and at a price they are willing to pay.

The net result from a practical standpoint is the formation of strategic alliances and partnerships between retailers and manufacturers. The goal is that by working together the manufacturer and retailer can accomplish more, namely the following:

- Increased cost efficiency
- Additional and sustained customer engagement
- Incremental revenue by driving in-store traffic and brand focus

Ultimately, the list that follows reflects the goals of each partner:

From the manufacturer's perspective

- Increase short-term volume
- Gain or retain retail distribution
- Counter-act competitive moves
- Obtain advertising and promotional support from retailers

From the retailer's perspective

Good as long as it helps the following:

- Increase store traffic
- Increase average sales volume per consumer
- Maintain or even increase profit margin

This partnership is reflective of the power shift to the consumer and has created a fundamental change in the marketing approach from a product-focused approach to a consumer-centric approach.

The concept of manufacturers and retailers working together has, in fact, been formalized into the following categories for shopper marketing:

- Joint promotions/Strategic partnerships
- Co-operative ("co-op") advertising and promotion

Joint promotions

A joint promotion is a promotion where two partners promote their brands together for mutual benefit.

In the joint relationship, one company is a manufacturer and the other is

- the retailer,
- a different manufacturer, or
- a different brand from the same manufacturer.

For example, the manufacturer is a manufacturer of shampoo. The joint partnership can be one of the following:

- CVS, the drug store chain
- A brand of hair conditioner from a different manufacturer

- A brand of conditioner from the same manufacturer

These types of promotions provide multiple advantages:

- The costs for creative development, advertising, and execution are shared between the partners. This, in turn, makes it theoretically easier for each partner to increase return on investment because it costs less to do the promotion
- The promotion has additional exposure because partners can build on one another's customer base, meaning the partners can share databases so that more potential customers are exposed to the promotion. This extends to cross advertising, meaning the advertising of the promotion is executed by both partners. In the case of the previous example, CVS would advertise the promotion in store and the shampoo manufacturer might advertise via social media or newspaper, driving customers to CVS. This, in turn, also theoretically increases the potential for greater revenues.
- Partners can gain beneficial support from the positive brand equity of each party, meaning if the brands have stronger brand affinity among consumers, then both brands benefit by being associated with each other.
- The risks of doing the promotion are shared between the parties as opposed to one company taking all the risk.

Examples

Retailer and Manufacturer—Joint Promotions

TARGET COUPON EXPIRES 6/30/10

Limit one item or offer per coupon. Void if copied, transferred, purchased, sold or prohibited by law. No cash value.

TARGET.

9856-0112-2540-8227-0329-1018-17

The above two (2) images reflect the joint partnership in terms of logo placement, color and font. More specifically, the Nickelodeon logo is on the front of the offer and the Target logo on the back with both logos relatively the same size. In addition, the creative use of blue and yellow makes the offer ($1.00 off) stand out. Importantly, the orange typeface for Nickelodeon and red typeface for Target work to clearly differentiate the brand names from the offer itself. The creative combination of colors works to motivate product purchase while simultaneously showcasing the partnership without making the partnership the central focus and instead making the offer the central focus. This in turn incentivizes consumer purchase and enhances both brands at the same time.

In the image above, the sponsor's name (Nickelodeon) stands out on the purple background. Once the eye focusses on the Nickelodeon name in both places (on top and then half way down), the Target logo stands out as it is in red and placed directly adjacent to the Nickelodeon name. This layout and design works to draw the consumer in both from a visual standpoint and also because the brand names are strong and there are two (2) of them, not just one (1). Once focused on the brand names the consumer can read the offer of a sweepstakes and take the action requested, i.e. to enter the sweepstakes at the URL provided. Also noteworthy is the fact that the URL has both sponsor names in it, again reinforcing the partnership.

Two Different Manufacturers—Joint Promotion

As shown in the image above, by placing a coupon directly on another product helps motivate purchase of both products. More specifically, the sponsors join together to share the benefits and costs of promoting to a similar target audience.

Co-operative Advertising and Promotion

Co-op advertising and promotion is manufacturers providing allowances, typically in the form of cash to retailers, in exchange for the retailer advertising the manufacturer's brand to the consumer. Importantly part of the "co-op allowance" arrangement is that the retailer places the sponsored brand in a prominent position in that advertising.

Manufacturers often make demands in terms of the creative direction for the advertising and the location of the advertising.

Manufacturers also provide allowances (cash) to retailers for promotion programs to be executed jointly for their mutual benefit. Importantly, the link between a "brand" and product(s) offered by the retailer should be one(s) that complement the sponsoring brand. Promotional costs are shared; this is an attractive set up for manufacturers and retailers.

Selecting the right partner

There are clear and powerful advantages to create partnerships. While this is true, it takes time and commitment to do so successfully. There are important considerations, as detailed next, that if followed, can increase success and revenues.

Look for partners that complement one another.

Partner selection involves thinking about synergies. Synergies deal with whether the partners good for one another. It means looking for brands where their images are complementary and work well together.

Ask yourself: Can working together achieve benefits in addition to cost savings? This is a very important consideration because although cost savings is the main reason to find a partner, partnering with the wrong company can have serious negative implications for the brand(s). Conversely, if the brands fit together naturally, the added benefits are many.

In addition to cost savings, a good fit will enhance the brand equity of both partners. It will also offer additional exposure for each brand. The relationship between the partners will be strengthened, which can lead to future partnerships and opportunities.

Negative implications include detracting from a brand's image. If the brands do not fit well together, that bad fit rubs off on the brands themselves. Negative implications also include eroding of confidence and trust in the brand; again, if the brands do not fit well together, the result can be a weakening of brand trust. Lastly, a bad fit can result in frictions among the companies' managers. This, in turn, can damage the overall working relationship.

Partnership has to make sense to the target customers

The fit between partners must be natural and logical. While it may be easy to find a partner who is willing to share costs, it is an entirely different mission to find an appropriate partner. Let's say the retailer is a sporting goods outlet and the manufacturer is a sock manufacturer. Even though they could very well partner, it may not make sense because the type of sock is not thought of by a consumer as a sporting sock but rather a casual sock. While it could be possible that these two companies could partner and sell the sock at the sporting goods retailer and share the cost of promotion, it would not be a good fit and could actually detract from brand images because consumers do not buy casual socks at a sporting goods retailer. If, on the other hand, the retailer is a department store, the fit would be better.

Stronger together?

After a partner is selected, be sure the partners are in fact, stronger together. What is meant here is that a partnership should be created so that the idea of "the sum is greater than the parts" is true. In other words, as will be explained in the next section, there is a considerable investment in terms of time and effort required to develop and execute joint promotions, so it is important to use resources properly to create partnerships that result in "more together" than each would alone.

Know when to wait

If there isn't enough time, it's better to wait until there is time to execute properly

Consumers are savvy, as discussed earlier in this book. They are able to execute research and compare products and offers. Similarly, they are able to detect nuances and offers that are illogical and/or poorly executed. If a joint promotion has been rushed, due to a lack of time, the resulting execution could be faulty in some way. This fault could be detected by consumers, which can result in negative publicity in addition to a weakening of the brand image, both of which are difficult to correct. A better solution is to create partnerships with the time required to do a good job.

Doing It Right

The process of setting up these partnerships/arrangements is cumbersome, largely because there are more people involved. Remember there are members of both companies who must review and agree on the joint partner creative and execution details. They must also jointly agree on the division of labor, that is, which partner is responsible to provide the manpower and which partner is responsible for the funding of which parts of the campaign.

These details take time to work through. It is also important that there is a commitment by both companies to see to it that the campaign is supported so that it has the greatest chances of success. If one partner is not as committed as the other, this could detract from success because of time delays and lack of attention to the project. Therefore, it is important that before the relationship is solidified, the partners make a commitment to the campaign's success.

Give-and-take

As is the case with any relationship, flexibility with a give-and-take attitude is a vital element in the formation of joint partnerships. Both partners must feel the partnership is beneficial to their end goals.

The members of the teams from both companies are best served to approach each other with an open mind, a willingness to collaborate and an eye toward success for *both* companies.

The negotiation of the specific terms of the arrangement will then be much easier to accomplish and hopefully, the partnership and resulting campaign will be more successful.

Here is an example from Friendship Dairies cottage cheese illustrating how they developed a consumer promotion campaign to revamp their sales at ShopRite and how they were able to have ShopRite fully supporting their Shopper Marketing campaign outside and inside the stores

Case Study:
Bringing Shopper Marketing To Life

CASE STUDY

2017 SILVER SHOPPER MARKETING EFFIE AWARD WINNER

"ShopRite Mix-In Matchmaker Program"

Friendship Dairies cottage cheese developed and led a multi-partner, cross-category shopper marketing program for ShopRite. Called 'Mix-In Matchmaker,' it encouraged the grocer's highly coveted healthy food shopper segment to discover surprising, new ways to combine Friendship Dairies cottage cheese with other healthy foods to expand their restless palates and enliven their food journeys. This resulted in a 12% increase in spending by health-focused shoppers. Brand sales grew 8.3%, with a 60% repeat rate by new customers. ShopRite loved the promotion so much they adopted their own recurring version of it.

COMPETITION:
Shopper Marketing Effie Awards

Ran in:
USA

CATEGORY:
Single-Retailer Program: Supermarkets

BRAND/CLIENT:
Friendship Dairies cottage cheese/ Saputo Dairy Foods

LEAD AGENCY:
Partners + Napier

CONTRIBUTING COMPANY:
Wakefern Food Corporation/ MyWebGrocer/ RDD Associates

PRODUCT/SERVICE:
Cottage Cheese

CLASSIFICATION:
Regional

DATES EFFORT RAN:
September 27, 2015 - October 24, 2015

PROGRAM ORGIN:
Brand Driven

CREDITS:
Rachel Ballatori
Carol Heyducek
Michael Kennedy
Ray Langton
Ron Manley
Jennifer Piper
Cindy Rogers
Greg Smith
John Tillstrom
Scott Wolf

Version: Original

Executive Summary

The Challenge

In spite of the cottage cheese category's 40-year, 50% decline, we needed to position Friendship Dairies cottage cheese as the unlikely hero to help ShopRite get a highly coveted, high-spending shopper segment who had been filling their healthy food needs at alternate food stores to shift spending to ShopRite.

The Idea

This shopper segment wants healthy, satisfying foods that allow for creativity and customization so we created the Mix-In Matchmaker - a partnership program that provides incentive and inspiration to try new healthy food combinations with an exclusive ShopRite offer.

Bringing the Idea to Life

Using digital, social and in-store activation, we launched the Mix-In Matchmaker promotion exclusively at ShopRite to open shoppers' minds to unique ways to eat Friendship Dairies cottage cheese and position it as the ideal base food for healthy eating experimentation and satisfaction.

The Results

Mix-In Matchmaker exceeded goals for new brand purchasers and post-program repeat rate while increasing total trip spending - inspiring ShopRite to adopt the program as a permanent promotion.

Effie Awards Category Context

Friendship Dairies cottage cheese – yes cottage cheese, your grandma's diet food – developed and led a multi-partner, cross-category shopper marketing program for ShopRite called the Mix-In Matchmaker that delivered an increase in spending among the retailer's coveted healthy food shopper segment. It brought new cottage cheese fans to the category and achieved significant repeat purchase rates by new Friendship Dairies brand purchasers. All of this was accomplished in a category that's been in decline for the last 40 years.

State of the Marketplace & Brand's Business

Too many think of cottage cheese as a dying category, an unappetizing diet food that grandmas eat. Since 1975 total consumed volume had dropped more than 50%. The category is now share-led by private label with shoppers buying on price alone.

In 2014, Friendship Dairies recognized consumers' changing eating habits, including a greater desire for healthy, simple snacks as meal replacement. Friendship Dairies determined the time was right to breathe new life into this dying category. Their efforts were working, with cottage cheese sales posting double digit growth, outpacing the competition, gaining category share and driving previously unseen upticks in category growth with each of its key retailers.

Except at ShopRite – an incredibly important retail partner responsible for a significant part of total brand volume. Here, Friendship Dairies cottage cheese sales had increased notably less than the double-digit growth achieved elsewhere. The national market leader was outperforming our brand on the back of its latest product introduction. While its sales were increasing, Friendship Dairies share had dropped at ShopRite.

At the same time, ShopRite was losing share of grocery-buying trips and shopper dollars to value channels and premium, health-oriented retailers like Whole Foods and Trader Joe's. Add to that, Friendship Dairies was pinched by its refrigeration- required dairy case location where the Greek yogurt wave had usurped virtually all co-marketing attention and opportunity. Against that backdrop, Friendship Dairies set out to create and execute a program that would change shoppers' minds about cottage cheese, deliver greater spending by ShopRite's coveted, defecting healthy food shopper segment and reverse our brand share decline.

Shopper Segment

The shopper segment targeted are selective in what they feed their families; they prefer to purchase high-quality, healthful foods. They are ShopRite's greatest "foodies." They also shop for groceries at Wegmans, Whole Foods, Trader Joe's and independent food channels.

Through third-party research, we uncovered a common motivation for this shopper: "Exploring food is one of the many ways I express who I am." They use snacking to fuel their day but also to relieve stress or boredom. They seek flavors that are different and new. Discovery is important and they are proud to promote "food finds" to others. They are not afraid to follow their own preferences and go against the mainstream.

Only 20% of this audience had purchased cottage cheese at ShopRite in the prior year. Considering the health benefits and customization possibilities of Friendship Dairies cottage cheese, we knew we had something for them to discover.

Reminder: Entrants will copy their answers into the entry form in the online entry area for judging purposes – this document will not be uploaded for judging. Use this form to draft your responses and collaborate with team members.

Objectives & KPI's

For ShopRite, our goal for the Mix-In Matchmaker program was to provide our target shoppers with an inspiring new eating alternative, capturing more total healthy food spending.

Not only did we want to encourage new purchasers to discover how Friendship Dairies cottage cheese fits into their healthy, creative eating lifestyle, we wanted them to repeat purchase after the program ended. We set goals for new Friendship Dairies cottage cheese purchasers and repeat purchase incidence.

By bringing these new, retained shoppers to the category we would achieve a reverse in our declining share, which we could attribute to category growth versus share stealing.

Shopper Insight

Shopper Insight: The foods I buy and eat are a big part of my overall journey to being the person I want to be.

This audience eats and shops for simple, healthy, satisfying foods with versatility. They have a restless palate, constantly looking to discover and try new things. They are also eating more, smaller, snack-type meals throughout the day, which in itself is an ongoing effort and expression of who they are working to be.

Friendship Dairies cottage cheese is well-suited to deliver in this high-requirement food routine, but these shoppers only saw barriers to purchasing it.

They did not consider it a worthwhile, newsworthy discovery or a platform for creative eating. They saw cottage cheese as a forgettable, unappetizing diet food for old folks on par with medicine.

We wanted their shopping action to reflect a radical mind shift: "Exploring food is one of the many ways I express who I am and I am proud to use Friendship Dairies cottage cheese as a new way to do that."

The Big Idea

In order to shift perception that Friendship Dairies cottage cheese is a forgettable old folks food to a surprisingly enlivened reflection of the person I want to be, we will create a partnership program that provides incentive and inspiration to try new healthy food combinations with an exclusive ShopRite offer.

Bringing the Idea to Life

The foundation for the Mix-In Matchmaker program was a partnership led by Friendship Dairies cottage cheese. We brought together Bear Naked Granola, Dole Wildly Nutritious Signature Blends frozen fruit, Dole Power Up Greens, Dole Pineapple and ShopRite Almonds with Friendship Dairies cottage cheese to inspire shoppers to discover and try interesting food combinations for delicious, quick, healthy snacks or mini-meals.

Pre-store:

ShopRite healthy food shoppers were targeted in pre-store planning mode where they accumulate inspiration and make shopping lists. Pre-store media included ShopRite subscriber emails, weekly circulars, digital displays, social media and a landing page feature at ShopRite.com. The goal of this outreach was to get the participating brands on the shopper's list and drive them to ShopRite to make a purchase. These elements were chosen because they are the primary communication vehicles used by ShopRite to announce offers and retailer programs to their loyalty card holders.

The program's landing page on ShopRite.com served as a program hub filled with inspirational content. Friendship Dairies cottage cheese recipes such as Protein Power Breakfast Bowls and Supercharged Green Smoothies were featured, each of which included a combination of Mix-in Matchmaker participant items as ingredients. All participant items were presented with an "add to shopping list" function to drive the pre-store behavior of adding the items to shoppers' lists. And in a highly engaging twist, the program's landing page on ShopRite.com included a content well that linked to a fun, branded interactive experience: the Friendship Dairies Superfood Generator. This tool inspired users to explore, create and share cottage cheese mix-in combinations using 99 different ingredient variables.

In-store:

In-store, shoppers were targeted via demos and case cards with take-ones at the in-store dietitian counter. Shelf signage at each item location also guided shoppers through the store to easily locate the participating items. The in-store elements drove trial, incentivized purchase, and guided shoppers to participating brands to fulfill their health-food shopping needs all at ShopRite.

Messaging:

To drive sales, each element included an offer to Save $5 with the purchase of any five participating Mix-in Matchmaker items. Shoppers redeemed the offer by purchasing these items with their ShopRite PricePlus Club loyalty card. This offer was good for the first week of the 4 week program.

Reminder: Entrants will copy their answers into the entry form in the online entry area for judging purposes – this document will not be uploaded for judging. Use this form to draft your responses and collaborate with team members.

Across print communications, a leading health benefit for each participating food brand was featured, along with creative suggestions to inspire shoppers to integrate the items into their everyday eating habits and onto their shopping lists. These communications were purposefully open-ended and non-prescriptive in advising how to combine the participant items, based on the insight that our healthy shopper segment looks to create and explore food in their own, unique ways.

Results

The program increased healthy food spending by ShopRite's target shoppers. Based on this success, ShopRite developed its own recurring, cross-category event modeled after the 'Mix-in Matchmaker' program. They liked the program so much, they wanted to make it their own!

We exceeded our goals to attract new purchasers and retain this target shopper to the Friendship brand.

Digital engagement results further demonstrate the program's success with the target shopper segment.

- The percent of 'Mix-in Matchmaker' ad clicks that resulted in an "add-to-shopping list" action outperformed benchmarks for ShopRite.com.
- Of shoppers taking the "add-to-shopping" list action, 46% added two or more 'Mix-In Matchmaker' participant items to their lists.

Ultimately Friendship Dairies cottage cheese achieved long-term category growth and brand impact. Driven by new and repeat users, the cottage cheese category at ShopRite was up vs. YAG and Friendship Dairies volume growth outpaced the category over that time period. Friendship Dairies also reversed its share of category decline at ShopRite.

To obtain all the Pre-store communications supports from ShopRite, Friendship Dairies had to offer at least some Advertising Allowances as Trade Promotion incentives to ShopRite. For the In-Store communications, Friendship Dairies had to offer some Advertising Allowances and Display Allowances to ShopRite.

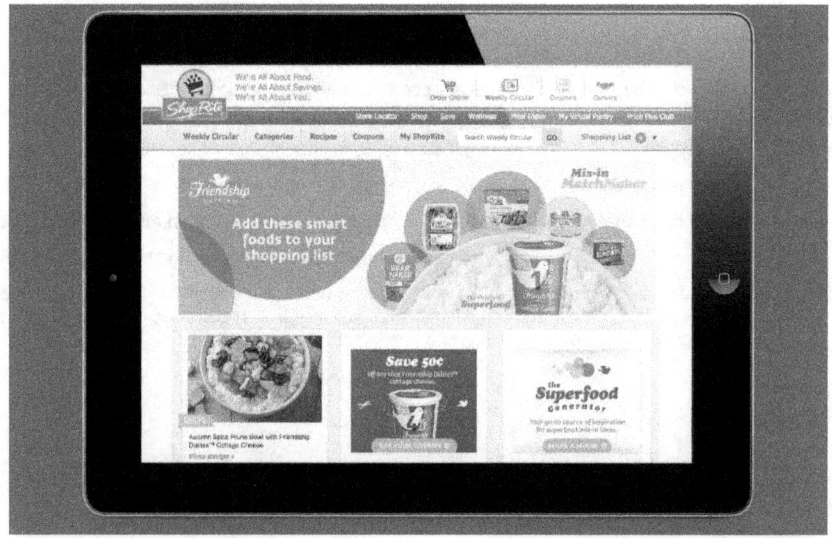

It is also probable that they also had to give to some buying allowance or off-Invoice allowance or Temporary Price Reductions (TPR) or even a cash rebate, to ensure that ShopRite will be motivated to have a high volume of their products in their warehouse and therefore, to push the products out of the warehouse as fast as possible.

Application Workshop

Throughout this book, you will have formal application workshops and exercises with supportive tools to help you apply the information from each chapter to your particular case or assignment. You will also have access to lists of key decisions to be made or capabilities that you need to have in place at each step of the shopper marketing planning process.

For this chapter, the workshop will expand on the analysis in which you have already engaged for your workshop in Chapters 4 and 5.

This workshop will focus on analyzing shopper marketing campaigns or activities examples by determining the consumer promotion techniques that were used as well as the communication activities selected to communicate an offer.

Now, for this workshop and based on what you have learned in this chapter, you will also assess the trade promotion techniques that you think were used for this shopper marketing promotion campaign.

To make things more insightful, we will ask you to pick a different consumer promotion example than the one that you selected for Chapters 4 and 5 workshops. So, pick a new example from one of your recent sales promotion or shopper marketing activities or by default (and if you are a student) by going to a grocery store and finding another example of sales promotion or shopper marketing.

To make the analysis applicable, be sure to pick a sales promotion example from a good consumer manufacturer at a retailer, not directly from a retailer.

As you have the Sales Promotion or Shopper Marketing offer example, to the best of your ability, do the following:

- Identify what product is the subject of the promotion
- Look at the sales promotion or shopper marketing offer example
  - What is the actual offer (Buy One Get One Free + a sweepstakes or just a price discount or a coupon with a refund offer for the next purchase, etc.)?
  - What are the communication activities used to promote this shopper marketing campaign outside and inside the store?
  - What specific consumer promotion techniques do they use for this promotion?
- Using your observations, what do you think were the possible trade promotion techniques used by the manufacturer for this shopper marketing promotion?

A good process to develop such analysis is to use the following table as your reference—where you identify the type of support that the manufacturer needed from the retailers (on the left side) and determine accordingly the trade promotion techniques that were potentially used with the retailer to obtain such support (on the right side).

IF FOR YOUR CONSUMER PROMOTION, YOU NEED...	THEN...
A new slot on the shelf	A slotting allowance or a failure fee will be applicable
An intense product presence in the store	-Buying allowance -Off-invoice allowance -Free goods -Price reductions

	-Temporary price reductions (TPR) -Dating -Scan down/Scan backs …will be applicable
A stockpiling—shelf space increase or a full product line display	A cash rebate will be appropriate
Special displays, a markdown offer advertised in the retailer's circular, or a price-off-shelf feature	An advertising or display allowance will be appropriate
An active support by the store staff	A spiff or mystery shopper program is applicable

Conclusion

As discussed in Chapter 5, given the proliferation of products and intense competition, coupled with the sophistication of the consumer as a buyer, the choice of what tactics to use to convince consumers to purchase has become challenging for shopper marketers.

That is precisely why strategic thinking and planning are at the forefront of shopper marketing. In addition, success relates directly to having a thorough understanding of what consumer and trade tactics are available as well as what each one can accomplish.

Adding further complexity is the fact that retailers are shopper marketers in their own right and execute campaigns as well as measure success. This, in turn, adds even more options for shopper marketers and increases the sheer number of potential tactics as companies compete for buyers. Furthermore, retailers and manufacturers pool resources and form partnerships in order to capture consumer attention, involvement, and, ultimately, sales. In doing so, selecting the right partner and creating the working arrangement requires time, commitment, strategy, and planning.

Ultimately, it is through the support of the trade to accept and showcase the shopper marketing campaign in combination with the incentive for consumers to make the purchase that a shopper marketing campaign has the greatest chances of driving sales.

(1) 2017 Shopper Marketing Survey with shopper marketing agencies representatives – Conducted by Professor Jean Marc Rejaud

Chapters 7: Shopper Marketing and Profitability Requirements

Learning Objectives

After completing this chapter, you will be able to do the following:

- Understand why profitability has become a requirement for any shopper marketing campaign
- Understand the various profitability calculation methods to estimate the profitability of a shopper marketing campaign
- Learn the decision criteria to make actual go/no-go decisions for shopper marketing campaigns
- Fully comprehend how to use such methods and decision criteria to make profitability-based decisions for new shopper marketing campaigns and analyze the actual results of the same campaigns once implemented
- Start practicing profitability analysis for shopper marketing campaigns

Introduction

What Is the Chapter About?

This chapter is about the requirement and goal that shopper marketing campaigns be profitable and about how profitability should be calculated and analyzed through a variety of methods.

This chapter will review the concept of profitability for a shopper marketing campaign and explain the different profitability calculation methods that can be used to decide whether to execute a particular campaign as well as analyze the results.

Why Is This Important?

As outlined earlier in this book, using sales promotions for tactical purposes has been replaced by the disciplined and strategic approach of shopper marketing and the use of many techniques. Along the same lines, the idea of seeing a quick boost in sales is no longer enough.

As companies face increased pressure from competition and the proliferation of new products coupled with lowering margins, shareholders are demanding a positive return on investment (increased profits). This requirement has extended to shopper marketing campaigns that are now looked at as investments where a positive return is expected.

In addition, the focus for measurement is no longer only on the short term, but also on the long-term impact. This is because the importance of relationship marketing and lifetime value has grown and continues to grow for an increased number of brands.

Therefore, it is of utmost importance for the shopper marketing professional to understand, master, and apply profitability calculations for all shopper marketing campaigns, both as tools to make the "go/no-go" decisions to execute the campaign as well as analyze campaign effectiveness.

Key Terms

- **Lifetime value:** Lifetime value is the dollar value calculated after all the revenues that a customer will bring and all the costs that will be generated by that same customer, over his or her lifetime with a product, are integrated.
- **Marginal profit:** Marginal profit is the profit calculated by subtracting the campaign costs (and just those costs; no cost for processing the order, for example, or no cost for providing customer service support to the customer, as another example) from the additional sales revenues generated by the campaign.
- **Variable contribution:** The variable contribution is basically the profit that a consumer will bring over time to a business or product when the fixed costs are considered sunk (happening anyway, so with no need to count them again for a specific campaign); therefore, only the variable costs are considered in the analysis. In that case, costs, such as production cost or other administrative costs directly linked to the products sold by the promotion, are included into the calculation as opposed to just the sales promotion costs as it is the case for the marginal profit calculation.
- **Net present value:** The net present value in the lifetime value calculation reflects the current (present) value of the future costs and revenues that a customer will generate over his or her lifetime. The difference between the "present" value of all revenues and

the "present" value of all costs is the net present value. The goal is for the net present value to be positive.

- **Return on investment (ROI):** "A performance measure used to evaluate the efficiency of an investment or to compare the efficiency of a number of different investments. ROI measures the amount of return on an investment relative to the investment's cost." (Accessed at https://www.investopedia.com/terms/r/returnoninvestment.asp?o=40186&l=dir&qsrc=999&qo=inve). Success is a positive ROI such that the revenue generated exceeds the costs.
- **Pay-back period:** Payback period in capital budgeting refers to "the period of time required to recoup the funds expended in an investment" or to reach the break-even point.
- **Benchmark:** A standard or point of reference against which activities may be compared or assessed. In the case of shopper marketing profitability analysis, this could be a certain level of ROI or a minimum variable contribution value against which future activities are compared.
- **Baseline:** A minimum or starting point used for comparisons. For shopper marketing, this could mean the last year's sales at the same time that the shopper marketing campaign is being run or the same promotion executed at a previous time (e.g., six months or a year ago). This is called a "baseline" for estimating the sales growth with the campaign.

An Expert's Perspective

The ultimate goal of any Shopper Marketing activity is to drive a change in people's behavior when they are in shopping mode, that results in increased conversion. But there's more to ROI than pure sales. We should also look to evaluate the impact of programs in terms of shopper behavior, customer/ channel variances, and tactic effectiveness. Beyond informing continuous improvement at a program level, it is also important to look at the impact in the longer term, through the broader lens of: commercial performance, brand impact and executional effectiveness.

- Jonathan Dodd, Global Chief Strategy Officer, Geometry

Key Concepts

Profitability Is a Requirement for Shopper Marketing

Sales promotion activities, such as those used in the past (often coupons), had a focus on a short-term sales volume boost, meaning to achieve immediate sales. No concern was expressed regarding sales gains (or losses) after the promotion period (i.e., in the long term).

The tendency was to use sales promotions to boost sales volume. An example of this might have been to use a coupon to show a good quarterly return to investors.

Another example might be to counter a competitor's move with a new product launch by increasing retail presence and shelf space at the time of the competitor's launch. But, in that case, the focus was on not losing market sales in the short term—without necessarily gaining profit or understanding the long-term impact of the promotion.

While those may have been good reasons to use sales promotion in the past, that is no longer true. This is due to the fact that sales promotion has morphed into shopper marketing and the responsibility for it has moved from sales departments to marketing communication departments, requiring financial contribution and brand building.

As a strategically-driven discipline, shopper marketing requires having pre- and post-campaign profitability analysis to ensure that while providing a boost in sales, a shopper marketing campaign actually contributes to the profitable growth of a product or a business over time. Said another way, it is not enough that the campaign drives a higher sales volume during the promotion period, but then sales drop off after the promotion period to what they had been before the promotion or even less than what they had been before the promotion. The promotion must optimally contribute to brand growth.

Importantly, with the increasing access to specific sales and consumer behavior data, the ability to calculate profitability has dramatically improved, thereby making analysis and the goal to be profitable a key shopper marketing imperative.

Short-Term and Long-Term Profitability

While the notion of profitability is now core to shopper marketing campaigns, the definition of profitability is "unique" in the shopper marketing context because these campaigns come on top all other marketing activities, with the goal of boosting sales during the time of the promotion. As such, shopper marketing profitability should be looked at in relationship to the specific **additional** sales and **additional** costs that a shopper marketing campaign generates.

The typical costs associated with a shopper marketing campaign are as follows:

- Time and manpower to develop the campaign strategy
- Time and manpower to develop the campaign creative assets

- Production costs for the communication materials (leaflets, etc.)
- Execution costs such as manpower to give out samples
- The cost associated with the offer (prizes for a sweepstakes or contest, samples, gifts, refunds, trade promotion costs, etc.)
- Legal expenses (for example, the rules for a sweepstakes or contest)

The first step in analyzing profitability is to determine the costs. Then the profitability of the campaign can be calculated.

Profitability of a shopper marketing campaign can be analyzed in two ways: short term and long term.

Short Term

Short term relates to the sales and profit impact of a shopper marketing campaign from the time it is launched until up to a few weeks or months after its launch. The short-term focus is typically what we call "during the promotion," meaning the sales results from immediately before the campaign launch until right after it ends. This is a measurement to show what the immediate impact of the campaign is on sales. It is focused on the incremental sales and costs generated by the campaign during the campaign. As stated earlier, while short term is important, it is not enough. Practitioners must be concerned with the impact of the campaign on the long-term results for the brand.

There is one key method to calculate the profitability of a shopper marketing campaign in terms of short-term focus: marginal profit analysis.

- Marginal profit is the profit calculated by subtracting the campaign costs from the additional sales revenues generated by the campaign. It is not desirable for the incremental sales revenues to be lower than the campaign costs, as this means monetary loss.

It is possible that a brand may face challenging situations and a shopper marketing campaign is used to boost sales for a short time period, even though the overall profit does not go up.

Long Term

Long-term relates to the sales and profit impact of a shopper marketing campaign after it has been executed and concluded.

- The long-term focus is typically what we call "after the promotion," meaning the sales results from before the campaign launch until a designated time period in the future after it ends. This is a measurement to show what the long-term impact of the campaign is on sales and profitability. It is focused on the incremental sales and costs generated by the campaign after the campaign is over.

- These effects might relate, for example, to the fact that the target shopper changes his or her purchase behavior for a longer period than just the shopper marketing campaign period—perhaps even permanently. As such, this change in behavior can be attributed to the shopper marketing campaign. The long-term impact could also be linked, for example, to the fact that a shopper marketing campaign brings new customers who, over time, start to purchase more products from the same brand.
- Taking a long-term profitability analysis, there are two methods to calculate the profitability of a Shopper Marketing campaign: variable contribution analysis and lifetime value analysis.

Variable Contribution Analysis

The variable contribution is basically the profit that an individual consumer will bring over time to a business when the fixed costs are considered sunk (happening anyway, so no need to count them again for a specific campaign that comes on the top of other marketing activities); therefore, only the variable costs are considered in the analysis. This method enables the shopper marketer to apply a simple calculation (as only the variable costs are included) while still integrating the long-term impact of a campaign.

This method is highly suitable for new customer acquisition and gauging the value of their purchases over time. An example would be the acquisition of new credit card members and then basing profitability on these customers using their credit card over time for multiple purchases so that profit will be generated. The variable contribution will be calculated to reflect the profit contribution that each new customer will bring over time—after variable costs.

There are different ways to calculate variable contribution, and they are easy to find on the Internet. In most cases, the variable contribution per customer will be calculated by your finance department.

For this method, you will simply subtract the cost of your shopper marketing campaign from the variable contribution (before your campaign costs). The goal is for this to be a positive number.

Lifetime (and Net Present) Value Analysis

Lifetime value is the dollar value of a customer based on the total revenue that this customer brings to your company over the course of his/her lifetime, minus the costs of selling and serving that customer over his/her lifetime.

The notion of lifetime varies by product category. For example, a consumer will keep his or her credit card for five years on average, so the lifetime value will be calculated for a five-year period. For an automobile, the lifetime value is much longer (thirty-plus years), with longer time intervals between purchases.

The value generated by the consumer over his or her lifetime will be calculated, taking into account all costs associated with that customer and all future revenues from repeat purchases of the same product and purchase of other products from the same business.

A present value calculation will then be applied to reflect the value of those future costs and revenues for that customer in "today's" money value terms, as you have to make the decision to invest in a particular campaign "today," and the value of money is not the same today and in the future. You will then end up with what is called the net present value of your customers where you subtract the net present value of the customer costs from the net present value of the customer revenues.

For the analysis of your shopper marketing campaign with this method, you will simply subtract the cost of your shopper marketing campaign from the calculated net present value per customer. The result of this calculation is simply called the net present value after shopper marketing costs. The goal, once again, is to generate a positive number.

Your finance department should be able to provide you with a net present value per customer before your campaign cost.

The profitability-based decision process has clear and distinct steps. These steps are detailed next.

Once the sales goals and estimated campaign costs have been established, decisions need to be made regarding the type of profitability analysis your team will use to determine whether the shopper campaign should be launched. These decisions are listed and then described in further detail.

- **Selection of short- or long-term analysis**
- **Profitability analysis selection** from among the following choices:
    - Marginal profit
    - Variable contribution
    - Lifetime value (and Net Present)
- **Identification of constraints and requirements**
- **Projections of sales and costs**
- **Determination of decision criteria or success metrics**, including the following:
    - Minimum value (For example, if you opt for a variable contribution analysis method, what is the minimum dollar value needed to launch the campaign?)
    - Pay-back period (When is the campaign cost re-couped?)
    - ROI (What is the return on investment?)
- **Identification of the benchmarks** to be used to determine what will be a successful campaign for the selected success metrics

Term Selection

Your selection of the analysis will depend on the type of business your product is in and the type of data to which the company has access.

It is preferable to analyze both the short-term and long-term impact, but if your product is not purchased repeatedly and/or you cannot access costs data at the customer level, then a long-term analysis will be difficult (as you need variable contribution or net present value at the customer level to be able to use such analysis methods.) In this case, the analysis would be short-term only.

Analysis Method Selection

Once you have selected the term(s) and you know the type of data that you can have access to, then you can decide which methods to use.

- **For short term:** Marginal profit analysis
- **For long-term:** Variable contribution or net present value-based analysis

Constraints and Requirements

Constraints are any business requirements that your campaign must follow and respect. They could be tied to a certain sales requirements, such as a minimum sales increase or a set sales volume to be achieved. Constraints are dictated by the strategic priorities of the business. Some examples of how these might be expressed are as follows:

- A minimum sales amount or volume has to be achieved
- Sales will have to be split at set percents between different products

They could also be linked to cost requirements where, for example, the marginal cost per sale cannot be more than a certain dollar amount.

Constraints can negate the need to calculate profitability. If, for example, the required additional sales volume increase is 10 percent during the promotion and the promotion generates only a projected additional 5 percent sales volume gain, there would be no need to calculate profitability simply because the requirement for the campaign is not met.

Remember, as outlined previously and stated as such in the previous example, the analysis of whether the campaign meets the requirements has to be done based on the additional sales and costs of the campaign.

Sales and Costs Projections

The campaign costs are specific and typically straightforward to calculate. They include the cost of the activities and communications linked to the campaign itself.

Sales projections are not that straightforward and depend on the product category, the specific product, the sales promotion techniques being used, and other factors that are specific to the business and campaign in question. The bottom line is to determine what sales boost is projected as result of the campaign.

There are many resources available online to develop sales projections for sales promotion and shopper marketing campaigns. One that we found useful is http://blueacorn.com/blog/roi-planner-and-promotion-projection-tools/. This is a free tool that can be a good place to start.

Regardless of the method being used to calculate sales, the shopper marketer must answer two major questions:

- **What are the baseline sales that you will use to compare against?**
- **What will be the baseline level of sales that you estimate will happen without the promotion?** (As this is what you will use to estimate your sales projections with the campaign.)

According to CrossCap.com (Accessed at https://www.crosscap.com/blog/3-strategies-for-measuring-sales-lift-in-a-retail-promotion), there are three options to estimate your baseline sales:

- Sales prior to promotion: What were the sales before the promotion began?
    - Pros: Simplest method. Here, the baseline used is the product sales right before the promotion began. Sales are calculated for the same amount of time the promotion will run, so, for example, if the promotion ran for one month, then the baseline sales using this option would include product sales for one month immediately before the promotion began.
    - Cons: Does not account for seasonality and/or trends, meaning if the product does not do seasonally well for the month you used as a baseline, your projected sales gain with your promotion (during the following month) will be artificially high.
- Fifty-two-week sales average—eliminating historical promotional periods: What are the average sales per week (over a year of sales data)?
    - Pros: Elimination of any promotional periods.
    - Cons: Difficult to find fifty-two weeks of sales and then eliminate any historical promotional sales.
- Last year (LY) seasonal average—eliminating historical promotional periods: What were the average sales the previous year at the same period?
    - Pros: Requires fewer data and measures baseline sales for an item just during a seasonal period.

- Cons: Requires a deep understanding of category seasonality.

Once again, according to CrossCap.com, "the best methodology would be to use your 'Last Year' seasonal average and even though it won't account for product trends, it'll give an accurate measure."

- **What is the expected sales lift from the promotion?**

  There are no straightforward answers to this question. This will really depend on the product category that you are in, the shopper types that your product attracts, and the particular shopper targets for which you aim in your campaign. The best is to test and learn, build your own database of results, and use those for future campaigns projections.

The charts from Nielsen Catalina Solution that follow give you a general sense of the sales lift amounts to expect per thousand impressions or households for an average shopper marketing campaign.

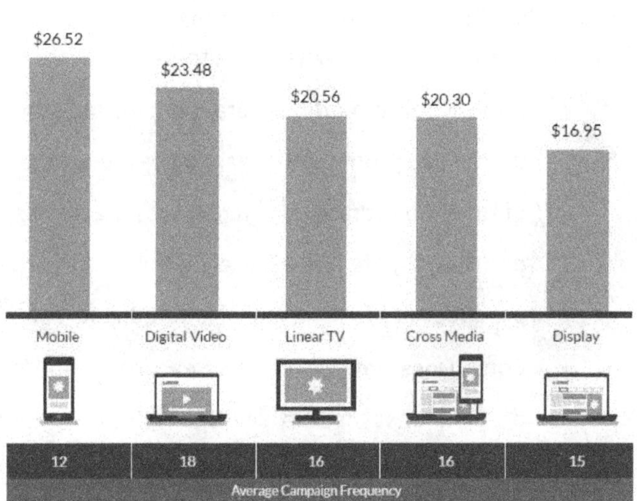

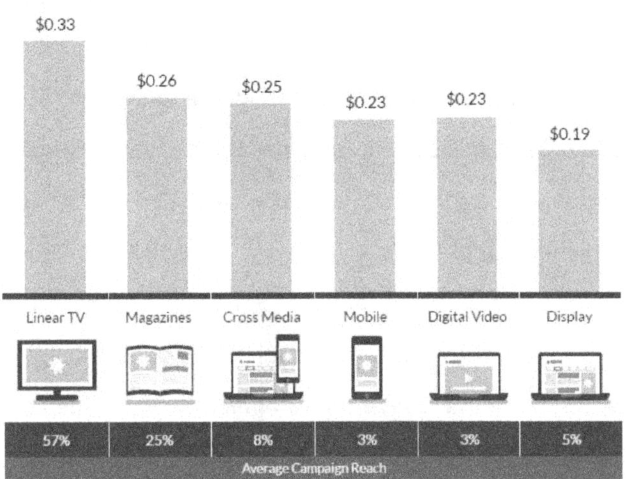

Decision Criteria or Success Metrics

Now that you have estimated your campaign costs, the expected sales lift, and your expected incremental sales, you will need to plug that data into your selected profit calculation methodology and decide on the success metrics to use. The purpose of doing so is to guide your team with whether to execute the shopper marketing campaign.

If you have chosen the marginal profit, or the variable contribution calculations, you can use different success criteria or metrics to decide if you should launch the shopper marketing campaign. The choices are listed.

1. **Straightforward minimum value:** If your shopper marketing campaign does not generate at least a pre-determined dollar value in profit or variable contribution, the campaign is not launched.
2. **Payback period:** In basic terms, payback analysis is the amount of time after the promotion ends in which the costs of the campaign are paid back or recovered. In the case of the variable contribution, and assuming that you can split this variable contribution by year or month, you could calculate your payback period, meaning when the variable contribution generated by your shopper marketing campaign will be at least equal to your campaign cost. You could determine, for example, that you will not fund campaigns where more than 1.5 years of variable contribution generation is needed to cover the cost of the campaign. In this case, 1.5 years is your payback period (i.e., your decision criterion on which you decide to move forward with the campaign). Using this same example, if the payback analysis reveals it will take two years to "payback" the promotion, you would decide not to execute it.

3. **Return on investment:** In the context of shopper marketing, ROI means the net profit a company makes from the shopper marketing campaign, divided by the amount invested in that company for that campaign. A company will typically decide what percentage ROI is necessary or acceptable in order to invest in the campaign. Therefore, if the generated marginal profit or variable contribution divided by your campaign cost is less than the percentage decided on by the company, the campaign is not launched. If it is above, the campaign is launched. For example, if your variable contribution is $10,000 and your campaign costs are $5,000, then $10,000 divided by $5,000 will be 2 or 200 percent. If your company does not invest in campaigns with less than 250 percent ROI, you will not invest in this campaign. If your criterion is to invest in campaigns with 200 percent or more ROI, you will.

If you have chosen net present value calculation, you can use the following success criteria to decide if you should launch your shopper marketing campaign:

2. **Straightforward minimum net present value:** If your shopper marketing campaign does not generate at least a set dollar value in net present value after shopper marketing costs, the campaign is not launched. If it is above, the campaign is launched.
3. **Return on investment:** If the generated net present value (after shopper marketing costs) divided by your campaign cost is less than a set percent, the campaign is not launched. If it is above, the campaign is launched.

Benchmarks

Once you have chosen your decision criterion, the next step is to formally decide what constitutes success. In the examples described in the previous section, we began to touch on this concept. For example, if you chose payback period as the success metric, then what will be the chosen payback period that will constitute success? Will it be one year? 1.5 years? Or just six months?

If you chose a straightforward minimum net present value, for example, will it be $200, $1,000, or another dollar amount?

Whatever the criterion you select, it is important to be clear on what defines success. For example, how does the company decide what the ROI needs to be or what the payback period should be? To make such decisions, companies use benchmarks.

Benchmarks could be a company's past campaign(s) where the actual results of the past campaign(s) can serve as the benchmarks.

This can also come from the competitors. Analyzing what the competitors are doing and using inputs both from the press as well as from retailers, who may share with you their experience about the competitors' campaigns, you could estimate their results of such campaigns and use such results as a benchmark of what to achieve (if the campaigns were successful) or what to avoid (if they were not).

You could also use benchmarks that are based on industry data. Such information is often gathered by research and analytics companies such as Nielsen and Catalina. Based on the data that they obtain from manufacturers and retailers, they calculate industry averages for various criteria that they then share with their clients.

Profitability Calculation Examples

Let's review a few examples to illustrate the profitability-based decision process.

Example #1: Short-Term Analysis

You plan a Shopper Marketing campaign that will have the following characteristics:

- **Term:**
  - Short term
- **Profitability analysis method:**
  - Marginal profit
- **Constraints and requirements:**
  - A minimum $250,000 sales amount
- **Sales and cost projections:**
  - A 5 percent sales lift from baseline (last year's seasonal average or $300,000)
  - Campaign costs: $300,000
- **Decision criterion or metric:**
  - Minimum value in marginal profit
- **Benchmarks for selected criteria/metrics:**
  - At least $20,000 in marginal profit

With these elements, we can calculate the following:

- The short-term sales generated by the campaign:
  - $300,000 (baseline sales) x (1 + 5% (expected sales lift)) = $315,000 in sales
- Marginal profit:
  - $315,000 (campaign sales) - $300,000 (campaign cost) = $15,000

In the scenario, the campaign should not be launched as the expected marginal profit ($15,000) is below the benchmark ($20,000).

Example #2: Short-term Analysis

You plan a shopper marketing campaign with the following characteristics:

- **Term:**
    - Short term
- **Profitability analysis method:**
    - Marginal profit
- **Constraints and requirements:**
    - A minimum $250,000 sales amount
- **Sales and cost projections:**
    - A 10 percent sales lift from baseline (last year's seasonal average or $300,000)
    - Sales to be distributed as follows:
        - Month 1: 35 percent of the total sales generated
        - Month 2: 25 percent
        - Month 3: 20 percent
        - Month 4: 10 percent
        - Month 5: 10 percent
    - Campaign costs: $200,000
- **Decision criterion or metric:**
    - Payback period
- **Benchmarks for selected criteria/metrics:**
    - Recoup of the campaign costs three months maximum after the campaign launch

With these elements, we can calculate the following:

- The short-term sales generated by the campaign:
    - $300,000 (baseline sales) x (1 + 10% (expected sales lift)) = $330,000 in sales
- The monthly sales distribution will be as follows:
    - Month 1: $115,000
    - Month 2: $83,000 (or $198,000 cumulatively)
    - Month 3: $66,000 (or $264,000 cumulatively)
    - Month 4: $33,000 (or $297,000 cumulatively)
    - Month 5: $33,000 (or $330,000 cumulatively)

When we look at this sales distribution and we compare the $200,000 campaign cost, we see that such costs will be recouped between the second and the third month. Therefore, the campaign should be launched as it is under the three-months payback period expectation.

Example #3: Long-Term Analysis

You plan a shopper marketing campaign with the following characteristics:

- **Term:**
    - Long-term
- **Profitability analysis method:**
    - Variable contribution
        - Variable Contribution (before campaign costs) is $10 per customer (provided to you by your finance department)
- **Constraints and requirements:**
    - A minimum 105,000 new customers
- **Sales and cost projections:**
    - A 15 percent new customer acquisition lift from baseline (last year's seasonal average or 100,000 new customers)
    - Campaign costs: $200,000
- **Decision criterion or metric:**
    - ROI
- **Benchmarks for selected criteria/metrics:**
    - At least 300 percent ROI

With these elements, we can calculate the following:

- The long-term new customers generated by the campaign:
    - 100,000 (baseline new customers) x (1 + 15% (expected lift)) = 115,000 new customers
- The variable contribution generated those new customers will be 115,000 x $10 = $1.15 million
- The variable contribution minus the campaign cost will be $1.15 million - $200,000 = $950,000
- Variable contribution (after campaign costs), or $950,000 divided by campaign costs, or $200,000 = 475% ROI

The expected ROI is superior to the benchmark ROI (300 percent). Therefore, the campaign should be launched.

Example #4: Long-Term Analysis

You plan a shopper marketing campaign with the following characteristics:

- **Term:**
  - Long-term
- **Profitability analysis method:**
  - Net present value
    - Net present value (before campaign costs) is $25 per customer (provided to you by your finance department)
- **Constraints and requirements:**
  - A minimum 105,000 new customers
- **Sales and cost projections:**
  - A 7.5 percent new customer lift from baseline (last year's seasonal average or 100,000 new customers)
  - Campaign costs: $500,000
- **Decision criterion or metric:**
  - Straightforward minimum net present value
- **Benchmarks for selected criteria/metrics:**
  - Net present value after campaign costs should be at least $2.5 million.

With these elements, we can calculate the following:

- The long-term new customers generated by the campaign:
  - 100,000 (baseline new customers) x (1 + 7.5% (expected lift)) = 107,500 new customers
- The net present value before campaign generated those new customers will be 115,000 x $25 = $2.69 million
- The variable contribution after campaign cost will be $2.69 million - $500,000 = $2.19 million

The planned net present value after campaign costs ($2.19 million) is, therefore, less than the benchmark ($2.5 million). So the campaign should not be launched.

Tracking The Results

Once the campaign has been executed, many actual data need to be gathered, for example, sales, costs and participation rates.

These actual data should replace the estimates calculated before the campaign. Naturally, the same calculation methods need to be used with the actual data to calculate actual profit contribution.

At this stage, it is important to compare the actual results to the estimates to identify discrepancies and plan for corrections in the future. This is also important to review the in-going assumptions and make adjustments to reflect actual data.

Lastly, the actual results can well serve as success benchmarks and sales baseline estimates to use for future campaigns.

Strong Communication Requirement for Long-Term Success

As discussed earlier in this book, shopper marketing campaigns cannot work in isolation and must be developed and aligned with other marketing functions. Communication between the departments is important for success. What could appear to be a successful shopper marketing campaign based on a positive long-term financial impact might not be as successful as it could have been, had the shopper marketing been more aligned with the other marketing activities.

To illustrate this point, let's look at a real example with American Express.

A few years back, American Express Europe was substantially behind budget in terms of acquisition of new America Express cardmembers in Europe for that year. Whatever were the reasons explaining that situation, the fact is that American Express Europe needed a strong boost of new members to counter those poor results and therefore decided to turn to aggressive sales promotions-based campaigns to do so. One of those campaigns was aimed at adding supplementary cardmembers on existing basic American Express accounts—where the basic cardmember would be giving some supplementary cards for his or her spouse and/or children under his/her main account.

To obtain that boost of sales, a one-year free membership offer was executed such that no fee would be imposed on the American Express cardmember for supplementary cards for one year. After one year, an annual fee will be charged for each supplementary card. This offer was selected as it had proven before to boost response rate and sales.

The optimization of this campaign was based on selecting the targets with the highest potential response to supplementary card offers (based on past results and profiling analysis) and on the average net present value (before acquisition costs) of supplementary cardmembers. This net present value had been calculated by the finance department at American Express Europe over many years of data.

The cost of the campaign itself (including the cost associated with losing the first-year fee for each supplementary card) was calculated as the acquisition cost.

This acquisition cost was then subtracted from the net present value to calculate a net present value after acquisition costs for each target segment scenario for this campaign.

As a key constraint, it was decided that any target segment scenario where the net present value after acquisition costs was negative was to be eliminated.

Then, two decision criteria (with their respective benchmark) were used to select the target segments that would be included in the campaign:

- The Return On Investment (ROI) was to be at least 200%
- The payback was to be no longer than 1.5 years

Given these clear decision criteria, the profitability of the campaign was established before launch.

Indeed, the campaign worked very well and even better than expected because the cost per acquisition was even lower than planned, adding to the profitability of the campaign (bigger ROI and a shorter payback period).

All was well up to when the concerned basic American Express cardmembers saw their bill one year after the campaign and they remembered that they had to pay for the supplementary card fees. This drove many of them to cancel the supplementary cards that they had applied to one year before.

Now the one-year-out cancellation was expected with the one-year-free offer, but not as much as it happened and, in all cases, it still took the marketing function in charge of loyalty and anti-attrition at American Express Europe by surprise.

As they were not prepared to handle that pick of attrition with special communications before, during, and after the one-year-free offer anniversary, they could not prevent as many cancellations as they would have liked, and this was not a good situation.

This situation pushed the finance department to recalculate the net present value per acquired customer, which ended up being lower than expected initially. They then subtracted the campaign costs against this new net present value. The result was still positive and above the benchmark but not as strong as initially thought.

While the supplementary card campaign was still profitable, even with that pick of attrition one year after the campaign, the process did not work well and many attritions could have been avoided if the shopper marketing function had interacted with the loyalty marketing function at American Express Europe, more formally and directly, as the campaign was conceived.

Hence, the need for formal alignment between shopper marketing, and all impacted marketing functions in a business, to ensure lasting success.

Lesson learned!

Here is an example from Mars Chocolate illustrating how a brand like Mars uses baselines, success metrics, and benchmarks to set Shopper Marketing objectives and assess how a campaign succeeds or not.

Case Study:
Bringing Shopper Marketing To Life

CASE STUDY

2017 SILVER SHOPPER MARKETING EFFIE AWARD WINNER EFFIE AWARD WINNER

"SAY THANK YOU WITH M"

"Say Thank You With M" unified three American icons — M&M'S, U.S. troops and Walmart — into one summer campaign.

When Walmart shoppers bought M&M's, we donated a bag to troops. We also provided meaningful engagement with our brand and our troops, and offered up inspiration for adding M&M's to summer celebrations.

Using shopper, brand and retailer insights, we created a fifth season for candy that saw $6MM in incremental sales, grew the category at Walmart by 2.4%. We also generated 13,000 letters to troops and donated 1.8MM pounds of chocolate.

COMPETITION:
Shopper Marketing Effie Awards

Ran in:
USA

CATEGORY:
Single-Retailer Program: Mass Merchants

BRAND/CLIENT:
Mars Chocolate North America

LEAD AGENCY:
Catapult Marketing

CONTRIBUTING COMPANIES:
Collective Bias/ Elevation Group

PRODUCT/SERVICE:
Candy

CLASSIFICATION:
National

DATES EFFORT RAN:
May 7, 2016 - July 8, 2016

PROGRAM ORGIN:
Brand Driven

CREDITS:
Sue Barkalow
Kaleb Doss
Ely Doval
Erin Dye
Jessica Gilbert
Crystal Putnam
Rick Schanz
Allisha Watkins
Cassie Wenger
Ashley Wright

effie worldwide

Executive Summary

The Challenge

Grow the category and drive incremental sales of Mars candies (including M&M'S, Snickers and Skittles) at Walmart during summer, when these brands are not top-of-mind.

The Idea

M&M's and Walmart are coming together to give America the biggest "Thank You" she has ever seen by donating chocolate to U.S. troops and veterans with every purchase of M&M's at Walmart.

Bringing the Idea to Life

A simple, powerful message — 1 for You = 1 for Troops — and meaningful ways for shoppers to engage via purchase-triggered donations and letters to troops were woven throughout their entire omnichannel path to purchase.

The Results

Over the course of just nine weeks, Mars donated 1.8MM pounds of chocolate (vs. 1MM goal) to active troops and veterans, grew the business by $6MM in incremental sales at Walmart (vs. $2.4MM goal), and achieved an 88.5% sell- through rate (vs. 85% benchmark).[1]

Effie Awards Category Context

"Say Thank You With M" unified three American icons — M&M'S, U.S. troops and Walmart — to create one simple shopper solution.

When Walmart shoppers purchased M&M's, a bag was donated to troops to say thanks. The program provided fun, easy ways for shoppers to engage with our brand and U.S. troops and delivered patriotic inspiration for adding M&M's to summer celebrations.

Using shopper, brand and retailer insights, we created a fifth season for candy that saw $6MM in incremental sales, grew the category at Walmart by 2.4%, and garnered 13,000 shopper-submitted letters to troops and 1.8MM pounds of donated chocolate.

State of the Marketplace & Brand's Business

Mars candy sees strong sales at Walmart throughout the year during the key gifting holidays of Valentine's Day, Easter, Halloween and Holiday — and coming out of Walmart's Q1 (February-April), the Mars candy business was strong once again.[2]

However, as Walmart transitions its focus from gifting to summer fun, Mars candy has traditionally underindexed vs. the rest of the category.

The lull in sales during this time can largely be credited to a favorite summertime staple: S'mores, of which Mars' top competitor, Hershey's, is a key player. Every summer, s'mores top billing with tab features, pallet trains, custom grocery endcaps and cross-department signage and displays. With so much focus and display dedicated to one solution, the rest of the category was left exposed.

Our strategic communication challenge: How do we keep Mars candy top-of-mind with Walmart shoppers during the summer?

We knew we had to think outside the campfire. We also knew that Walmart fully embraces a patriotic thematic for summer, dedicates prime display space to red, white and blue merchandise, and actively supports its own veteran initiatives, which are paramount to the retailer's corporate reputation strategy. At the same time, M&Ms – a candy created as rations for U.S. troops – was celebrating its 75th Anniversary.

Leveraging this information, we tested concepts with Walmart shoppers and learned they had a strong affinity for patriotism and supporting U.S. troops. Based on these insights, we created a new, fifth season for buying Mars candies built around summer's natural theme of patriotism as well as a different kind of giving — giving back to those who have served our country.

This new reason to gift was designed to drive incremental sales, category growth and loyalty during a season dominated by a competitor.

2 Source: Internal Sales Data, Retail Link, August 2016

Shopper Segment

The campaign targeted Millennial shoppers who have purchased Mars candies at Walmart within the past 3 months. Contextually, they are enticed by messaging that disrupts and grabs their attention. They are more likely to buy a product if it's tied to a good cause, especially if their participation is turn-key.

Beyond purchase behavior, our shopper is someone who has a love for America, and Americana. They are also Walmart Busy Families seeking to save time and money who need easy solutions and ways to give back. They enjoy entertaining during the summer months, and they actively embrace and celebrate patriotism.

As an additional program overlay, we leveraged our partnership with NASCAR to spread the word to its fans, who overindex as Walmart shoppers[1], with custom messaging and events, knowing that patriotism is a top priority for them.

By appealing to their patriotism and offering them a simple way to support their military, "Say Thank You with M" gave Walmart shoppers an entirely new reason not only to entertain with M&M'S, but also to give to someone they consider a hero.

1 Source: Internal Sales Data, Retail Link, August 2016

Objectives & KPI's

BUSINESS OBJECTIVES[3]

Brand:

- Drive a 10% lift in incremental sales of M&M'S and other Mars confections brands at Walmart, which equates to $2.4MM
- Grow the Mars share of category at Walmart by 1 point

Retailer:

- Grow the candy category as a whole by 1%
- Meet Walmart's sell-through benchmark of 85%

Importance:

- Expanding the summer focus beyond just one usage occasion will help grow the category as a whole at Walmart
- Meeting or exceeding retailer benchmarks helps gain retailer confidence in the brand

BEHAVIORAL OBJECTIVES3

- Generate over 10,000 shopper-submitted letters for U.S. troops and veterans
- Convert shoppers and donate 1MM pounds of chocolate
- Achieve more than 44MM impressions and 2,500 engagements with our digital and social media tactics

PERCEPTUAL/ATTITUDINAL OBJECTIVES

- Grow shopper loyalty and affinity for the brand and retailer
- Make Mars candy top-of-mind with shoppers for summer usage occasion

3 Source: Agency Shopper Insights, Jan. 2016

Shopper Insight

Shopper Insight: Americans are proud of their military, want easy ways to say thanks, and are more likely to buy a product if it's tied to a good cause.

Observations:

Shopper: Insights show that 76% of Americans have "a great deal of confidence" in the military[4]. We also know that 67% of Total U.S. have shopped in Walmart in the past month.[5]

NASCAR fans: 95% of NASCAR fans (68% of whom have shopped at Walmart in the past month[5] say patriotism is important and that they're proud to see NASCAR support the military and their families[5].

Brand: M&M'S is a candy that was created 75 years ago as rations for U.S. troops.

Retailer: Walmart's corporate reputation strategy includes the support of U.S. military troops and veterans with programs such as Veterans Welcome Home and Greenlight a Vet. This level of support garners loyalty for the retailer.

Shopper Barriers: Because of Walmart's focus on s'mores during the summer, Mars candies were not top-of-mind with shoppers. We also know that shoppers are hesitant to participate in promotions if the work outweighs the reward.

Behavior Change Objective: Convert shoppers to purchasing more Mars candies at Walmart during the summer months by giving them new usage occasions that also helps a good cause.

4 Source: Gallup Poll, "American's Confidence in Congress Falls to Lowest on Record," 2013

5 Source: GfK MRI 2015 Doublebase

Reminder: Entrants will copy their answers into the entry form in the online entry area for judging purposes – this document will not be uploaded for judging. Use this form to draft your responses and collaborate with team members.

The Big Idea

By appealing to shoppers' patriotism, we'll create loyalty for Mars candies and drive sales at Walmart by transforming summer into a "fifth season" of giving.

Bringing the Idea to Life

Idea and Overall Strategy

Our idea was to create a fifth season for giving candy at Walmart during summer. Our strategy was to create a simple, powerful and disruptive omnichannel customer experience that appealed to Walmart shoppers' patriotism along their entire path to purchase.

Our Communication Strategy was two-pronged:

- Speak not only to our core shopper segment (shoppers who have purchased chocolate at Walmart in the past 3 months), but also to a much larger portion of the American population who live near Walmart locations and have a love for the U.S military.
- Leverage Mars' corporate partnership with NASCAR to reach fans who overindex as Walmart shoppers.

Because these groups are large and diverse, we employed an army of tactics that spanned all channels that targeted them based on context, geography and affinity. This wide reach made it crucial for our campaign to be consistent and compelling across all platforms. No matter where shoppers encountered this campaign, they were greeted with our simple yet powerful conversion message: "1 for You = 1 for Troops".

The Tactics

Awareness

- To reach past Walmart purchasers, we employed WMX media banners both on Walmart.com and offsite. (Accessing Walmart's first-party data via WMX allowed us to carefully hone our targeting to this core group.)
- Because 74% of consumers use social media to make purchase decisions[6], we used social buzz to get people talking. Bloggers created original content about the campaign, which we then amplified via content ads. We also had a series of targeted Facebook posts. We created continuity across channels with the hashtag #CelebrateWithM.
- For maximum reach, we also published a print FSI (35.8MM circ.)[7]
- As an additional overlay, we enlisted Kyle Busch, M&M's NASCAR driver, to specifically target NASCAR fans with a custom messaging that ran on Gas Station TV, Walmart Promo Radio and Facebook. (68% of NASCAR fans shop at Walmart)[8]
- NASCAR-themed Retailtainment events in key markets featured letter-writing stations and the creation of care packages courtesy of Operation Gratitude. In addition, we painted the M&Ms car red, white and blue, and we convinced Walmart to add its logo as well – the first time it's appeared on a NASCAR track in over a decade.

Conversion

- To help funnel such a wide range of shoppers down the path to purchase, all media pointed to an engaging, interactive landing destination on Walmart.com where shoppers could purchase product, track donations, view a Kyle Busch video and write letters to the troops.
- Because of our strong partnership with Walmart, we were able to hit a large number of disruption points with in-store signage and displays including in-aisle blades and shelf strips, a front endcap, a saddlebag display and Checkout TV.
- Retailtainment events at 405 military-traited stores featured M&M'S characters, letter-writing stations, a wrapped vehicle and attendance by military personnel.

6 Source: Digital Marketing Agency Research, 2011

7 Source: Agency Partner Data, 2016

8 Source: GfK MRI 2015 Doublebase

Communication Touch Points - All

Branded Content
During

Digital/Interactive
During
Developed Retailer Site Content
Digital Video
Display Ads
MRF/Retailer Website

Packaing
During

PR
During
Post

Print
Post
Custom Publication
Magazine - Print

Radio
During
Spots

Retail Experience
During
In-Store Merchandizing
In-Store Video/Kiosk
POP
Retailtainment

Sampling
During
In-Store

Shopper Involvement
During
Consumer Generated
Viral

Social Media
During

Sponsorship
During

Paid Media Expenditures

Current Year: September 2015 – August 2016
$1-2 million

Year Prior: September 2014 – August 2015
Not Applicable

Budget
Less than other competitors.
More than prior year's budget.

The budget for this program was a new spend this year, because there was no specific program activation the year prior. We received a challenge from the buyer to develop a new "fifth season" for candy.

Owned Media & Sponsorship

We had a variety of owned media which included

- Red, white and blue packaging and M&M lentils: Developed to celebrate the "Say Thank You With M" thematic at Walmart all summer long
- Mars social-media content hub (myconfectioncorner.com): Served as a central destination for all of our social-media posts, aggregated under the hashtag

#celebratewithm.

- Promotional content on the M&Ms Facebook page: The national M&Ms Facebook page helped spread awareness about our retailer-specific program.
- Branded retailtainment wrapped vehicle: Vehicles placed outside participating Walmart stores helped draw attention to events happening inside.

The M&Ms & Kyle Busch NASCAR vehicle sponsored the campaign. Sponsorship elements included:

- Wrapping the NASCAR with red, white and blue M&Ms and the Walmart logo
- Tented events at NASCAR races throughout the campaign
- Videos and radio spots featuring Kyle Busch

Reminder: Entrants will copy their answers into the entry form in the online entry area for judging purposes – this document will not be uploaded for judging. Use this form to draft your responses and collaborate with team members.

Results

BUSINESS / KPI RESULTS[9]

Brand:

- During the campaign timeframe (5/21/16–7/8/16) the brand sold $6MM in incremental sales at Walmart (vs. $2.4MM goal)
- This equates to a sales lift of between 25-30% (vs. 10% goal) vs. YA (with no program activation)
- The program helped grow the Mars share of the category at Walmart by 1.75 points (vs. 1 point goal)

Retailer:

- The program helped grow the candy category at Walmart by 2.4% (vs 1% goal)
- The program enjoyed an 88.5% average sell-through rate (vs. 85% benchmark). Select M&M'S and Snickers SKUs saw a 95-100% sell-through.

BEHAVIORAL RESULTS

- Shoppers wrote over 13,000 thank you letters (vs. 10,000 goal) in-store and online[10]
- Over 1.8MM pounds of chocolate (vs. 1MM goal) were donated to U.S. troops and veterans[9]
- Achieved 104MM campaign impresions (136% vs. 44MM goal) and 34,500 social engagements (1280% over 2,500 goal) with our digital and social media tactics[10]
- Significance: Almost 2 for 1 campaign ROI for social media[10]

PERCEPTUAL / ATTITUDINAL RESULTS[10]

- "That is so nice for Mars/Wrigley to donate to the troops when a bag is bought at Walmart. I did not know that!"
- "My kids love M&Ms. We also bought them this Memorial Day from Walmart to show our support for the troops."

SHOPPER SEGMENT RESULTS[10]

- Achieving far over benchmark impressions and engagements exposed 33% of NEW shoppers to the brand

9 Source: Mars Internal Sales Data, Retail Link, May 7-July 8 2016

10 Source: Social Media Agency Partner, Social Media Metrics Final Campaign Reports, May 7-July 8, 2016

Other Contributing Factors

This campaign coincided with M&M's 75th anniversary campaign. However, this was a national campaign was not specifically targeted to Walmart and its shoppers.

Reminder: Entrants will copy their answers into the entry form in the online entry area for judging purposes – this document will not be uploaded for judging. Use this form to draft your responses and collaborate with team members.

Application Workshop

Throughout this book, you will have formal application workshops and exercises with supportive tools to help you apply the information from each chapter to your particular case or assignment. You will also have access to lists of key decisions to be made or capabilities that you need to have in place at each step of the shopper marketing planning process.

For this workshop, you are going to simulate a shopper marketing campaign analysis. A fully functional incremental sales estimation, profitability calculation, and criteria-based decision tool are provided to you with the Chapter 7 – Shopper Marketing – Investment Analysis Tool.

Look at this tool (https://drive.google.com/file/d/1yLAaVVWq0RmpQ1e2-GdGb48kMgaS-3Ck/view?usp=sharing), download the excel file and familiarize yourself with its functions, and provide the inputs as directed so that you will be able to assess the calculated ratio to make investment decisions.

Now, read the following shopper marketing campaign scenario.

For each scenario, use some of the key information provided to add key data inputs into the various simulation spreadsheets:

- One for sales and costs estimations
- One for profitability analysis
- One to make the investment decision

As you have captured the proper inputs into the simulations, the investment decision analysis will provide you with key ratios. Based on those ratios, *would you decide to invest in the shopper marketing campaign presented in each scenario?*

Analyze one scenario at a time. Be sure to clear the inputs (by using the Cleaner button on steps 1 and 2 in the worksheets) as you go from one scenario to another.

Go for it!

Scenario 1:

- **Description:** You want to launch a rewards promotion for one of your new products
- **Analysis term:** Long term
- **Profitability analysis method:** Variable contribution
    - Variable contribution (before campaign costs) is $25 per customer (provided to you by your finance department)
- **Constraints and requirements:**
    - A minimum $500,000 in sales

- **Sales and cost projections:**
    - A 7.5 percent sales lift from baseline (last year's seasonal average or $750,000 in sales)
    - Sales/customer: $75
    - Campaign costs: $450,000
- **Decision criterion or success metric:**
    - Straightforward minimum variable contribution
- **Benchmarks for selected criteria/metrics:**
    - Variable contribution (after campaign costs) should be at least $100,000
- **Your analysis results:**
    - Campaign variable contribution (after campaign costs): ______________________________
- **Your decision (go/no-go):** _______________

Scenario 2:

- **Description:** You want to launch a price promotion for your main product
- **Analysis term:** Short term
- **Profitability analysis method:** Marginal profit
- **Constraints and requirements:**
    - A minimum $100,000 in sales
- **Sales and cost projections:**
    - A 10 percent sales lift from baseline (last year's seasonal average or $300,000 in sales)
    - Campaign costs: $50,000
- **Decision criterion or success metric:**
    - ROI
- **Benchmarks for selected criteria/metrics:**
    - ROI at least 150 percent
- **Your analysis results:**
    - ROI: ______________________________
- **Your decision (go/no-go):** _______________

Scenario 3:

- **Description:** You want to acquire new customers for a new product in a new market segment with a coupon and a sample offer
- **Analysis term:** Long term
- **Profitability analysis method:** Net present value
    - Net present value (before campaign costs) is $55 per customer (provided to you by your finance department)
- **Constraints and requirements:**
    - A minimum $250,000 in sales
- **Sales and cost projections:**
    - A 6 percent sales lift from baseline (last year's seasonal average or $250,000 in sales)
    - Sales/customer: $25
  - Campaign costs: $150,000
- **Decision criterion or success metric:**
    - Straightforward minimum net present value
- **Benchmarks for selected criteria/metrics:**
    - Net present value (after campaign costs) should be at least $100,000
- **Your analysis results:**
    - Campaign net present value (after campaign costs): ______________________________
- **Your decision (go/no-go):** _______________

The correct answers can be obtained at [Chapter 7 Workshop Answers. (https://drive.google.com/file/d/1mju96VaGzrgBUjccpUh_pAXd-KxAnNwj/view?usp=sharing)](https://drive.google.com/file/d/1mju96VaGzrgBUjccpUh_pAXd-KxAnNwj/view?usp=sharing)

Conclusion

Profitability is a critical component of all marketing activities and it is also the case for shopper marketing.

While it might not have always been true for sales promotion, the requirement to generate incremental profits with shopper marketing campaigns is a must. Merely demonstrating an immediate sales volume increase with no impact on future brand building is not enough.

Shopper marketing professionals need to plan shopper marketing campaigns with this profitability requirement in mind and analyze such campaigns post-execution, with the same profitability focus.

It is also important to understand that shopper marketing campaigns have both short-term and long-term impacts. Both need to be using the proper analysis methods and with adherence to the established decision criteria.

The requirement for profitability and formal analysis is clearly an additional sign of maturity of the shopper marketing discipline.

This profitability accountability also requires that shopper marketing professionals align themselves with the other marketing functions to be sure that any potential side effect of a shopper marketing campaign is fully understood and integrated into the analysis.

Chapters 8: The Shopper Marketing Planning Process

Learning Objectives

After completing this chapter, you will be able to do the following:

- Further your understanding of why planning a shopper marketing campaign requires as much discipline as any other marketing communications method.
- Understand in more detail the key steps, milestones, and deliverables that are required for effectively planning a shopper marketing campaign
- Fully comprehend how such steps, milestones, and deliverables (and their sequencing) ensure a proper alignment of a shopper marketing campaign, with the specific marketing and communication objectives and strategies that have been established for the product or service.
- Fully comprehend the activities and tools that are necessary for each planning step in order to develop and implement a coherent, aligned, and properly focused shopper marketing campaign.
- Learn how to apply those key steps, milestones, and deliverables to properly plan a successful shopper marketing campaign as well as analyze its effectiveness.

What Is the Chapter About?

This chapter is about the planning steps/activities, milestones, and deliverables that are required to develop an effective shopper marketing campaign. It is also the need for more effective planning that accelerated the transformation of sales promotion into shopper marketing.

This need was and continues to be driven by the required alignment between marketing, marketing communications, and shopper marketing. In order to develop and maintain this alignment, a disciplined planning approach is required.

In this chapter, the planning process used for developing an effective shopper marketing campaign will be described inclusive of its nine steps. For each step, there are unique requirements and activities to ensure planning is optimized within each step as well as between the various steps.

This chapter will provide detailed directions for proper planning of a shopper marketing campaign.

Why Is This Important?

As we have learned, the alignment among business, marketing, marketing communications, and shopper marketing is critical to ensure that each element (for example, shopper marketing) is established to assist in achieving the objectives of the element at the previous level (in this example, marketing communications). These elements must ultimately align with the strategic goals of the brand (such as targeting and branding, etc.).

Without such alignment, and as we have also learned, the resources will be wasted on mediocre results. And to make matters worse, without proper planning, it will be impossible to know what the problems were that led to the failure of a campaign or what contributed to its success.

Not only do the selected shopper marketing objectives for any campaign need to help achieve the marketing and communication objectives of the product, but the target for the shopper marketing campaign must be aligned with and actually derived from the marketing target. Said another way, this means that if the marketing target is a millennial aged eighteen to twenty-four, the shopper marketing campaign must also be targeting the millennial aged eighteen to twenty-four, but this time focusing on the shopper types within the marketing target, that will be the most appropriate to help achieve the shopper marketing objectives.

And this doesn't end here. The big creative idea behind a shopper marketing campaign also has to be aligned with the brand personality of the product or service—and it has to be focused on helping achieve the shopper marketing objectives against the targeted shopper types.

In fact, the exact consumer promotion techniques that will be selected to make the big creative idea a reality have to be effectively aligned with the change of purchase behavior that is expected for the shopper target for the campaign. This extends to the trade promotion techniques in terms of selecting which ones to use based on what specific type of support is needed from the trade partners to make the consumer promotion a success.

Therefore, this is important that all elements are linked and planned using a highly disciplined approach.

Key Terms

- **Big idea:** A big idea in marketing and advertising is a term used to symbolize the most powerful and effective campaign message idea to convey a major selling point for a brand or a product. When applied to shopper marketing, this refers to the most powerful and effective idea to obtain the expected change of purchase behavior from the target shopper.

- **Client brief:** A client brief (or project brief, if it is not part of an on-going relationship between an agency and a client) is the first document where all the key information is shared (by the client) with the agency to start the planning process for the campaign. It gives information including but not limited to the marketing objective, the actual campaign assignment, the shopper marketing goal, the shopper marketing campaign strategy statement, specific requirements, etc.
- **Creative brief:** "A creative brief is a unifying document that identifies the important key benefits of a campaign. It tells the story and explains why it is important to the audience," and it serves as a creative "guide for the creation of new materials." (Accessed at https://cglife.com/blog/importance-creative-brief). This is, in fact, a brief (built on the initial client brief) for the creative professionals who will be in charge of actually creating the message and the related assets for a campaign.
- **Creative process:** A creative process is a process of generating, developing, and communicating new ideas.
- **Buyer or shopper persona:** "A buyer persona is a semi-fictional representation of an ideal customer based on market research and real data about existing customers. When creating your buyer persona(s), customer demographics, behavior patterns, motivations, and goals" should be reviewed and incorporated. (Accessed at https://blog.hubspot.com/marketing/buyer-persona-definition-under-100-sr)
- **Shopper marketing goal:** A high-level formulation of what a shopper marketing campaign should aim at achieving.
- **Shopper marketing objective(s):** The actual objective(s) that the shopper marketing campaign should achieve (e.g., increase purchase frequency) to help achieve the marketing objective and, the shopper marketing campaign goal, as well as properly address the challenge or the opportunity that justified the shopper marketing campaign in the first place.
- **Shopper marketing target(s):** The specific shopper type(s) (within the marketing target or the communication audiences) that will be targeted for the shopper marketing campaign and of who the campaign aims at obtaining a certain change of purchase behavior (during the time of the campaign) in order to achieve the selected shopper marketing objectives.
- **SWOT:** A strategic planning technique used to help identify the strengths, weaknesses, opportunities, and threats related to a product or service; used in project planning. Strengths and weakness are derived from internal factors, such as specific product features, whereas

opportunities and threats are derived from external factors, such as competitive new product entries.

An Expert's Perspective

In Shopper Marketing planning, the problem is that all too often, initiatives are created by the brand team and therefore do not meet the needs of a retailer, so the shopper team has to retrofit the program in order to get the retailer's support. This retrofitting wastes an immense amount of internal resources. To fix this, retailer and shopper needs must be pulled to the very beginning of the planning process and given the same strategic weight as the consumer and brand inputs.

– Christopher Brace, Founder & CEO, Syntegrate Consulting

Key Concepts

A thorough and complex nine-step shopper marketing planning process

As with any other business or marketing-related activities, shopper marketing campaigns require proper planning so that the right offer is communicated to the right target at the right time through the right channels and touchpoints, and for the right purpose. As stated previously in this book, there is a need for a key set of steps to be managed in a particular sequence to ensure that the campaign will be efficiently and effectively conceived and implemented.

There are nine steps that we have identified from many examples of effective shopper marketing campaigns development and that are covered in this chapter:

- Step 1: The shopper marketing campaign (client) project brief
- Step 2: Defining the shopper marketing objectives
- Step 3: (Shopper) market and past shopper marketing campaigns analysis
- Step 4: Selection of "best" shopper marketing targets and development of a shopper persona
- Step 5: Identification of the desired change in purchase behavior of targeted shoppers
- Step 6: The shopper marketing creative process and the "big" campaign idea
- Step 7: Creation of the Communication Plan for the Campaign
- Step 8: Financial projections
- Step 9: Control, evaluation, and measurements

This planning discipline applies not only to the inputs that are required for the shopper marketing planning to start but also within the process itself from one step to another. Without proper planning, under the pressure of politics, misunderstanding, or ignorance, a shopper marketing campaign can easily end up focusing on the wrong offer to the wrong target at the wrong time through the wrong channels and touchpoints, and for the wrong purpose.

As you can imagine, under these circumstances, it is very unlikely that your shopper marketing campaign will ever succeed.

Let's go through each step of the planning process.

Step 1: The Shopper Marketing Campaign (Client) Project Brief

When correctly done, a shopper marketing campaign starts with a brief. This can be from a client if you are an agency (and this will be called a "client brief" in that case). The brief typically originates in the marketing department, as they are responsible for providing brand directives to all groups working on the brand.

No matter what, you need a brief that will set the stage for what is needed from you as a shopper marketing professional. The formalization of this brief can also help you determine if shopper marketing is an appropriate marketing communication discipline for the challenge at hand. For example, if the communication objective stated in the brief is for a campaign designed to boost the appeal of a brand, it is unlikely that shopper marketing will be the best discipline to help achieve this. It is more likely that a public relations or advertising campaign would drive brand appeal.

It is important to understand that it is unlikely that the specifics of what you would need for the shopper marketing campaign (e.g., shopper marketing objectives, shopper marketing targets, and the expected change of purchase behaviors) will be enumerated in the brief. It is more likely that the brief will contain a mix of marketing and marketing communications elements that will provide the stage for the planning of your shopper marketing campaign. What the shopper marketer will need to do is to ask questions in order to obtain the necessary information to develop and plan a successful shopper marketing campaign.

The information that is necessary to have is listed next. If it is not included in the project brief, it should be ascertained and then added to the brief.

Overview of the Required Components of a Shopper Marketing Campaign Project Brief

The initial brief should contain several key elements to assist in 1) determining if shopper marketing is really the appropriate discipline to use and 2) starting the actual shopper marketing planning process.

Basics of the Assignment:

What are you actually being asked to develop for this project? (i.e., What is the marketing team asking you to do?) See the following examples:

- Develop and execute a summer promotion

- Activate multiple retailers using a month-long promotion
- Support the launch of a new product

Background:

The brief should cover background information so as to provide the appropriate context for understanding the product situation and the need for a shopper marketing campaign. This information can include, the following:

- Where is the product in its life cycle? Is it new? Growing? Declining? Under siege by the competition?
- Are there important consumer trends in the product category? What are they? Are there negative or positive consumer trends? What are they?
- What is the marketing objective of the product or service (for this campaign)?
    - Is the marketing for this product focused on acquisition, loyalty, retention or win-back?
    - Remember the marketing objectives should be SMART, which stands for specific, measurable, achievable, relevant, and with a timetable
        - For example, a SMART acquisition objective could be to acquire 1500 new customers within six months for a new service, from a target customer defined as female—forty to fifty years old—upper executive management role in top key cities in the US
        - An example of a SMART win-back objective would be to obtain a new (one item) purchase from past customers (inactive for at least six months) by end of the year
- Who is the target customer for the marketing objective?
    - Prospects, current customers or past customers?
    - What information is there about this customer?
        - Demographics
        - Psychographics
        - Geographics
        - Behavioral characteristics (in relation to their use of the product)
- What is the value proposition of the product or service?
    - Remember, this is what the campaign is being designed to alter temporarily
    - How would you summarize the value proposition? Is it based on specific product features? If so, what are those features and resulting benefits to the customer?
    - What is the pricing strategy for the product in relation to the price side of the value proposition? If your value proposition is more benefits for a lesser price, how is it formally converted into your actual pricing strategy?
- Will this shopper marketing campaign be part of a larger marketing campaign or will it be a stand-alone effort?
    - If part of a larger campaign, what are the details of that campaign? See the following examples:

        - Major selling idea
        - Big idea and message
        - Media plan
        - Timing
- Details on the product such as how and when it is used by consumers, season, price points, and competitive information are necessary to obtain

Opportunity or Challenge:

What is the actual opportunity or challenge that justifies the need for a shopper marketing campaign?

- Below are several examples of appropriate opportunities or challenges:
    - A competitive product that is directly aimed at your top-selling retailer is being launched and its impact needs to be minimized or even nullified
    - You are in the soft drink business and soft drink consumers are dramatically shifting to healthy options when purchasing products like yours. You have a new healthy soft drink product that you need to support the launch of sales
    - You have a new companion product (such as a conditioner for a shampoo product) that you want your current shampoo customers to use as well

Shopper Marketing Campaign Goal(s)

This particular section would be the overall goal of the shopper marketing campaign expressed as SMART goals.

Examples of shopper marketing campaign goals include the following:

- Boost sales of the product during summer months by a certain percentage
- Have product B purchased with product A for 50 percent of the purchases during the last two weeks of a given month

The Shopper Marketing Campaign Strategy Statement

A brief statement is needed on how the campaign should be achieving the shopper marketing campaign goal.

This statement is a direction from the product manager or the marketing communication manager regarding how the shopper marketing campaign can accomplish the goal.

More often than not, this is set up very much like a communication strategy statement but with a shopper focus/ twist. For example, see the following statement:

- **GET** the targeted shopper with his or her shopper characteristics
- **TO** engage a certain act of purchase as expected with the shopper marketing campaign goal
- **BY** communicating a key argument/message to generate the expected purchase behavior

- **BECAUSE** of a particular reason linked to the product or an offer.

For example, for a shopper marketing campaign for Reebok Classics several years ago, Reebok provided this shopper marketing campaign strategy statement to its agency:

- **GET** men who wear lifestyle sneakers as a punctuation to their style
- **TO** choose Reebok as a relevant style accessory
- **BY** inspiring them to follow the passions that move them
- **BECAUSE** Reebok unites people together through music, art, and fashion and their classics line

Communication Objectives

What are the communication objectives that the shopper marketing campaign should ultimately help achieve?

A strong shopper marketing practitioner should ask the marketing team for the communication objectives for which the shopper marketing campaign will support the achievement. This is even more needed when the shopper marketing campaign is one element of a bigger marketing communications campaign and shall be integrated into and supportive of an on-going brand positioning strategy.

Remember that communication objectives are not shopper marketing objectives. Communication objectives are one level up. In chapter 4, using the hierarchy of effect response model, these objectives are stated as awareness, knowledge, liking, preference, conviction, and purchase.

So while they are not shopper marketing objectives, they help detect if shopper marketing should be used, and if so, for what purpose.

For example, if the communications objective is to build awareness for a new product, shopper marketing will not be the most obvious marketing communication method to use. Advertising or PR will be far more appropriate. This does not mean that shopper marketing cannot play a role at some point, but shopper marketing is here to generate a boost of sales, so awareness of the product need to be established first before attention can be directed toward this boost.

On the contrary, if the communication objective is to push for actual conviction and purchase, shopper marketing will then be a perfect marketing communication method to use.

If the shopper marketing campaign is not part of a bigger marketing campaign, (and whenever possible, overall communication objectives for the product or brand should be provided by the marketing manager, as a general reference to respect), the communication objectives should be communicated in the "constraints and requirements" section of the project-client brief.

Communication Audiences

If the shopper marketing element is part of a bigger campaign, who is the target for that campaign?

In the case of a bigger marketing campaign, the communication audience for that campaign should be the baseline for selection of the shopper marketing target. Again, the goal is to align shopper marketing activities with the overall brand marketing activities.

If there is no bigger campaign, then the marketing target will be the direct baseline for selecting the shopper marketing target.

Shopper Marketing Campaign Partnerships

- Are there any partnerships that the shopper marketing campaign should incorporate?
    - The partnership could be with one or several retailers or with one or several other manufacturers that sell complementary products. For example, a peanut butter manufacturer might create a campaign in partnership with a jelly manufacturer.
- If so, what are the expectations and specifics to be respected for the partnership?
    - For example, the marketing team includes in the brief that the shopper marketing campaign should be developed as an exclusive offer with one particular retailer. The brief should include what this means in terms of the ability to communicate with the retailer's consumers, what type of access will there be to the retailer's database, and what access will there be to advertising space outside and inside the store.

Constraints and Requirements

- Are there any constraints and requirements that should be respected as the campaign is conceived and developed?
- What are the brand values that the shopper marketing campaign must seek to support?
- Who are the retailer(s) to engage the campaign with (if not mentioned already in the partnership section)?
- What are the key dates for the campaign, including launch and end dates, as well as deliverables of creative materials and the review/approval process?
- What is the budget for the campaign? Knowing the budget, which can be expressed as a dollar range, is critical because campaign expenditure can vary tremendously based on the specifics of the execution. Therefore, a project brief must contain a budget in order to direct proper development of the campaign and avoid a great deal of wasted time and energy.

Importantly, obtaining the required information is to some extent an iterative process. The initial brief may not contain all that you need. However, with patience and perseverance, the information can be obtained. What is key for a shopper marketer is to, in fact, strive to secure as much of this information as possible, because the more you know, the closer your team can be to develop a strong campaign that will be successful in generating the type of incremental revenue that is expected.

Let's Take a Look at a Good Example of a Shopper Marketing Client Brief Received by the Shopper Marketing Agency Tracy Locke from Pepsi Cola, for a Summer Promotion Campaign.

Assignment:

Create a national shopper marketing program and sales promotion at CVS that links Diet Pepsi to fashion.

Background:

The Pepsi Brand as the foundation:

- "Live for Now" is not a description of current affairs; it is a motto that speaks to a belief system (mind-set). At the heart of this belief system is the view that the world is an amazing place.
- "Live for Now" is a call to arms for all who want to explore this world and are open to the possibilities it offers.
    - *It is an expression of optimism.*
    - *It stands for an effervescent engagement with everyday living.*
    - *It is about a desire to be fully present and truly experience the joys of life.*
- Diet Pepsi believes life should be lived fully and in the moment—less worry, more lightness—and anchored around the people who matter the most. Diet Pepsi's crisp, bubbly refreshment re-centers you so you can reconnect with your vibrant NOW.

Marketing Objective and Target: Loyalty and Current Customers

- Obtain more sales from current customers of Diet Pepsi

Opportunity or Challenge:

Leverage the natural association of the Pepsi Brand with a fashion-oriented lifestyle by partnering with a fashion retailer leader (CVS).

CVS is a convenient easy-to-shop luxury retailer where women can go to pamper themselves. It is moving its position from a drug store to a trusted advisor for health and wellness ("Reinventing Beauty" platform, new-life format of stores with beauty in the front of the store and on lower aisles, beauty club offers and rewards through ExtraCare loyalty program).

Communication Objectives:

Diet Pepsi is *THE* diet soda associated with fashion

Communication Audiences:

Upbeat and connected woman (aged thirty-five to fifty-four), all incomes levels and household sizes

- She is upbeat and connected
- She leads a full life—a lot of responsibilities, a lot of running around
- She has a lot of personality and is comfortable in her own skin
- She has a light, optimistic view on life
- People like being around her because she is upbeat and fun

Shopper Marketing Campaign Goal(s):

- Boost Diet Pepsi purchase frequency of current customers during the promotion

The Shopper Marketing Campaign Strategy Statement:

- GET fun, connected women who like to look great and feel great
- TO buy Diet Pepsi at CVS
- BY linking Diet Pepsi with fashion through CVS's health and beauty offerings
- BECAUSE we can leverage the culture-forward message of "The Excitement of Now" by linking it with Diet Pepsi's fashion assets.

Shopper Marketing Campaign Partnership:

CVS and Diet Pepsi

Constraints and Requirements:

The campaign has to do the following:

- Respect the Pepsi brand identity and promise
- Leverage Pepsi's assets, including, for example, celebrity endorsements, concerts sponsorships, etc.)

Step 2: Defining the Shopper Marketing objectives

Once the stage is set through a proper campaign brief and it has been decided that a shopper marketing campaign is a proper solution, the next step is to define the most appropriate shopper marketing objectives for the campaign.

Definition and Options

As stated in chapter 4 and in the overview earlier in this chapter, shopper marketing objectives should be linked to the shopper and therefore defined in shopper terms. This is because (as we have learned), shopper marketing is designed to ultimately drive sales and change purchase behavior, so the related objectives should be stated in those terms to generate the expected incremental sales at the time the promotion is executed.

Examples of common shopper marketing objectives used by businesses are as follows:

- Increase purchase frequency
- Generate product trial
- Increase transaction size
- Increase usage occasions
- Increase the number of distribution outlets
- Increase shelf space
- Increase in-store presence
- Expand the selling season

As stated in chapter 4, this list is not exhaustive. You can create your own shopper marketing objectives, as long as they relate to increasing sales for a particular product or service and imply a shift in shopping behavior at the time of the promotion.

The link with marketing (and communication) objectives

As mentioned before in chapter 4, the shopper marketing objectives must be aligned with the brand marketing objectives.

As illustrated by the following chart, the marketing objectives (and targets) give the foundation for selecting the shopper marketing objectives from the list of potential objectives.

Examples of alignment and selection can be found next.

If your marketing objective is acquisition targeting prospects (i.e., new customers), the following shopper marketing objectives could potentially be appropriate:

- Generate product trial
- Increase usage occasions (so new customers try the brand for this new occasion that might be more attractive to them)
- Increase the number of distribution outlets (if new venues for sale would increase the likelihood new customers would try the brand)
- Increase the shelf space and in-store presence (if the product is a new launch)
- Expand the selling season (if expanding to a new selling season would attract new customers)

If your marketing objective is loyalty targeting current customers, the following shopper marketing objectives could apply:

- Increase transaction size
- Increase purchase frequency
- Generate product trial (for a new product manufactured by the same company aimed at the same current customers)
- Increase usage occasions (if additional usage occasions would stimulate current customers to buy more of the same product)
- Increase the number of distribution outlets (if, for example, by increasing where the brand is available might increase sales as these new retail outlets are locations where your current customer is now shopping)
- Increase the shelf space and in-store presence (if it is related to supporting the launch of a new product)
- Expand the selling season (if expanding to a new selling season would result in current customers to purchase more of the brand)

Similarly, if your marketing objective is retention targeting current customers who are purchasing less than before (i.e., "going away"), the following shopper marketing objectives could also be applicable:

- Generate product trial (for a new, improved version of your product aimed at the "going-away" customer target)
- Increase usage occasions (if the new occasion attracts "going-away" customer target to use the product "again")

- Increase the number of distribution outlets (if, for example, increasing where the brand is available might increase sales as these new retail outlets are locations where your "going-away" customer target is shopping)
- Increase the shelf space and in-store presence (if it is related to supporting the launch of a new improved version of your product for your "going-away" current customers)
- Expand the selling season (if expanding to a new selling season would result in your "going-away" current customers purchasing the brand again as they used to)
- Re-increase purchase frequency or transaction size (if, for example, the decline in frequency or transaction size is linked to the lack of special offers directly aimed at your "going-away" current customers—who might be aggressively targeted by your competition)

In contrast, if the marketing objective is win back targeting past customers, the following shopper marketing objectives might be applicable:

- Generate product trial (of a new and improved version of the product to stimulate past customers to purchase the brand again)
- Increase usage occasions (if this means that the new usage occasion aims at bringing past customers back)
- Increase the number of distribution outlets (if this means that the new distribution aims at bringing past customers back because this is where they now shop for products like yours)
- Increase the shelf space and in-store presence (if it is related to supporting the launch of a new product aimed at bringing past customers back)
- Expand the selling season (if this means that the new season will help bring past customers back)

Development of specific Shopper Promotion objectives

In order to establish clear and actionable objectives, it is important to apply the following two principles:

1. *Select the objectives that are most aligned with the achievement of the campaign goal, communication objectives, and ultimate marketing objectives.* This is highly important because any given shopper marketing campaign should focus on two to three objectives and not more. Being able to prioritize a "wish list" of objectives requires discipline to select the ones most aligned with achieving the marketing objectives overall.
2. *SMARTize the selected objectives.*

Next, are a few examples to help illustrate these two principles.

If your marketing objective is acquisition of new customers for a new product and your communication objectives are to build brand awareness, knowledge, and liking, along with creating preference and conviction for the brand, a set of appropriate shopper marketing objectives might be the following:

- Generate trial for the new product through sampling
- Increase the in-store presence of the product with special displays, posters, etc.
- Increase shelf space of the product during the promotion

The examples of these objectives when they are SMARTized are as follows:

- The generating trial objective might become "Achieve 30 percent effective (actual) product trial on 20,000 distributed samples by the end of the two-week campaign" (This would mean that 30 percent of the 20,000 samples would be used during the two weeks of the campaign).
- The in-store presence objective might become "70 percent of daily store visitors shopping for your product category are exposed to the shopper marketing campaign message in retail stores during the time of the campaign."
- The increase-shelf-space objective might become "50 percent of shoppers shopping for your product category in aisle X will see your new product and the associated offer during the time of the promotion."

As another example, if your marketing objective is retention (because your surveys and sales data indicated that your (or some of your) customers are on their way out) and your communication objectives are focused on rebuilding preference, conviction, and purchase, a set of good shopper marketing objectives might be one of the following:

- (Re)increase purchase frequency and transaction size (as the issue seems to be linked to a reduced purchase frequency and transaction size trends that you want now to reverse).
- Increase usage occasions (if based on your research, you found that your customers have identified a "better" alternative product for the first usage occasion (that justified their initial purchases of your product) but they have another usage occasion that they do not associate your product with yet and that you could leverage to make them purchase again). A good way to imagine such a scenario would be to think of baking soda. While it might be selling less for actually baking, a cleaning/ air freshener usage application for baking soda offers (as we know) some great sales potential.

The examples of these objectives when they are SMARTized are as follows:

- An "increase-purchase-frequency" objective might be expressed as "increase the purchase frequency from one to two purchases per week during the promotion."
- An "increase-transaction-size" objective might be expressed as, "Move transaction size per purchase back to $50 during the three-week promotion—with 25% of the purchasers continuing at that transaction level after the promotion."
- The "increase-usage-occasions" objective might be expressed as "by the end of the three-week promotion, 20 percent of purchases will have been made with the newly identified usage occasion as the purchase reason – with 30% of the concerned purchasers continuing to purchase for the new occasion after the promotion"

Step 3: (Shopper) Market and Past Shopper Marketing Campaigns Analysis

Once the shopper marketing objectives have been defined, the next step is to thoroughly understand the category your brand competes in and the environment surrounding that category and your brand in particular. This knowledge will assist the shopper marketer in formulating an effective campaign, using this information as the context surrounding the brand.

- This knowledge is gathered and compiled as a SWOT analysis.
- SWOT, as previously discussed, stands for strengths, weaknesses, opportunities, and threats. The information that helps build the SWOT consists of the areas described next and on the following pages.

Internal and External Environment Analysis

As mentioned in chapter 4, effective shopper marketing planning requires a thorough analysis of the following:

- The target customer and his or her behavior
- The competition
- The environment surrounding the product or service
- Past shopper marketing campaigns results

The Target Customer and His or Her Behavior

For shopper marketing, this research and analysis focus on the purchase and shopping behavior of the target customer outlined in the initial project brief.

The shopper marketing objectives that have been established imply a certain purchase behavior for those objectives to be achieved. For example, if the shopper marketing objective is to "increase purchase frequency," that means your marketing target, when he or she has reached the shopping stage, must come purchase at the store more often during the promotion.

In this scenario, it would be important to start with a shopper target whose current purchase behavior will be the easiest to influence (i.e., to get that target customer to buy more often). Objectively, consumers who already purchase the product regularly could be a very good shopper marketing target as they might be more easily convinced to increase their purchase frequency during the time of the promotion.

Understanding who is the best target customer would involve analyzing the types of shoppers that you have in your product category and for your product or brand, particularly.

- Are they price sensitive or value sensitive?
- Are they loyal to brands? If yes, which ones?
- Are they creatures of habit?
- Are they switching brands?

These answers will tell the shopper marketer which shopper types are in your market (non-users, loyal users, competitive loyals, switchers (with different subcategories), or price buyers) and what the proportion of each is in the mix.

The next step would be to define the type of specific purchase behavior of each target. Using the previous example, the "loyal user" segment of your product, users who purchase the product do so 70 or 80 percent of the time. This will be your baseline for the purchase behavior change that you expect from your campaign.

The Competition

Analyzing the competition is another critical piece of the puzzle in terms of creating an accurate and powerful shopper marketing campaign. Without a thorough understanding of the competition, the shopper marketer can easily waste valuable assets and create a campaign that is ineffective.

This analysis should include the following:

1. Who are the competitors, what are their products and offerings, where do they sell their product, and at what price points do they sell?
2. What type(s) of shopper targets does each competitor attract?

   For example, if one of your competitors has a high proportion of loyal users in its shoppers base, it will be very difficult for you to "steal" them away. If, on the other hand, your competitors tend to attract primarily price buyers, it would be important to consider if it is desirable to go after its shoppers as it will certainly mean a price and discount war that might not be worthwhile to engage in, and, moreover, might be counterproductive to achieving the shopper marketing objectives for the campaign.
3. What types of shopper marketing campaigns do each of the competitors execute? Are they all about discount, sweepstakes, or cause-related promotions?

4. Which retailer(s) does each competitor execute campaigns with? For example, you might want to avoid the retailers the competitors work with or, on the contrary, you might decide to "attack" the competitors by engaging bigger shopper marketing campaigns than they do and do so on their turf with "their" retailers.
5. What consumer and trade promotion tactics does each competitor use?

   Whatever it is for consumer or trade-promotion tactics, you might decide to come up with the same techniques they already used but create even larger campaigns, or you might decide to propose other incentives (that have never been used by your competition) to be sure to generate an interest from the retailers that the competition partners with and from the targeted shoppers at those retailers.
6. What activities are being planned by each competitor?

   This information may be difficult to obtain, but it can be very helpful. For example, a competitor might be planning the launch of a new product that will be directly aimed at your best customers and will be supported by an aggressive shopper marketing campaign. This information can be valuable as you plan for your own campaign, but it will also help you decide what specific action you should take to counter the competitive move. The counter-attack could involve consumer promotion elements and/or trade promotion elements (to make the retailers the competitors count on to launch the new product less supportive of the launch, for example).

The Environment Surrounding the Product or Service

Gaining an understanding of the "environment" surrounding the product category can provide meaningful and actionable information on the specifics of the shopper marketing campaign to be created.

For example, a societal tipping point might have been reached where people are systematically considering the health impact and sustainability of products when making purchase decisions. Not only would this impact the type of products your company develops, but it might also impact the type of offers that you should consider as part of your shopper marketing campaigns.

For example, if you manufacture car sound systems and having an understanding of the importance of sustainability for your target, your shopper marketing campaign could include sweepstakes in which the grand prize is an electric car.

Past Shopper Marketing Campaigns Results

Using past campaign results is a powerful way to guide future campaigns. This type of analysis can illustrate what worked and what did not work, as well as show how to improve future initiatives.

The learning could be linked, for example, to the reaction of certain shopper types to certain techniques in your product category or to the lack of collaboration of certain retailers for certain types of promotions.

The learning you extract will depend on the nature and the intensity of your past shopper marketing campaigns.

The Shopper Marketing SWOT Analysis

With the information outlined on the previous pages, the shopper marketing SWOT analysis can be completed.

As it has been stated, strengths and weaknesses relate to your business, and opportunities and threats related to the environment surrounding your brand and category.

For the purposes of shopper marketing planning, those strengths, weaknesses, opportunities, and threats **have to relate to the shopper marketing strategies and activities.**

This is very important to remember as people tend to SWOT brands or business situations in general, even when the exercise is supposed to focus on shopper marketing. So, things can very easily go off tangent and while you might end up with a good SWOT, it will not be related to shopper marketing.

Additionally, a SWOT analysis for shopper marketing can be tricky in terms of what statements belong in which category.

Here are two tips to help achieve a solid SWOT analysis for a shopper marketing campaign:

- A first key question to ask yourself as you analyze the insights is "how related and relevant is each insight to develop the planned shopper marketing campaign?"
    - For example, an asset, such as having a well-known brand with access to celebrities, might be relevant to a shopper marketing campaign. This strength could be leveraged through a national sweepstakes, giving away concert tickets and/or a meet-and-greet with the celebrities.
    - Another asset, such as product durability, might not be relevant to your shopper marketing campaign as this is not something you are asked to focus on to stimulate the purchase.
    - A "slow production cycle" (while is clearly a weakness for the business) might not be relevant to your shopper marketing campaign because it has always been the case for your product and your company was able to launch successful promotions in the past.
- Another key question to ask yourself is, "in which SWOT category does this insight belong in terms of helping you actually achieve the shopper marketing objectives?" Where the insight will be placed in the SWOT analysis will depend on the contribution of that insight in achieving the campaign goal(s).
    - For example, the insight is "the current brand is strong and recognized by the shopper target." This might be perceived as a strength, but only if the promotion is focused

on that same brand. This might be a weakness if the goal of the company is to replace this brand with another—with the support of your shopper marketing campaign.

- Another example might be the insight "consumers are purchasing more and more in bulk quantities." This might be an opportunity if the shopper marketing objective is to increase transaction size. However, it could be a threat if the campaign goal is to generate trial for a new product as the shoppers might not consider bulk purchase for new products.

Example

What follows is an example of a properly developed and formulated shopper marketing-focused SWOT analysis. A new product from one of your key competitors is being launched—with a direct aim at your best selling product. So, you decide to engage an immediate shopper marketing campaign with the objective to "increase the transaction size" of your loyal users for your product. This will make your loyal users stock up your product and, therefore, be off-market when the competitive product is launched.

STRENGTHS:	WEAKNESSES:
• Great relationship with retailers for building in-store promotions • Past BOGO offers performed well in increasing transaction size	• Not large enough inventory of products at targeted retailers to support BOGO offer • Shopper marketing budget is cut by 10 percent
OPPORTUNITIES:	THREATS:
• Overall, consumers are increasingly interested in BOGO offers • Retailers' sales are stagnant and they are looking for opportunities to grow sales before the end of year	• Key competitor is known for providing large trade promotion incentives to its retailers • Retailers are more and more resistant to overstock products

Step 4: Selection of "Best" Shopper Marketing targets and development of a Shopper Persona

Executing a SWOT analysis has provided the following:

- The context within which you will have to develop and implement the shopper marketing campaign
- Clear indications of the type of purchase behavior of the target consumer and the shopper types to which those behaviors correspond

With this information, the most effective shopper marketing target(s) to focus on can be established for optimizing the shopper marketing campaign.

Selection Logic

As we know, according to Don Schultz, there are five main types of shoppers (loyal users, competitive loyals, switchers (with many sub-categories), price buyers and non-users).

The shopper marketing objectives that you have selected gave you an idea of the type of purchase behavior that you should expect to achieve with the shopper marketing campaign.

Based on your analysis in Step 3, you also know the type of shoppers you have in the market in which you aim.

At that stage comes the practice to match that information to select the best shopper marketing targets—meaning the "best" shopper types within the targeted market segment that will be the most inclined (based on their current purchase behavior) to have the expected behavior change and, therefore, help achieve the shopper marketing objectives.

The Link between Shopper Marketing Targets and Marketing Targets Communication Audiences

As stated before, everything is linked. So, you have to select the shopper targets from within the marketing target that has been given to you or, if the shopper marketing campaign is part of a bigger marketing campaign, the communication audience for the bigger campaign.

How to Select and Formulate Your Shopper Marketing Targets

As illustrated by the chart, within the context of the marketing objectives and targets that are at the foundation of the campaign, shopper marketing objectives will dictate which shopper target is most appropriate to achieve those objectives.

Let's look at each possible shopper marketing objective and assess what such objective implies in terms of best shopper targets:

Increase Purchase Frequency

- The best shopper types—if applicable to your campaign and available in your market—will be the loyal users, followed by switchers (as long as those switchers switch to your brand from time to time). The selection could also depend on if the marketing objective is loyalty or retention as loyalty will call for loyal users and retention will certainly call for switchers first.
- Price buyers might be the third option—if loyal users and switchers are not present in the market (or there is not enough of them) and as long as they purchase from you already (meaning that you are a low price brand or product and you attract such shopper type).

Generate Product Trial

- All shopper types might be applicable here. This will all depend on the context and the justification for the shopper marketing campaign.
- Now, it might be easier to make your loyal users or even your switchers try a new product from you than it is to have switchers (who switch between competitive brands), competitive loyals, or non-users do so. It might be that the new product is aimed at stealing consumers

away from the competition. In this case, the choice will be between switchers (who switch between competitive brands) and/or competitive loyals.

Increase Transaction Size

- The best shopper types—if applicable to your campaign and available in your market—will be, of course, the loyal users followed by switchers (as long as those switchers switch to your brand from time to time).
- Price buyers might not be an easy option if loyal users and switchers are not present in the market. Now, price buyers might be interested in bulk purchase.

Increase Usage Occasions

- Depending on the genesis of the campaign from the client-project brief, the selection of the shopper targets can go in many directions.
- If the usage occasions' expansion is linked to having more applications of the same product with the same consumers, loyal users will be the first choice for loyalty and switchers (as long as those switchers switch to your brand from time to time) for retention—even though switchers might not be an easy shopper target in this context.
- If the usage occasions' expansion is linked to acquiring new customers, switchers, (who switch between competitive brands),competitive loyals, and, in the last position, non-users will be better choices.

Increase the Number of Distribution Outlets

- Once again, depending on the genesis of the campaign from the client-project brief, the selection of the shopper targets can go in many directions.
- If the goal is to generate more sales from the current customers by being present in more outlets, then loyal users will be the first choice—once again followed by switchers (as long as those switchers switch to your brand from time to time).
- If the goal is to gain sales back from current customers through the multiplication of the distribution outlets at new retailers, then switchers (as long as those switchers switch to your brand from time to time) will be the most obvious shopper target choice.
- If the goal is to gain sales back from past customers or to acquire new customers through new distribution outlets, then switchers, (who switch between competitive brands), competitive loyals, and, in the last position, non-users will be better choices.

Increase the Shelf Space/ Increase the In-Store Presence

- If the goal is to generate more sales from the current customers by increasing the shelf space and/or the store presence, then loyal users will be the first choice—once again followed by switchers (as long as those switchers switch to your brand from time to time).
- If the goal is to gain sales back from current customers by increasing the shelf space and/or the store presence, then switchers (as long as those switchers switch to your brand from time to time) will be the most obvious shopper target choice.
- If the goal is to gain sales back from past customers or to acquire new customers by increasing the shelf space and/or the store presence, then switchers (who switch between competitive brands), competitive loyals and, in the last position, non-users will be better choices.

Expand the Selling Season

- If the selling season expansion is linked to having more purchase justifications for the same product with the same consumers, loyal users will be the first choice for loyalty—once again followed by switchers (as long as those switchers switch to your brand from time to time), even though switchers might not be an easy target.
- If the selling season expansion is linked to acquiring new customers, switchers, who switch between competitive brands), competitive loyals, and, in the last position, non-users will be better choices.

The Shopper Persona

In order to develop a strong shopper marketing campaign that changes purchase behavior, a deeper understanding of the target customer is necessary.

The understanding should be as detailed as possible to formulate a "persona" describing that particular person. The information should be gathered in terms of the consumer and shopping behaviors as it relates to your specific product and for the product category your brand is in.

Examples of key questions to obtain appropriate information on your shopper target for building a persona are as follows:

- What are their goals, issues, and concerns as individuals and consumers?
- What is their lifestyle? What do they like to do? What are their activities and interests, hobbies, and opinions?
- What brands do they trust?
- How and where do they shop?
- What retailers do they use?

- What are their online purchase habits?
- What or who are they influenced by?
- What media do they consume? Offline? Online?

You should also focus your analysis on your product category and your product, in particular.

Based on this information, a persona can be derived. It is best to try to make the description as realistic as possible, even giving him or her a name and a face is suggested.

The following figures are examples of shopper personas.

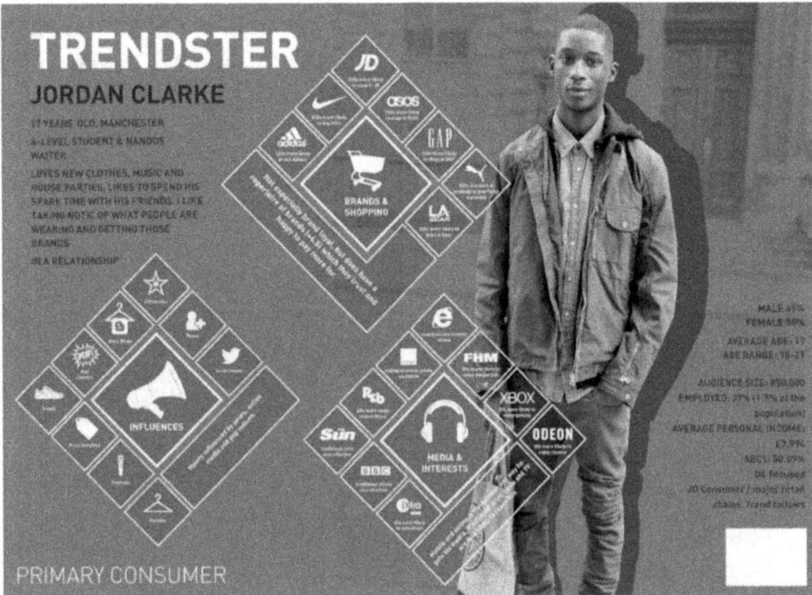

The above example of customer persona has all the elements of a power shopper persona with demographic information, a name and key insights on his influences, brands & shopping preferences as well as his media consumptions and interests.

In this other example, the shopper persona descriptions are more based on quotes and simples facts but the baseline information is identical and covers the same key elements of a shopper personality and behavior like his or her goal as well as his or her frustration and satisfaction when shopping.

As discussed later in this chapter, this persona and related insights will be critical to find the most effective solution for the shopper marketing campaign as outlined in the project brief.

A persona is also a powerful tool for developing the creative assets for the campaign—copy and visuals—that will hopefully resonate with the shopper target for the shopper marketing campaign.

Examples of How Agencies Develop and Formulate Customer Personas

The agency TPN uses a slightly different format to build their personas but has the same goal: to provide a life- and insights-based perspective of the targeted shopper in order to build an effective shopper marketing campaign.

The following are two examples by TPN:

7 Eleven Case

The image is a good illustration of a well-formulated campaign Ask with a picture of the product that the client would like to leverage for this promotion.

Source: TPN

This brief by 7 Eleven led to the development of the following shopper persona by TPN.

With 60% of convenience store "mission trips" being beverage related, 7-Eleven saw frozen carbonated beverages as a difference maker. But with so many choices it was going to take a truly unique experience to break through and connect.

M Shopper Mindset
When it comes to beverages, there are millions of choices. I can afford to be selective and pick the ones that get me.

B Shopper Behavior
I am always on social media. It's the way I communicate and how I capture all my day's biggest moments.

S Shopper Surroundings
I don't watch tv or pay attention to ads. Il get my entertainment from my friends and all my devices.

For this example, the agency that was in charge of the promotion decided to communicate the shopper persona to focus on with 3 profiling categories: Shopper Mindset, Shopper Behavior, and Shopper Surroundings. This is another way to structure and present shopper persona. This helps to provide useful insights to the creative staff to help them develop a powerful campaign idea.

Source: TPN

Sally Beauty Case

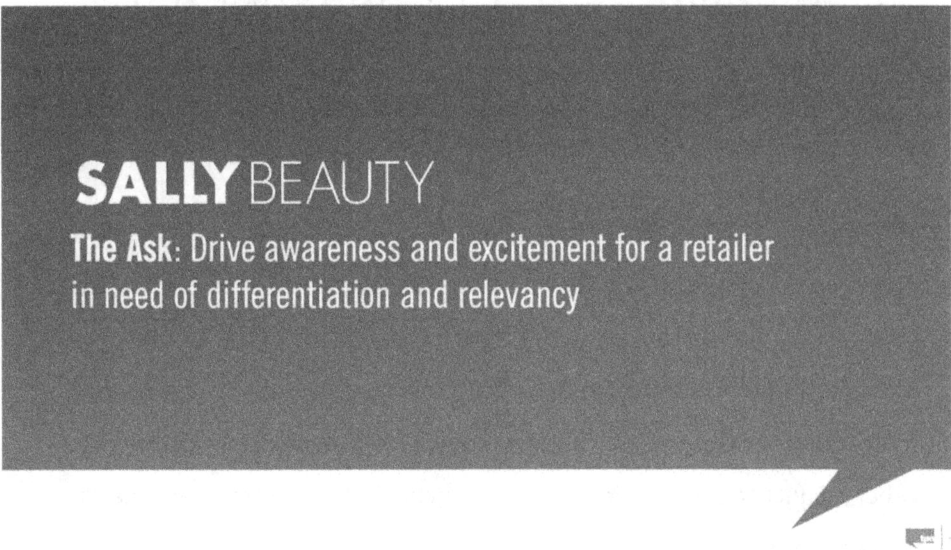

The image is another good illustration of a well-formulated Ask with a clear indication of the focus of the campaign in terms of driving awareness and excitement for a retailer brand.

Source: TPN

This brief by Sally Beauty led to the development of the following shopper persona by TPN.

SALLY BEAUTY wanted to create a unique and unexpected customer experience to entice DIY beauty lovers to consider Sally over their competitors such as Walmart, Sephora, Target and drugstores.

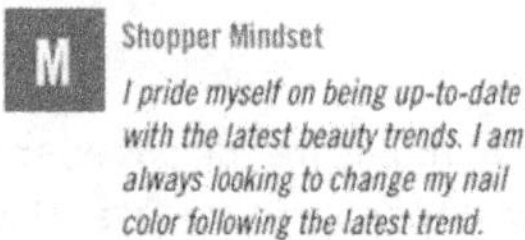

B Shopper Behavior
I am constantly on-the-go with little time to shop multiple retailers. It is important to have a variety of product options wherever I'm shopping.

S Shopper Surroundings
The majority of the retailers I shop have nail products scattered throughout the store.

For this example, the agency that was in charge of the promotion decided to use the same shopper persona profiling categories than the ones it uses for the 7 Eleven project: Shopper Mindset, Shopper Behavior, and Shopper Surroundings. This structure provides clear insights on the shopper target and how to communicate with him or her.

Source: TPN

Step 5: Identification of the Desired Change in Purchase Behavior of the Target Shoppers

Having selected the target shopper and developed a persona, the next step is to identify the specific change in purchase behavior that the campaign will be designed to accomplish, in order to achieve the selected shopper marketing objectives.

A Review

By way of a brief review, and as detailed in chapter 4, the expected changes of purchase behavior are listed next.

- More purchases being made of the same product on each shopping occasion
- More frequent purchases of the same product made by the same consumer
- Other products from the same company purchased by the same consumer
- Change in purchase timing
- Breaking loyalty-based purchases
- Forcing a switch to your brand
- Making the purchasers "stay" with your brand

This list is not exhaustive. The point is that the change in behavior should be based on purchase and immediacy of the required shopper action.

Of course, you could also aim at achieving no change in purchase behavior if, for example, you face a competitor's move to steal your customers away from your brand and, therefore, achieving an "unchanged" purchase behavior from your customers could be an appropriate accomplishment from your shopper marketing campaign. In that case, the desired change in purchase behavior will be to "reinforce your customers' behavior."

Selection of the Most Appropriate Desired Change in Purchase Behavior

Again, by way of a review, and as covered in chapter 4, the following table illustrates the connection between shopper targets and expected changes in purchase behavior.

Depending on the shopper marketing objective and selected shopper target, the most appropriate change in purchase behavior can be identified.

Shopper Marketing Target	Description	Expected Purchase Behavior Change(s)
Current Loyals	People who buy your product most or all of the time	•*Reinforce behavior* •*Increase consumption* •*Change purchase timing*
Competitive Loyals	People who buy a competitive product most or all of the time	•*Break loyalty* •*Switch to your product*
Switchers	People who buy a variety of products in the category	•*Persuade to "switch" to your product more often*
Price Buyers	People who consistently buy the least expensive brand	•*Match their value requirements to make them stay with your product*
Nonusers	People who don't use any product in the category	•None for Sales Promotion •Advertising & PR focus

Formulating the Specific Desired Change in Purchase Behavior

The desired change in purchase behavior should be expressed in specific terms and follow the SMART principles.

The following two examples will illustrate the process:

- Let's assume that your marketing department launches a new complementary product (for example a new conditioner to complement your shampoo product) that is aimed at your current customers. The shopper marketing objective is to "increase transaction size" and you know there are enough loyal users as shoppers to achieve this shopper marketing objective.

In this case, the expected change of purchase behavior for the loyal users' shopper marketing target should be "increasing consumption with more products purchased by the same consumer" during the promotion period.

- As another example, your marketing department indicates that there is a decline in purchase frequency from some current customers and they need a shopper marketing campaign to reverse this trend. Your analysis shows that many loyal users of your brand shifted to a switcher mode under the pressure of the competition with new products. Therefore, you select the switcher shopper target within the current customer base and identify the desired change in purchase behavior as "switching more often to your brand," with the ultimate goal of making those customers loyal users again.

As previously learned, it is important to optimize the effectiveness of the campaign by making the expected change in purchase behavior "SMART." Using the previous example, if the desired change in purchase behavior is to "increase consumption with more products purchased by the same consumer during the promotion period," the actual number of products to be purchased has to be stated, meaning, how many products have to be purchased at the same time by the same consumer? This then is making the desired change in purchase behavior a "SMART" change.

And, this specific expectation has, of course, to be aligned with the shopper marketing objectives. In the previous example, the shopper marketing objective is to "increase transaction size" among loyal users. This objective could become "increase transaction volume size by 100 percent during the promotion period." This will imply the expected change of purchase behavior to become SMART as well. For example, this could become "increasing consumption with an average of one more product purchased by the same consumer during the promotion period."

Using the previous second example, the process would be same. If the shopper marketing objective is to "increase purchase frequency" among a switcher target, the SMART version of this objective could be "increase purchase from 25 percent to 50 percent of the targeted purchase occasions during the promotion period." This objective could be expressed as follows in terms of a specific change in purchase behavior: "Convince switchers to switch **two times_more often** toward your brand during the promotion period."

Step 6: The Shopper Marketing Creative Process and The Selection of the Big Idea

The foundation is now set for a proper formulation of the campaign. The first step in doing so is to prepare a shopper marketing creative brief.

As the title indicates, a creative brief is a brief for the creative professionals who will work on the campaign. The creative team members can be part of an agency or they can be employed by your company. Either way, based on the client brief and all the steps that you have engaged in the shopper marketing planning process, the key is to incorporate the decisions made, the information gathered, and the Insights extracted to create a powerful, focused, and insights-based brief. A creative brief could be looked at as a "conversion" of the client brief into a document on which creative professionals can actually build their creative work.

Overview of the Shopper Marketing Creative Process

The steps listed next represent an overview of the shopper marketing creative process, where the ultimate goal is to develop a powerful and strategically-based shopper marketing campaign:

1. Execute research and analysis to understand the context, opportunities, and challenges associated with this campaign project and identify key insights that should be used for the conception and development of the campaign.
2. Identify the "best" shopper marketing objectives and target customer (and shopper persona) as well as the "best" change of purchase behavior to be expected.
3. Begin writing the shopper marketing creative brief.
4. Formalize and share the creative brief with the creative team. Be sure to update the creative brief based on their inputs. Details about what should be in a creative brief will be discussed later in this chapter.
5. Based on the approved creative brief, the assignment for the creative team is to develop big (creative) ideas. Details about what the "big idea" means will be discussed later in this chapter.
6. The "best" big idea is selected and the creative team is tasked with developing actual creative examples for the selected idea.
7. Assuming the examples are acceptable to the decision makers, the formal development of the campaign begins.

It is important to understand that multiple rounds of revisions are typically needed for the proper formulation of the creative brief, identification of the winning big idea, and the selection of the best creative executions for the winning big idea. Although these descriptions may appear straightforward and "simplistic," the actual process is "complex" and requires patience and perseverance.

Required Resources

Typically, the creation of a shopper marketing campaign involves multiple team members to assist with the analysis, preparation of the creative brief, and actual development of the campaign.

These key resources are as follows:

- **Research support** that will execute and analyze the research. Specifically, the research, as discussed earlier in this chapter, will include shopper market analysis (Step 3), past shopper marketing campaigns analysis (Step 3), identification of the best shopper marketing target (Step 4), and expected change in purchase behavior (Step 5)
- **A strategic planner** who will provide key insights (based on the gathered research) that will drive the development of the campaign "big idea" and its execution
- **A creative team** of graphic designers, copywriters, and digital technologists
- **A legal counsel** that will ensure the campaign is legally compliant

The Shopper Marketing Creative Brief

Before delving into the creative brief, it is important to note that the creative staff, and more often than not the creative director, will be involved in the formulation of the creative brief.

The creative brief stems from the initial client brief and parts of the initial client brief are included in the creative brief. The formulation of the creative brief is the foundation of the campaign because it serves as a roadmap that answers the who, what, how, when, where, and why of the campaign. It also includes how the campaign will be measured. The main goal of the creative brief is to keep the client and agency team members aligned and focused on "getting the job done."

The eleven components of the shopper marketing creative brief are next, along with an example to illustrate how the components could be actually expressed in the creative brief.

The Key Ask

The key Ask is a reminder of what you have been assigned to deliver. For example, consider these possibilities:

- A summer promotion
- A two-week campaign exclusive to one retailer
- A month-long multi-retailer activation campaign

This information comes from the project (client) brief.

Looking at a past shopper marketing campaign for a Quick Serve restaurant chain (QSR) in the US, which partnered with a large soft drink brand, this is what was written as the ask:

Create a national promotion campaign that will do the following:

- ***GET** current soft drink brand, lapsed QSR chain's consumers, ages eighteen to thirty-four*
- ***TO** purchase again at the QSR chain (where the soft drink brand is sold)*
- ***BY** leveraging the soft drink brand promise to "turn the everyday into something exciting and new" (also at the QSR chain)*
- ***BECAUSE** as for the soft drink brand, the QSR chain also has a uniquely exciting cravable positioning*

The Key Issue (or Opportunity) Justifying the Campaign

What is the justification for the campaign? This information also comes from the project (client) brief.

Using the same example for the (QSR) Quick Serve restaurant chain, **the key issue** *was stated as follows:*

- *The lapsed (past) consumers do not know that*
    - *their meal can be customized at the QSR Chain, and that*
    - *the food at the QSR Chain is freshly prepared*

Brand/Product Truth

- What is the brand promise? What does the brand stand for? What are its values? What is the brand personality?

This section has become increasingly more important as sales promotion has evolved into shopper marketing because of the necessity to have strategic alignment required with brand marketing and a longer-term view.

Taking this one step further, it is critical that the shopper marketing campaign being developed not only is aligned with the brand truth but also works to support it beyond just the short term.

*Using the same example of the QSR restaurant chain, this is what was written as **the brand truth**:*

- *QSR chain uniquely has the speed of a QSR and the customization of a deli.*

Buyer Persona (Profile and Shopping Habits)

Who is the precise target customer? What is the persona of that shopper?

*Using the same example of the QSR restaurant chain, this is what was written as **the buyer persona**:*

- *The target customers are MILLENNIALS wanting a quick meal and something new.: The shopper persona is LAPSED USERS (switchers who switch between competitive QSR brands and competitive loyals).*

Key Insights

This section is very important because here is where the creative team will be given information to help them brainstorm for ideas that will help achieve the shopper marketing objectives, connect with the targeted shopper, and obtain the expected change in purchase behavior.

The mind-set to use for providing key insights is to consider all data gathered and select the top two or three insights that are unique and best able to leverage in order to create the campaign idea.

*Using the same example of the QSR restaurant chain, this is what was written for **key insights:***

- ***Consumer Insights:***
    - *Millennials feel entitled to influence the world around them*
    - *Millennials live in a non-stop world that focuses on convenience and personalization. They have been enabled by parents to ask those in authority to*

bend the rules. Brands have started allowing Millennials to decide the future of their products

- ***Shopper Target Insights:***
    - *They seek instant gratification*
        - *Too busy to finish everything in a day*
        - *Fast food fits their lifestyle*
    - *They love to experiment with food*
        - *Like to try new food, drinks, and recipes*

Key Solution

In this section of the creative brief, the solution is stated in words. The solution needs to effectively address the key issue justifying the campaign and be linked to the key insights identified in order to address this issue properly.

Importantly, the solution serves as the foundation for the development of the big idea for the campaign. What this means from a practical standpoint is that the creative team should not be coming up with the solution but rather creative expressions of the solution. This is most successfully accomplished when the shopper marketing practitioner collaborates with the creative director to develop the solution so that the solution has creative potential.

*Using the same example of the QSR restaurant chain, this is what was written as **the solution**:*

- *Let QSR chain's visitors (who are soft drink brand drinkers) create their own personalized experience*

Shopper Experience, Key Touch Points, and Retail Partners

This section delineates the experience that the targeted shopper should have when exposed to the campaign as well as the touch points (inside and/or outside the store) where the campaign is communicated and with, if any, specific retail partners. The touch points could be, for example, a web page, a store shelf, just outside the store, on social media, etc.

*Using the same example of the QSR restaurant chain, this is what was written as **the shopper experience**:*

- *Fun and creative in-store experience as the consumers build their own food experience*

Key Partners (Retailers, etc.)

In this section, the partners are described in terms of who they are and what, if any, requirements they may have. These requirements could include, for example, what type of support they agreed on, what type of in-store promotional materials they will permit (if a retailer), and what type of brand alignment they may require. This is also the section where you will present any assets or insights on the partners (and/or their consumers) that might be relevant to the campaign and the shopper target.

Using the same example of the QSR restaurant chain, this is what was written as ***the key partner****:*

- *A very large soft drink company with a strong brand and strong celebrity endorsements to leverage*

Success Measurement

What defines success? This section spells out specific measurement evaluation criteria. Remember that you had to SMARTize your goal and objectives as well as be specific with your expected changes of purchase behaviors.

Using the same example of the QSR restaurant chain, this is what could have been written as ***the Success Measures****:*

- *Having 30% of the targeted shoppers trying again the QSR restaurant chain during the time of the promotion*

Considerations: Legal and Compliance Requirements and/or Constraints

What, if any, are the legal considerations, restrictions, and/or other requirements that the creative team must adhere to when developing the big campaign idea?

This could be legal requirements or linked to brand policies. It could also be connected to relevant perspectives on the shopper target. No matter what, if it is relevant to the campaign, it must be communicated to the creative team.

Using the same example of the QSR restaurant chain, this is what was written as ***the considerations****: Millennials love to*

- *listen to music and*
- *attend concerts*

The soft drink partner has key sponsorship and celebrity endorsement opportunities linked to music and concerts and will need to obtain permission from soft drink company on the creative material before it is produced.

Timeline

This section is about the expected timing for the development and revisions of the big idea campaign and subsequent executions and also includes the start and end date of the campaign.

Case Study of a Creative Brief

This case study will be used during the remainder of this chapter. It is to illustrate the creative process for development of a shopper marketing campaign. This case study is from the agency Tracy Locke and executed for Publix, which is an American supermarket chain.

The Key Ask

Develop two unique shopper marketing platforms that are inspired by Publix customer insights and embrace wellness and portability trends.

The Key Issue (or Opportunity)

How can Publix attract more of its Millennial shopper who prioritizes health and wellness in his or her grocery selection and is increasingly making smaller, more frequent, less planned trips?

Shopper Marketing Objective:

Increase Purchase Frequency with our Millennial shopper

Brand/Product Truth

Ours is to be the premier quality food retailer in the world.

Buyer Persona

- Older Millennials, twenty-five to thirty-four, (loyal users and switchers who switch to Publix from time to time)
    - Multitasking pulls them in many directions
    - They lead a more on-the-go, impulsive, and mobile lifestyle
    - They love environments that allow them to browse and discover
    - They want tools and approaches that inspire them to make better choices
    - They are significantly more likely to be influenced by single-serve packaging to purchase one food product over another

Key Insights

- The traditional way of shopping—once-a-week stock-up trips—is becoming less common as Millennials use varied retailers and quick fill-up trips.
- Calories, food, steps, heartbeats, miles, sleep—for Millennials, nearly every element of their daily lives can be tracked, and many are embracing this trend in order to optimize their health and wellness.

- As a generation that is making more meals at home than ever before, Millennials are constantly looking for inspiration, creativity, and useful solutions to help simplify meal preparation.

Key Solution

Inspire discovery in-store while empowering wellness at home

- Convenience
- Fitness tracking
- Meal planning, prep, and portability

Considerations: Legal and Compliance Requirements and/or Constraints

The program should be grounded in the following trends:

- Portions and portability—with a change in eating habits, consumers are snacking in between meals and looking for on-the-go options
- Living well—a holistic approach to health and wellness with a focus on attaining a longer, higher quality of life

Development of the Big Idea

The creative brief will be used by the creative team to develop the big idea. There are two main parts to the development of the big idea. The first is the campaign idea (also called concept statement) and the second is how the idea works.

The creative team will likely develop two to three ideas, and therefore two to three concept statements, with a section on how each one works. It is from this that the big idea will be selected (the best concept statement) and the campaign built.

Two main components:

Concept Statement

A shopper marketing concept statement is formulated as a pitch to the target shopper with the aim to have the shopper positively react to the campaign idea (and its related offers) and ultimately demonstrate the desired change in purchase behavior.

This is an actual pitch of the idea to the actual shopper. It is typically two to three short paragraphs and may include a slogan.

"How Will It Work?"

This section is briefly providing key elements on the construct of the idea so that readers can understand quickly how the idea will/could work. It should include what consumer promotion and trade promotion techniques will be used as well as a rough timeline. Ultimately, it should convince readers that the idea can be implemented and has some success potential.

Brainstorming Techniques

To assist in the development of big idea concept statements, brainstorming is commonly used. There are multiple techniques; below is one that works well to develop shopper marketing campaign concepts.

To illustrate this approach, let's imagine that the shopper marketing campaign brief is about developing a summer campaign to promote a new healthy soda for Hispanic millennials in the US.

Step 1: From the creative brief, you identify key categories or components on which the campaign will be focused. Using the previous example, the key components or categories could be the following:

- Summertime
- Healthy
- Soft drink
- Hispanic
- Millennials

Step 2: For each category, the team then comes up with words or short sentences describing what each component or category means for them. This is supposed to be done spontaneously, without thinking. The words should be what comes to mind right away and can be images, ideas, people, places, etc. Quantity is what matters here.

For example, "summer" might mean beach, sun, music, flirting, sports etc.; "healthy" might mean natural, organic, exercise, etc; "soft drink" might mean thirst, tasty, activities, etc; "Hispanic" might mean family, parties, heritage, etc.; and "Millennials" might mean entitled, confident, adventurous, etc.

Step 3: In this step, the words for each category should be re-grouped into themes. Using the previous example, the words could be re-grouped into the following themes:

- Beach time
- Concert scene
- Hispanic heritage theme
- Family theme
- Adventure theme
- Natural theme

Step 4: In this step, the embryo of the idea is created from the themes by associating the themes to form an idea. For example, a campaign idea might be one in which a Hispanic family wins a private party for their immediate family (Family theme) at a beach destination of their choice (Beach time) with music and natural products (Natural theme) from their original culture (Hispanic heritage theme).

This brainstorming process can be done multiple times for the same assignment and is recommended to be repeated as the team becomes more knowledgeable about the product, the shopper, and the retail environment.

Concept/Big Idea Selection

If you are the agency pitching ideas to a client, the big idea will be ultimately selected by the client. The client will often request a point of view from the agency on which idea they prefer and why.

In general, there are characteristics that define what the best idea should look like.

The selected big idea will the one that is the most

- insight-based,
- simple and succinct,
- focused on the shopper,
- effective at providing a solution to the issue from the creative brief,
- effective at providing an attractive solution for the shopper to obtain the expected change in purchase behavior,
- aligned with the achievement of the selected shopper marketing objectives for the selected shopper targets,
- aligned with the brand and the path to purchase of the targeted shopper,
- effective at providing opportunities to engage the targeted shopper along the path to purchase,
- ready for strong creative executions, and
- (if applicable) aligned with the selected retailer's shopper and objectives.

From the list, you could select the criteria that are the most applicable to your particular campaign, and you can also decide to use a scorecard approach where you can give different weights to each selected characteristic so that this better reflects the uniqueness of your situation.

Case Study of the development of big ideas:

Using the previously mentioned case study for Publix supermarkets, the proposed solution to obtain a purchase frequency increase from loyal users and possibly switchers was stated as "inspire discovery in-store while empowering wellness at home."

- Convenience and savings
- Fitness tracking

- Meal planning, prep, and portability

Based on this solution from the creative brief, the agency came back with some campaign big ideas. Two of them are listed. Each idea is comprised of a concept statement and "how it works" section.

Idea #1

Concept Statement:

- Nothing is more valuable than your health So, when something is better for your body, you want to gran as much as possible. Publix is going to make stocking up on good stuff more convenient and valuable than ever, so it is putting savings right in the bag.

How Will It Work?

- As shoppers search for easy solutions that help their on-the-go lifestyle, Publix offers a bag full of living well value all month long
- OFFER: Fill the "Bag a Good Deal" bag with $15 in participating Publix products and receive an automatic 10 percent discount

Pre-Shop Communications:

- Program and participating products announcements through weekly flyer, reminding shoppers to plan ahead for the valuable in-store offer
- Targeted direct mailer to top Publix shoppers to include a "Value on the Go" bag, to encourage shoppers to participate. Bag can be a grocery recycle bag

At-Shop Communications:

- "Bag a Good Deal" bags
- Bag includes a shopping list of participating products for easy navigation as well as a scannable barcode for instant savings off all products, no additional coupons needed
- In-store POS including in-aisle interrupters and shelf tags

Post-Shop Communications:

- Digital shopping bag: Shoppers can go online all month long and fill a digital Publix "Bag a Good Deal" bag and receive a shopping list, tips, and tricks on packing the perfect snacks

Idea #2

Concept Statement:

- The struggle in packing your meals is actually packing your meals. There are baggies and dishes and they just end up sliding around your purse, getting crushed to a pulp. Publix wants meal packing to be as easy as it is good for you, so they're giving shoppers products and packaging to simplify the struggle.

How Will It Work?

- Shoppers are preparing more meals and snacks at home and taking them on the go, so Publix wants to make things easier by giving shoppers what they need to keep their food and drinks cool or hot.
- **OFFER:** Buy $20 participating Publix products and receive a "Pack Better" item—branded cooler bag, branded thermos, etc.

Pre-Shop Communications:

- Homepage carousel ad on Publix.com to announce the program, with a link to the program microsite
- Bloggers' tips on the microsite, on how they make their snacks and meals easy and portable

At-Shop Communications:

- In-store end cap display with "Pack Better" premium coolers or info on how to redeem
- Take-ones on display with a list of participating products and information on premium
- "Snack Better, Pack Better" tags throughout the store

Post-Shop Communications:

- Shoppers upload a picture of their "Snack Better, Pack Better" tip on social media
- Users who use the #snackbetterpackbetter hashtag are entered for a chance to win a Publix gift card, along with additional savings on their next purchase of Publix products

In total, the client was presented with four campaign ideas (including the two described), and the client selected the first one as the big idea for the campaign.

Selection of promotion techniques

Once the big idea has been selected, the next step is to formally select the consumer promotion and trade promotion techniques that are best suited to make the concept/big idea "come to life".

The Selection Logic

As stated in chapter 5, the selection logic is simple. Select the consumer promotion techniques that will be the most effective at making the big idea succeed and will be best judged as ones that will help achieve the campaign objective(s).

In terms of selecting the best trade promotion techniques, please refer to chapter 6. The techniques should be selected based on their ability to obtain the required retail support for ensuring consumer participation in the shopper marketing campaign being developed.

Review of Consumer Promotion Techniques

As stated in chapter 5, listed below are the main consumer promotion techniques/tactics:

- Price promotion tactics
- Product promotion tactics
- Free gifts and premiums tactics
- Sampling
- Prizes promotion tactics
- Cause-related promotions
- Reward and continuity programs

Please refer back to chapter 5 to have a more detailed sense of what each consumer promotion technique or tactic is best suited to accomplish in terms of shopper marketing objective for what type of shopper target

Review of Trade Promotions Techniques

As given in chapter 6, listed below are the main trade promotion techniques/tactics and under what circumstances, they are the most applicable.

If for your consumer promotion, you need. . . .	*Then . . .*
a new slot on the shelf	a slotting allowance or a failure fee will be applicable.
an intense product presence in the store	a buying allowance, off-invoice allowance, free goods, price reductions, Temporary Price Reductions (TPR), dating, scan down/ scan backs will be applicable.
shelf space increase or a full product line display	a cash rebate will be appropriate.
special displays, a markdown offer advertised in the retailer's circular or a price-off shelf feature	an advertising or display allowance will be appropriate.
active support by the store staff	a spiff or mystery shopper program is applicable.

Please refer to chapter 6 to have a more detailed sense of what each trade promotion technique is best suited to accomplish.

Legal Compliance Steps

As discussed previously, before the actual development of the creative materials and the implementation of the campaign, you need to confer with legal counsel (the internal legal department or outside legal counsel) to be sure that the campaign is legally compliant and will contain and/or meet any disclaimer, registration, and/or permission requirements. They are quite complex as beside the federal rules, they vary by state.

Illustration of Consumer and Trade Promotions Selection

Going back to the shopper marketing example for Publix supermarkets used earlier in this chapter, the consumer and trade tactics are as follows:

- **Big idea #1 offer:** Fill the "Bag A Good Deal" bag with $15 participating Publix products and receive an automatic 10 percent discount.

  This is a price promotion (a discount offer with minimum purchase).
- **Big idea #2 offer:** Buy $20 of participating Publix products and receive a "Pack Better" item—branded cooler bag, branded Snackeez snack/cup, branded thermos, etc. (item can change).

  This is a gift-with-purchase promotion.

Publix does not accept trade promotion; however, the following could have worked if they did accept trade promotions from the products that wanted to be involved in the promotion: a buying allowance, an off-invoice allowance, free goods, and price reductions (for insuring that the product will be on the shelf and in enough quantity in the store...with an attractive price to have the support of the financial manager at Publix), and an advertising allowance (for obtaining from Publix that the product be mentioned in all their communications for this campaign).

Step 7: Creation of the communication plan for the campaign

With the selected big idea and tactics, the next step is to develop and create the actual communications (also known as the creative executions). Besides the impact of the creative work itself, it is critical to creating a strong communications plan that will appeal to and reach the shopper target because, without it, the campaign will fail. That is, of course, because the target customer would not be exposed to it or will not respond to it based on a lack of relevance and/or appeal.

More specifically, the focus of a shopper marketing communications plan is to communicate the campaign idea through an attractive message to motivate the target shopper to

1. come to the store;
2. once there, remain focused on the promotion/offer; and
3. ultimately select and purchase the product on promotion.

Shopper Marketing Communication areas

In that context, the shopper marketing communication plan should encompass the following three areas:

- **Outside-the-store communications** to drive shoppers into the store. Examples of this media are e-mails, billboards, print ads, TV commercials, direct mail, weekly circulars, or social media. This should be focused on driving the target customer into the store.
- **Inside-the-store communications**, designed to ensure that when the target customer is in the store, he or she does not lose focus on the offer. Examples are posters, counter displays, window clings, sampling tables, special displays, or coupon dispensers—any in-store media that will ensure that when the shopper gets into the store, he or she doesn't lose focus on your offer.
- **At-the-shelf communications,** designed to ensure the target customer selects the product from the shelf and purchases it. Examples are on-shelf display, on-shelf coupon dispensers, on-pack stickers/advertising, etc.

In order to stimulate additional purchases of the product and build loyalty and/or promote the sale of other related products, the shopper marketing campaign communications should include **post-purchase communications** so that if at all possible, the shopper is sent communications after having made the purchase, with a coupon for a future purchase, for example.

In terms of communications to the retailers, their management and staff, the goal of these communications is to inform the selected retailers of the exact consumer offer(s) and what is involved from them, including the consumer communications that they should support and where they should be featured in the store. Also, if store employees need to play an active role in the promotion, instruction and directions for the staff would be part of the retailer communications.

Examples of these communications might include actual visits to the stores by the brand's sales force to present the consumer promotion and ensure that all in-store communications are in place.

Example of Creative Executions

Using the Publix case study again, below are creative executions for the two presented ideas.

- **Big idea #1 offer:** Fill the "Bag A Good Deal" bag

- **Big idea #2 offer:** Buy $20 participating Publix products and receive a "Pack Better" item

Step 8: Financial projections

As stated in Chapter 7, a financial analysis of the feasibility of the proposed shopper marketing campaign must be calculated. While this is presented as Step 8, you should not wait "that long" to engage your profitability analysis. As soon as you have enough elements to start your analysis, you should engage and you fine-tune it as you go and have more precise elements.

As a brief review of Chapter 7, the financial analysis encompasses the following:

- Selection of short- or long-term analysis
- Profitability analysis selection from among the following choices:
    - Marginal profit
    - Variable contribution
    - Lifetime value (Net Present)
- Identification of constraints and requirements. For example, see the following:
    - A minimum sales amount or volume that has to be achieved

    - Sales split at set percentages between different products
- Sales and cost projections
- Determination of decision criteria or success metrics including the following:
    - Minimum value (For example, if you opt for a variable contribution analysis method, what is the minimum dollar value needed to launch the campaign?)
    - Pay- back period (When is the campaign cost re-couped?)
    - ROI (what is the return on investment?)
- Identification of the benchmarks to be used to define success

Step 9: Control, evaluation, and measurement

Once the campaign is launched, results must be tracked, and ,as stated in chapter 7, the actual results must be compared to the assumptions that were made prior to the campaign. This analysis will then assist in the refinement of projection models for subsequent shopper marketing campaigns.

Here is an example from Coca-Cola illustrating how a well-planned Shopper Marketing campaign with an up-front integration of the selected retailer into the campaign at the concept development stage (and a clear shared focus on increasing purchase frequency and transaction size with loyal users and switchers) helped delivered historical sales lift results.

Case Study:
Bringing Shopper Marketing To Life

COMPETITION:
North American Effie Awards Shopper Marketing Effie

Ran in:
United States

CATEGORY:
Single-Retailer Rollout

CLIENT:
Coca-Cola, Walmart

LEAD AGENCIES:
Shopper Events
Collective Bias

PRODUCT/SERVICE:
Sparkling Soft Drinks

CLASSIFICATION:
National

DATES EFFORT RAN:
June 30, 2014 - August 2, 2014

CREDITS:
Amanda Whittaker
James Beck
Cookie Parker
Brandan Parker
Billy Courtney
Steve Weir
Jerra Nalley
Jared Delaney
Sarah Clinard
Sarah Mhoon

CASE STUDY

2015 GOLD SHOPPER MARKETING EFFIE AWARD WINNER

"COCA-COLA SHARE IT FORWARD"

In the summer of 2014, two of the world's most inclusive brands, Walmart and Coca-Cola, teamed up to inspire shoppers to share over a million icy cold Cokes to get the happiness started and then Share It Forward, thus connecting retailer, shopper and brand for something powerful. The Walmart Exclusive Share it Forward Event succeeded with an unprecedented commitment to execution excellence. The millennial targeted, socially supported plan surpassed expectations, resulting in distributing 1.2MM icy-cold coke and drive double digit lifts on 20oz months following.

State of the Marketplace & Brand's Business

Over the past ten years, the carbonated soft drink category has endured severe competition from categories like water, energy drinks, tea, and sports drinks. Even the category leader, Coca-Cola, has been affected. Milienniais and teenagers, so important to sales in this category, **were** losing identification with the brand, and with the category overall.

A key barometer of category health is sales of the single-serve, immediate consumption category, more specifically the 20-ounce bottle. At Walmart, 20 oz. sales in the 9 months leading up to our program were averaging a 3.4% sales decline vs. prior year (source: Retail Link, see chart below). Furthermore, Walmart had experienced multiple quarters of flat to declining comp store sales and customer traffic (source: http://stock.walmart.com/financial-reporting/quarterly-results/). We needed a **Big Idea** to bring some fun to Walmart's stores and boost sales for 20-ounce bottles of Coca-Cola in Walmart stores nationwide.

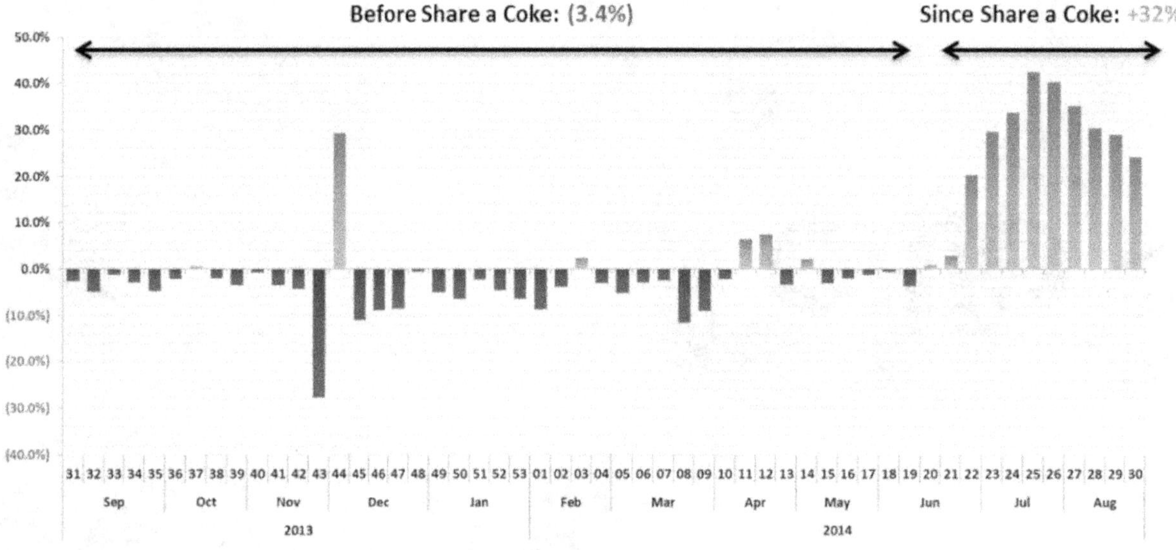

Strategic Marketing Challenge

While teenagers represent a key advertising target for Coca-Cola overall, the brand and retailer's messaging to Walmart shoppers has historically and consistently been mom-targeted. With millennial and teen consumers representing such an important component to both Coca-Cola and Walmart's future success, we needed to change up our messaging and media approach with a game-changing idea to motivate those consumers to shop for Coca-Cola products at Walmart. Our goal was to increase sales of 20-ounce bottles of Coca-Cola in Walmart; to do that we needed to encourage shoppers to not only purchase 20-ounce bottles for themselves, but also for friends, family and co-workers. Brand awareness among teens and millennials was not the key problem. Converting that awareness to purchase was the clear challenge.

Objectives & KPIs

We set out to increase revenue over a 4-week period and drive shopper traffic on a traditionally slow day without discounting the product. Specifically, we wanted to grow our immediate consumption business (20-ounce single serve bottles) by +8 to +10% during the 4-week marketing period and bring some fun to Walmart's stores. To appeal to teenage and millennial shoppers, we knew we needed to create an event, something that would get people talking about Coke and Walmart and sharing it across their social circles, spontaneously (and virally) repeating the phrase, "I shared an icy-cold Coke." We also wanted to be sure our results (sales, in-store traffic, social media hits) were measurable, so we knew we needed to draw on analytics that would precisely measure the distinct impact of this program.

Shopper Segment

We were trying to reach the younger **millennials, as young people's** purchasing power has traditionally driven the carbonated beverage category. This generation's upbringing with hyper-involved parents, constant feedback from peers and adults and exposure to a wide variety of experiences (both physically and digitally) has shaped their attitudes and behaviors. They're optimistic, socially sensitive and aware, inclusive and not hierarchical, always connected to their mobile device and human networks. They value authenticity and have grown accustomed to being able to have a 2-way dialogue with anyone or any corporate entity. Finally, a challenging economic environment has especially affected millennials.

Reminder: Entrants will copy their answers into the entry form in the online entry area for judging purposes – this document will not be uploaded for judging. Use this form to draft your responses and collaborate with team members.

Shopper Insight

Teen and Millennial shoppers represent a huge opportunity for both Walmart and Coca-Cola. Approximately 80MM strong, these shoppers spend over $300B in retail and are set to outspend Boomers within the next ten years. And surprisingly for many people at Coca-Cola, Walmart not only provides perfect access to the American Mom, but is also teeming with Teens and Millennials. While Millennials make up roughly 25% of the population, they actually represent 30% of Walmart's weekly shoppers. Throw in Teen shoppers and the total comes up to 34%. (SOURCES: Retail Net Group and Coca-Cola's proprietary iSHOP survey)

If we could give the young Millennial shoppers a simple, easy, and affordable way to make someone's day while giving them a moment of discovery, a moment of fame, and moments worth sharing, we knew we could significantly grow brand love and brand value for both Walmart and Coca-Cola.

The Big Idea

By teaming up to share over 1MM icy-cold Cokes with Americans during one big, highly social event, Coca-Cola and Walmart got shoppers to "share it forward" by buying personalized Cokes for their friends, family, and co-workers all summer long, thereby connecting shoppers, retailer, and the brand for a summer of sales growth and brand adoration.

Bringing the Idea to Life

By working closely with Walmart, their in-store events agency, and our social media partner, we collectively executed the following 4-part communications strategy:

1) Ensure the 20-ounce bottles were **readily and easily accessible in all stores**
    a. All checkout coolers were loaded with icy-cold cokes with proper names on them
    b. The tops of coolers carried ambient 20-ounce bottles - perfect for quickly finding names to give to others later
    c. Share Bins were shopable from 4 sides, typically found along check-out action alley near both entrances and self-checkout locations because millennial shoppers over-index in use of self-checkout (source: APT)
    d. WOW and Lobby Displays
    e. In-aisle reminders via floor graphics
    f. All with simple, consistent, eye-catching, and persuasive messaging
2) **Create and drive awareness** for a big, bold and exciting kick-off event
    a. Ryan Seacrest radio shout-outs the week of the event drove awareness. His show over-indexes with the target and also allowed us to utilize an already-owned Coca-Cola media asset
    b. A Twitter Party 3 days before the in-store sharing event drew dense traffic In tweets and generated enough conversation to become a top trending topic in the United States. The Party highlighted uses for Coca-Cola that would appeal to young Millennials and urged people to share their Coke stories while building excitement about the in-store event.
    c. An unpaid Walmart Facebook post drove traffic to the event and built excitement among their 1.4MM associates and 30MM+ Facebook fans
3) **Share 1MM icy-cold Cokes at Walmart** on Sunday, July 6th
    a. Informed and outfitted the in-store event team with key sound bites, hashtags, and awesome Coca-Cola gear to make for a terrific brand experience and make it easy for shoppers to start sharing in 3,200 Walmart stores
    b. Further energized this event group to over-achieve by executing a sales incentive contest for "the most 20-ounce Cokes, Diet Cokes, and Coke Zeros sold during the event"
    c. Made a huge impression on Walmart store associates nationwide by showing them firsthand the sales they could expect to see in the coming weeks if they stayed engaged
4) **Keep the sharing going**
    a. Bloggers created an engaging online campaign in which the new occasions for drinking Coca-Cola were emphasized for young Millennial shoppers.
    b. Bloggers introduced the "Share It Forward" message by not only showing their readers how they had creatively shared Cokes with their friends and family, but by also encouraging their readers to "Share It Forward" with select Coca-Cola products from Walmart.
    c. We leveraged key Facebook, Twitter, Instagram, and Pinterest social networks pre-demo, during-demo, and post-demo knowing that's where young Millennial Walmart shoppers look for Inspiration.

In summary, #shareitforward was a cohesive, synergistic program: the social media drove awareness for the event and provided lots of ongoing sharing ideas; the big event energized shoppers and associates in store; and the incremental, inspiring points of in-store display made it easy for Walmart shoppers to share Cokes and happiness all summer long.

Reminder: Entrants will copy their answers into the entry form in the online entry area for judging purposes – this document will not be uploaded for judging. Use this form to draft your responses and collaborate with team members.

Path to Purchase Communications & Marketing Components

Pre	During	Post
Retail Experience	**Retail Experience**	**Retail Experience**
-In-Store Merchandizing	-In-Store Merchandizing	-In-Store Merchandizing
-Retailtainment	-Retailtainment	-Retailtainment
Radio	**Sampling**	**Shopper Involvement**
Progam/Content	-In-Store	-WOM
Social Media	**Shopper Involvement**	-Consumer Generated
	-WOM	-Viral
	-Consumer Generated	**Social Media**
	-Viral	
	Events	
	Social Media	

Paid Media Expenditures

September 2013 – August 2014

Under $500 thousand

September 2012 – August 2013

Not Applicable

Budget

Less than/as other competitors.

More than/as prior year's budget.

Header Touchpoint		Specific Touchpoint (if applicable)
Touch Point A:	In Store Merchandising	Share Bins, tops of coolers, front-end coolers
Touch Point B:	Retailtainment	Share it Forward event on July 6, 2014
Touch Point C:	Social Media	Bloggers, Facebook, Instagram, Twitter

Owned Media & Sponsorship

Radio – Ryan Seacrest radio shout-outs for the July 6th giveaway the week of 6/30/14.

Not applicable sponsorships.

Results

The Coca-Cola #shareitforward marketing program at Walmart far surpassed performance expectations on several, tangible fronts:

- Walmart's 20-ounce soft drink sales growth was DOUBLE the growth experienced by all other large store retailers combined during the 4-week program
- Greatly exceeded projected sales lifts (+8-10%) derived from previous Share-a-Coke executions in other countries with sales peaks as high as +40% along with sustained growth significantly higher than +8-10% for many more weeks to come.

- Greatly exceeded social projected social media impact:
  - Blog page views - 3.4MM vs. 2.3MM benchmark *(48% greater than goal)*
  - Syndicated Impressions - 28.9MM vs. 19.7MM benchmark *(47% greater than goal)*
  - 8,484 pieces of content and 10,603 blog page engagements
  - Twitter Party alone - US Trending; 7,241 tweets: 14.2MM impressions

Other Contributing Factors

- Coca-Cola ran a national TV campaign, digital, and social media for Share a Coke in July and August outside of the Walmart "Share It Forward" campaign.
- The campaigns generated lot of buzz; it was a self-reinforcing, exciting message.

Reminder: Entrants will copy their answers into the entry form in the online entry area for judging purposes – this document will not be uploaded for judging. Use this form to draft your responses and collaborate with team members.

Application Workshop

Throughout this book, you will have formal application workshops and exercises with supportive tools to help you apply the information from each chapter to your particular case or assignment. You will also have access to lists of key decisions to be made or capabilities that you need to have in place at each step of the shopper marketing planning process.

For this chapter, the workshop will focus on developing shopper marketing campaign idea recommendations based on an actual shopper marketing client brief.

Remember the shopper marketing client brief received by the shopper marketing agency Tracy Locke from Pepsi Cola for a promotional campaign for Diet Pepsi at CVS? **This is now your turn to work on it as a shopper marketing professional and develop two shopper marketing campaign ideas.**

- Read the client brief (on the next page)
- Execute the appropriate research and gather data
- Develop a shopper marketing SWOT analysis based on this research
- To the best of your ability, leverage your analysis and your SWOT to build your own shopper marketing creative brief with at least the following sections:
    - The key ask
    - The key issue (or opportunity) justifying the campaign
    - The brand truth
    - Buyer persona (profile and shopping habits)
    - Key insights (two to three maximum)
    - Key Solution
    - Shopper experience and key touch points
    - Key partners (retailers, etc.)
    - Considerations/Constraints
    - Success measurement

Important: The point of this workshop is to gain practical experience. Since the full array of data that would be available in the real world is likely not available to you at this time, focus on applying whatever data you can gather and use your best judgment.

Based on this creative brief, develop two shopper marketing campaign idea recommendations. Each idea should contain the following:

- A concept statement (two paragraphs and one slogan)
- A short and clearly written "how it will work" section

Which of the two campaign ideas will be your big idea recommendation? Why?

The Client Brief

Assignment:

Create a national shopper marketing program and sales promotion at CVS that links Diet Pepsi to fashion.

Background:

The Pepsi Brand as the foundation

- "Live for now" is not a description of current affairs; it is a motto that speaks to a belief-system (mindset). At the heart of this belief system is the view that the world is an amazing place.
- "Live for now" is a call to arms for all who want to explore this world and are open to the possibilities it offers.
    - It is an expression of optimism
    - It stands for an effervescent engagement with everyday living
    - It is about a desire to be fully present and truly experience the joys of life
- Diet Pepsi believes life should be lived fully and in the moment—less worry, more lightness, and anchored around the people who matter the most. Diet Pepsi's crisp, bubbly refreshment re-centers you so you can reconnect with your vibrant NOW.

Marketing Objective and Target:

Loyal and current customers-> Obtain more sales from current customers of Diet Pepsi

Opportunity or Challenge:

Leverage the natural association of the Pepsi Brand with a fashion-oriented lifestyle by partnering with a fashion retailer leader (CVS)

Communication Objectives:

Diet Pepsi is *the* diet soda associated with fashion

Communication Audiences:

Upbeat and connected woman (aged thirty-five to fifty-four), all income levels and household sizes

- She is upbeat and connected
- She leads a full life, a lot of responsibilities, a lot of running around
- She has a strong personality and is comfortable in her own skin
- She has a light, optimistic view on life

- People like being around her because she is upbeat and fun

Shopper Marketing Campaign Goal(s):

Boost Diet Pepsi purchase frequency of current customers during the promotion

The Shopper Marketing Campaign Strategy Statement:

- GET fun, connected women who like to look great and feel great
- TO buy Diet Pepsi at CVS
- BY linking Diet Pepsi with fashion through CVS's health and beauty offerings
- BECAUSE we can leverage the culture-forward message of "the excitement of now" by linking it with Diet Pepsi's fashion assets.

Shopper Marketing Campaign Partnership:

CVS and Diet Pepsi

CVS is a convenient easy-to-shop luxury retailer where women can go to pamper themselves. It is moving its position from a drug store to a trusted advisor for health and wellness.

Constraints and Requirements:

The campaign has to do the following:

- Respect the Pepsi brand identity and promise
- Leverage Pepsi's assets, including celebrity endorsements, concerts sponsorships, etc.

Leverage fashion-related CVS assets:

- "Reinventing Beauty" platform
- New store format with beauty in the front of the store and on lower aisles
- Beauty Club offers and rewards through the ExtraCare loyalty program

Conclusion

Shopper marketing planning is a thorough and complex nine-step process that requires a disciplined approach to be effective.

It is critical to follow the steps in the proposed order and with the required depth to be sure that the right inputs are obtained and the right outputs are generated for each step.

Since shopper marketing is part of marketing and, more specifically, marketing communications, vital input is required from these marketing teams. Not only does the shopper marketing practitioner rely on this input, full alignment and integration with marketing are essential. This alignment is required for all nine steps of the planning process.

By formally applying a fully aligned and integrated planning process, a shopper marketer will optimize his or her ability to develop and implement a shopper marketing campaign that will be focused on the right shopper marketing objectives, the right shopper target with the right campaign idea, the right offer, the right mix of consumer and trade promotion techniques, and the right communication plan. This, in turn, will optimize the likelihood that the campaign will be successful at delivering on the goals set for it.

Chapter 9: Shopper Marketing, An International Perspective

Learning Objectives

After completing this chapter, you will be able to do the following:

- Learn why companies look to build global brands
- Understand the complex nature of extending a brand to multiple countries
- Comprehend why shopper marketing has to go international
- Start understanding the challenges in developing shopper marketing campaigns internationally
- Gain "hands-on" experience with analyzing how to extend a shopper marketing campaign to other countries

Introduction

What Is the Chapter About?

This chapter focuses on the challenges associated with going global and, in doing so, the considerable research required to extend brands internationally. The necessary alignment of shopper marketing initiatives with global sales and marketing strategies is making the job of a shopper marketer even more complex. Not only does shopper marketing have to find the best ways to align itself with global branding and communications, but it has to do so while shopping behaviors are far more diverse and specific for each country than ever before. Simply said, there are no easy ways for shopper marketing to avoid globalization and there are no shortcuts to making this happen!

Why Is This Important?

The idea of globalization whereby a brand seeks to increase sales by selling in multiple countries around the world has been a mainstream phenomenon for quite some time. As such, being able to extend shopper marketing campaigns to other countries is now part of the requirements for a competent shopper marketer. The core challenge of any globalization effort is to be as standardized as possible among countries, with enough adaptations for each market so that the targeted consumers positively react and make the purchase. Since shopping behavior differs dramatically from country to country, knowing what research is necessary to detect those differences, as well as being able to adhere to the legal framework country by country are a must for success.

Key Terms

- **Ethnographic research or cultural research:** The study and systematic recording of human cultures
- **Global brand:** A global brand is one that is sold in a very large number of national markets on the basis of a single unique *brand name*, rather than using different brand names for each separate national market.
- **Global promotion:** A promotion whereby the sponsoring company executes a promotion that residents of multiple countries can enter or participate.
- **International promotions:** A promotion whereby the sponsoring company executes a promotion internationally such that residents of multiple countries can enter or participate
- **Standardization versus customization**: Going "global" comes down to defining the most effective balance between standardization (where elements are identical between countries) and customization (where elements are customized to the local market including, for example, culture, attitudes, and consumer behavior)

An Expert's Perspective

Shopper research is challenging enough in the United States, as the complexity in channels continues to increase; however, understanding shoppers internationally is even more difficult as you layer on differences in motivation, retail availability, societal triggers, and cultural values and norms.

-Carrie Friend, President, Friendsight, LLC

The heart of shopper marketing is providing shoppers with the right amount of information they need at the right point in time when they are ready to buy. Understanding what motivates shoppers is the crux of the shopper marketing challenge for all brands and requires deep insights on human behaviors in the context of their culture. Great global shopper marketing is more than taking a campaign and translating it to the local market language in a toolkit, it is about uncovering a human insight in the context of shopping and bringing it to life in culturally relevant ways.

- April Carlisle, VP Shopper Marketing, Coca-Cola

Key Concepts

Globalization Is a Mainstream Phenomenon

According to the Organisation for Economic Co-operation and Development (OCDE), in the past ten years, global trade has continued to grow from $10.5 trillion in 2006 to $14.6 trillion in 2016 for exports. This is not going to stop. (Accessed at OCDE Data 2017—https://data.oecd.org/trade/trade-in-goods-and-services.htm#indicator-chart).

According to the World Bank, global trade will continue at grow between 2.9 percent and 3.1 percent per year until 2020. (Accessed at https://www.worldbank.org/content/dam/Worldbank/GEP/GEP2016a/Global-Economic-Prospects-January-2016-Global-Outlook.pdf)

Not surprisingly, companies have caught onto the idea that gaining customers in the global marketplace is important for brand growth. According to Ben Snider from Goldman Sachs, "foreign sales accounted for 33% of aggregate revenue for the S&P 500 in 2014," and "the median stock reported 29% of sales outside the US." (Accessed at http://www.businessinsider.com/foreign-revenues-by-region-2015-7)

The Internet has further connected people and made it easy to obtain brand information and purchase product from that brand for anyone, from anywhere.

According to data from Statista in 2018, "As of the most recent reported period, the number of internet users worldwide was 3.58 billion, up from 3.39 billion in the previous year. Easier access to computers, the modernization of countries around the world and an increased utilization of smartphones has given people the opportunity to use the internet more frequently and with more convenience." (1)

Similarly, the number of digital purchases has increased, and growth is expected to continue. Also according to a 2018 study by Statista, "in 2021, over 2.14 billion people worldwide are expected to buy goods and services online, up from 1.66 billion global digital buyers in 2016." (2)

(1)https://www.statista.com/statistics/273018/number-of-internet-users-worldwide/
(2)https://www.statista.com/statistics/251666/number-of-digital-buyers-worldwide/

Shopper Marketing Must Align with Global-International Marketing Strategies

As discussed throughout this book, shopper marketing plans must align with the overall brand marketing strategies of a product or service in order to succeed and grow the brand. This is also true from an international perspective. The direction of the brand, its core marketing strategies (target market, value proposition, and positioning strategies), and resulting marketing tactics in each country will dictate the shopper marketing initiatives.

As defined by Martin in a Cleverism article: "Global marketing is defined as the process of 'adjusting' the marketing strategies of your company to adapt to the conditions of other countries. Of course, global marketing is more than selling your product or service globally. It is the full process of planning, creating, positioning, and promoting your products" in each country. (Accessed at https://www.cleverism.com/global-marketing-strategies/)

The way a brand is marketed internationally or globally is a reflection of the international business strategy behind the brand.

According to Business-to-you (B2U, 2017) and as illustrated in the chart that follows, a business has four possible international business strategy options, depending on the attractiveness of going global (either for cost reduction reasons, for sales growth potential reasons, or both) and the need for customizations by the local population or target. (Accessed at http://www.business-to-you.com/international-business-strategy/).

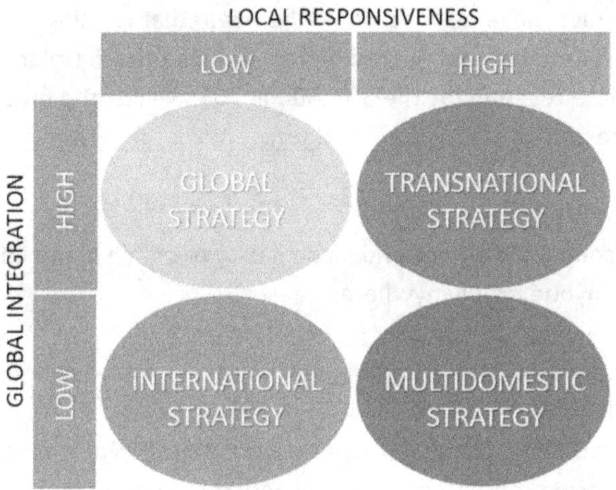

These four strategic options lead to four types of global or international business types as follows:

- **Companies with a multi-domestic strategy:** Such businesses aim at meeting the specific needs and requirements of local markets through an intense products and services customization. An example is Netflix, where the content is mostly localized.
- **Global companies:** On the other hand, these companies offer a standardized product worldwide with the goal to maximize efficiencies in order to reduce costs as much as possible. Pfizer or Uber could be considered global companies.
- **Transnational companies:** Transnational companies combined characteristics of both the global and multi-domestic companies. They want to maximize local responsiveness but also achieve costs reduction through globalization of production. Unilever could be considered a transnational company.

- **International companies:** These companies have little need for local adaption and global integration. and are satisfied with a simple exporting strategy. A company like American Express could be considered international.

Therefore, the way the brand is managed internationally will be reflective of its international business strategy.

And, ultimately, shopper marketing campaigns must align with the international marketing strategies.

Let's illustrate this point with a few scenarios:

- If your business opts for a multi-domestic business strategy, you will need to align the brands and corresponding strategies for each country you are in. Said another way, each country should have a brand and marketing adaptation suitable for that local country.
- If your business opts for a global business strategy, you will need a global brand with one set of marketing objectives and strategies for all countries it operates in with a global shopper marketing approach that is standardized to work in all the countries.
- If your business opts for a transnational business strategy, you will need a brand strategy that fits with this direction, with maybe some of your brands that are global (with global marketing objectives and strategies) and some that are local (with localized marketing objectives and strategies). Furthermore, you will have to develop, to the extent possible, a shopper marketing approach that will fit the direction taken for that brand in each country, whether global or local.
- If your business opts for an international business strategy, you will need an "exporting" brand and will have to develop a shopper marketing approach that fits this exporting brand status. This might lead you to prefer localization and adaptation of your shopper marketing to compensate for the "foreign" status of your brand.

Global-International Shopper Marketing Must Align with Customer Preferences

Consumers preferences can substantially vary from one country to another and this is creating a significant challenge for the internationalization of shopper marketing campaigns.

In a June 2, 2016, Brandman University interview by Gustav Deutsch , Kevin Bailey, President of VF Action Sports and CEO of Vans (VF Corporation) spoke to a group of business students at the Irvine campus. Here's what he had to say when asked to pick one of the top challenges of operating globally: "YI think the biggest, one of the biggest challenges is really learning to learn the culture first. We shared in the beginning that how important it is to put your consumer at the center of the choices you make." (https://www.brandman.edu/news-and-events/news/2017/08/17/03/46/ep-16-and8211-vans-ceo-kevin-bailey-shares-insight-from-managing-a-global-brand)

Proponents of this theory further argue that a brand holds its value in whichever market it occupies but the reason for purchase may differ.

For example, Dunkin Donuts sells donuts all over the world but varies its products offerings based on the country and the specific desires of the local customer. (Accessed at https://www.boston.com/culture/travel/2014/06/30/dunkin-donuts-you-cant-get-in-america).

- Fruit-loving Germans want the option of cherry banana, plum and green apple stuffed donuts, all topped with colorful frosting. Cherry banana seems like an odd flavor combination, but Thrillist recently named it the chain's "must-get donut."

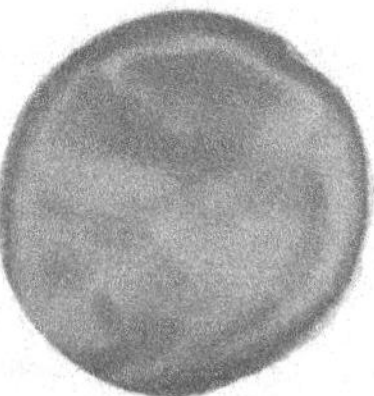

- In China, customers enjoy savory options like a dried pork and seaweed donut ("a classic glazed donut topped with dried pork floss and seaweed," as Dunkin' Donut's public relations manager Justin Drake described it).

- The *ube* is a purple yam that's very popular in the Philippines, while *chicha* is made from purple corn, which has to taste better than it sounds.

- Koreans get to snack on green tea-flavored bagels stuffed with a sweet red bean paste and bulgogi-jalapeno-cheese sandwiches. (Bulgogi is a thinly sliced, marinated beef.)

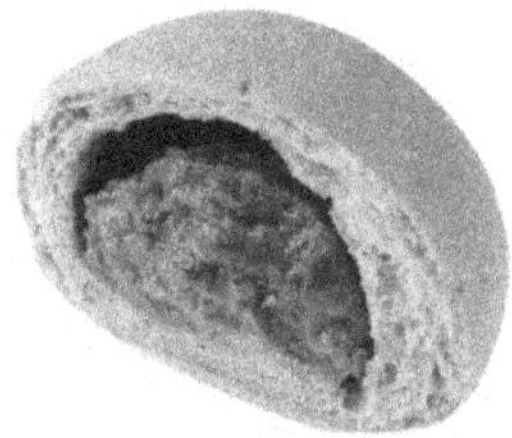

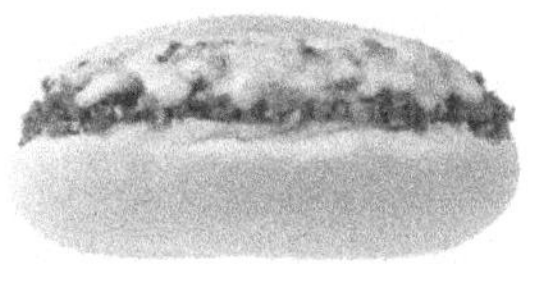

The potential variations of marketing targets, marketing strategies, and marketing mix between countries (due to the differences of consumers preferences) lead to of the need for variations in the shopper marketing approaches between countries as the starting point in shopper marketing campaign planning. This means that the marketing objectives and marketing targets for the product might differ by country.

The variations due to cultural preferences between countries are amplified when it comes to the actual shopping habits and customer purchase motivations. This makes the internationalization of shopper marketing even more challenging.

Here is an example to illustrate this concept.

Previous research from Klaus Wustrack (1999) (for the telecommunication company Alcatel) (1) has cited various reasons why women purchase mobile phones depending on the country they are from or live in:

- In the UK, women purchased them for security reasons.
- In China, women bought them as a status symbol.
- In South Africa, women purchased them because they were easier to use based on the country's wire infrastructure.

To be effective in each country, the type of shopper marketing campaign would have to be inclusive and the specific communication elements would have to be vastly different in order to achieve success.

Using the previous example, in China, the mobile phone company might offer a free fashionable phone case with a purchase of a phone to activate trial.

In South Africa, the same mobile phone company might offer a certain number of free minutes each month for a twelve-month subscription.

To further illustrate the variations of purchase drivers and motivations between consumers from different countries, let's look at the luxury consumer market.

According to the Boston Consulting Group, and as illustrated by the below table, we can observe similarities as well as differences in consumers' purchase motivations, depending on the country in which they live. Similarities might be a focus on product quality as a key driver for purchase, whereas differences might be a stronger focus on exclusivity for the South Korean consumer as compared to the relative importance of customization for the Russian consumer.

Clearly, these insights can have a dramatic impact on the way a brand is marketed and what shopper marketing initiatives are executed.

For example, for the South Korean consumer, the offer might be a high-quality gift with product purchase, whereas, for the Russian consumer, a limited edition customized product would be the appropriate offer.

1

Quality and Exclusivity leading

"What is luxury to you?"

Intro values / Extro Values

% of respondents

	Total	EU 4[1]	US	Japan	S. Korea	China	Brazil	Russia
Quality	57	58	68	55	45	63	40	61
Exclusivity	35	36	22	25	59	26	38	46
Craftsmanship	30	28	43	32	34	27	12	33
Timeless	29	27	44	37	18	37	11	23
Adorned aesthetics	31	34	24	37	17	34	33	36
Brand	19	22	11	11	38	11	23	16
Customization	13	12	8	12	7	16	24	22
Being Cool/Sexy	12	9	7	16	20	8	21	15

Note: Multiple answer possible; 1. IT, FR, DE, UK
Source: BCG 2013 specific survey (10 000 core luxury Consumers in 10 countries)
20140124 Final Document FINAL SENT.pptx

Fondazione Altagamma The Boston Consulting Group 20

As a final example, Statista indicates that the primary purchasing behavior for cosmetics consumers in the US is their preference for shopping at stores that offer good deals on their products. (Accessed at https://www.statista.com/study/38769/cosmetics-consumer-behavior-in-the-us-statista-dossier/)

In China, though, the purchase behaviors for cosmetics products are mainly driven by the preference for international brands, the lack of loyalty of the Chinese consumers, and their stronger willingness to buy cosmetic products online instead of physical stores. (Accessed at http://cosmeticschinaagency.com/10-trends-chinese-consumers-cosmetics/)

Once again, we detect substantial differences that should lead the shopper marketer to different shopper marketing constructs.

In this last example, a discount offer might be the most appropriate for motivating the US cosmetics consumer, while a loyalty program might be a better approach to fight the lack of loyalty of the Chinese consumer. Furthermore, the offer should be valid for online purchases in China (as opposed to being valid in-store for the US consumer).

In summary, it is critical to understand and integrate purchase and shopping behavior differences between countries in the planning of international shopper marketing campaigns to resonate with the target audience in each country. Otherwise, the shopper marketing objectives, targets, and expected changes in purchase behaviors might be inappropriate for each country and the campaign will not succeed. Ultimately, the campaign will not only fail to sell the product, it may also negatively impact the brand image.

That is why it is critical to executing appropriate research to identify the similarities and differences of shopping and purchase behaviors between countries.

Global-International Shopper Marketing Is Complex

It is time-consuming, complex, and costly to create and develop effective international shopper marketing campaigns.

In order to maximize the impact of a shopper marketing effort, market research will help.

Conducting behavioral research, for example, an attitude, and usage study or shopper behaviors analysis among target customers in each market can provide highly valuable information about the shopping behaviors and local market nuances.

Before executing the shopper marketing campaign, the research helps the marketer gain a formal understanding of the shopping and purchase habits of the consumers in each country.

This should be a country-by-country analysis. Questions to be answered are as follows:

- What are the purchase drivers and shopping habits of consumers?

- What is the degree and nature of loyalty (or lack of) of the shoppers for the product category and your product in particular?
- What is the distribution of shopper types between loyal users, competitive loyals, switchers, price buyers, and non-users for your product category and for your product in particular?

Using this information, the shopper marketer will be able to decide what is most appropriate for each country. For example, which shopper targets would be the most effective to focus on? What is the best objective to focus on in terms of a change in purchase behavior?

It would be important to also use ethnography or cultural research to understand the core cultural differences between countries. Ethnography, according to the Department of Sociology at Columbia University, "is a sociological method that explores how people live and make sense of their lives with one another in particular places". (Accessed at https://publicsociologytoolkit.com/public-sociology-toolkit/ethnography/)

In terms of its application to marketing—according to Study.com, "at the core of everything they do, marketing professionals seek to understand their potential consumers. Successful marketing is based on a solid understanding of why consumers make the decisions they do: how they identify a need or a want, how they gather information about their options, and how they decide what, or what not, to buy." (Accessed at https://study.com/academy/lesson/what-is-ethnographic-research-in-marketing-definition-methods-examples.html)

For example, perceptions of color and symbols vary by country. In the West, white is associated with weddings, but in China, India, and Japan, white is a symbol of mourning. In the West, green represents health, but in India, green is forbidden, and Arab countries favor green. In China, red represents good fortune, but it represents death in Turkey.

As another example, collectivism is much stronger in China than in the US (where people are more focused on individualism). For example, if the shopper marketing campaign includes a sweepstakes, it will make sense to develop a prize structure in China that involves people enjoying the prize together, such as a family trip for ten people.

It is important to additionally research common trade practices in each country. This can be done by executing formal research or by talking to the local retailers in each market.

As a practitioner, it is key to understand, again on a country-by-country basis, the differences between markets regarding consumer and trade promotion practices.

From a consumer standpoint, it would be extremely helpful to know what sales promotion techniques are used and which ones have historically been successful at achieving change in purchase behavior.

From a trade promotion standpoint, you'll need to know which tactics are acceptable to use, which ones work best, and which ones are unique to a particular country.

On the top of understanding local buying behavior and sales promotion practices in each country, conducting research on a country-by-country basis can also provide necessary information on the following:

- Payment methods, advertising practices, and privacy laws
- Each country's infrastructure: transportation, communications, utilities, and banking
- Postal/delivery services, and other communication infrastructures (mobile, Internet coverage, etc.)

Visiting the local country is also a powerful way to learn. Interacting with the people, asking questions, and visiting retailers, distributors, and fulfillment centers should be part of the visit.

At the end of the day, the goal is to be able to identify the following for each country:

- The most effective shopper marketing objectives
- The best shopper targets to focus on to achieve the shopper marketing objectives
- The most appropriate change in purchase behaviors to obtain from this target, in order to achieve the shopper marketing objective
- The most effective consumer promotion techniques to use in order to obtain the desired change in purchase behavior
- The most effective trade promotion techniques to "motivate" the retailer for the desired change in purchase behavior

Understanding the local infrastructure and legal framework to assess the level of shopper marketing readiness of each country is vital.

The following are the cost and time impediments that contribute to the challenges of global shopper marketing programs:

1. **The legal framework, requirements, and restrictions** are the largest impediments to international promo execution. What is legal in one country may not be legal in another. It is important to contact legal counsel in each country to be sure your promotion is legal there. That can add up to a significant amount of money. Companies may decide to consult a lawyer in the US who specializes in promotion law and who can advise on a country-by-country basis but to be certain the program you'd like to execute is legal, it is necessary to work directly with legal counsel in each participating country.

2. There are **language and translation requirements** for execution of international shopper marketing programs. For example, Mexico, Puerto Rico, and the Province of Quebec are three places that a promotion must be translated to the language of that country. In these examples, it would be French for the Province of Quebec, and Spanish for Mexico and

Puerto Rico. Importantly, the translation requirement is for all material that advertises the promotion.

   a. There are thousands of languages in the world, making it difficult to execute in multiple countries. More specifically, there are approximately three thousand current languages in use, and, in India for example, there are two hundred dialects.

3. **Packaging requirements and space allotment on labels** vary from country to country. First of all, multiple languages on the same package mean there is less space for each language, which means fewer words can be used. In addition, there are different requirements depending on the specific country regarding what specific information must be disclosed.

4. The **actual out of pocket costs** to execute in different countries is high for a multitude of reasons:
   a. Market maturity: Given that brands may be at different points in their brand life cycle in different markets, what works in one market may not work in another, so the program may have to be adjusted in order to resonate with each audience.
   b. The actual perceptions of consumers and trade personnel toward promotional activity may be different in different countries, so again the program may need to be tweaked accordingly.
   c. The retail landscape varies from country to country, increasing the need for customization of trade promotion activity. Even a concept as basic as how far the stores are from one another can directly impact the cost to ship materials to each store.

5. It is complex to thoroughly understand and establish **payment and fulfillment protocols.** Some of the considerations are as follows:
   a. Are credit cards available?
   b. How do products get to the stores? Can you ship products from home location (United States Postal Service (USPS)), employ consolidators within the US, such as FedEx, or establish a bulk distribution operation overseas?
   c. What are the options for payment, customer service, and distribution/storage facilities?

6. **Development and execution of media plans** are time-consuming and complex. The shopper marketer must determine the most effective media mix based on consumer preferences, as well as the country-specific factors present in each foreign market.

   Some considerations would be as follows:
   a) What is the quality of the local postal service? (Are there standardized addresses and postal codes? What are the average postage costs?)
   b) What is the infrastructure? (For example, no mailboxes may exist in Argentina, and telemarketing is seen as too aggressive in Japan.)
   c) What, if any, are the legal restrictions on media?
   d) What are the privacy laws?
   e) What media is usable and available?
   f) What types of lists are available?

g) What are the literacy rates?
h) What response media are available (e.g., direct response television)?
i) Is inbound or outbound telemarketing available?

7. **Creative development and execution** are challenging.
As explained earlier in this chapter, each market has its own culture and language. It is important for the success of a shopper marketing program to research the audience thoroughly and test the campaign and copy before full execution. Obviously, the campaign must be translated and adapted to the local nuances of the different cultures. Again, it is critical to understand these nuances and word choices because words that are appropriate in one country may be insulting in another (e.g., the word "diet" has a negative impression in Japan; Diet Coke changed its name to "Coke Light" in Japan).

It is clear that shopper marketing from an international perspective requires careful planning and significant investment, both monetarily and from a time standpoint.

Here is an example from Unilever illustrating how a brand like Magnum Ice Cream leveraged the same Shopper Marketing Campaign in several countries.

Case Study:
Bringing Shopper Marketing To Life

CASE STUDY

2016 BRONZE EURO EFFIE AWARD WINNER

"PINK AND BLACK"

Pink & Black has been one of the most successful ice cream product launches in history. The launch has not only achieved an outstanding awareness, it did it with a relevant message to Pleasure Seekers, a message that made them feel identified. A perfect channel strategy that made every touch point relevant and efficient in conquering results. The success was such that in a world full of novelties and product launches, sales and trial was overly accomplished.

COMPETITION:
Euro Effie Awards

Ran in:
Austria, France, Germany, Portugal, Switzerland, United Kingdom

---

CATEGORY:
Product/Service Launch

Brand/CLIENT:
Magnum/Unilever

LEAD AGENCY:
Lead Agency

CONTRIBUTING COMPANY:
LOLA-MULLENLOWE S.L.U.

PRODUCT/SERVICE:
Food

CLASSIFICATION:
Multinational

DATES EFFORT RAN:
January 2, 2015 - December 31, 2015

CREDITS:
Caio Del Manto
Neil Gledhil

Executive Summary

This case illustrates the challenge of catching pleasure seekers' attention and wanting them to try seasonal limited editions.

Magnum is the unquestionable leader in the premium ice cream segment, selling more than one billion units annually worldwide.

Magnum has always been focused on the territory of pleasure. The innovative Magnum Gold campaign in 2010 started to present the new Magnum point of view via "The Pleasure is Yours for the Taking". This step away from a passive POV, waiting for pleasure to come, to a new, active attitude towards pleasure, was further reinforced in 2011 and 2012 with the new campaign idea of being "For Pleasure Seekers".

Latest successes with concept driven products, such as Magnum Gold or Magnum's 25th anniversary have supported the brand's ever-increasing growth rate. Over the years, Magnum has been a brand that constantly innovates in 'limited edition' summer SKUs that consumers anticipate:

"I expect to see new products, especially from Magnum, my favourite premium and innovative brand. I still remember Gold..."

Pink&Black Magnum was presenting two new irresistible, contrasting, sophisticated and stylish ice creams, raising the bar of its already premium and contemporary positioning. However, these launches faced significant challenges as to how to:

- Sustain and push forward the growth rate trend.
- Satisfy the high expectations from both consumers and the market due to previous successful launches.
- Communication-wise, ensure pleasure seekers identify with Magnum Pink&Black to actively embrace pleasure.
- Play out stereotypes without being prescriptive, exclusive or cliché.

(Source: Unilever – Nielsen POS Sales data GMI)

Objectives

We needed to develop a campaign to drive variant sales and brand perceptions. Objectives were:

Communication objectives

- Drive brand equity credentials on 'leadership' and 'innovation'. KPI brand tracking attributes:
- 'Are modern and up to date'
- 'Is a brand that always surprises and excites me'
- Generate awareness and talkability about the new SKU and our Pink&Black campaign.

Marketing objective

- Drive trial of this variant. An ambitious sells target was set.

Business Objective

- The ultimate goal was to raise sales and achieve a very ambitious turnover figure.

NB: Targets were based on previous limited-edition summer launches.

(Source: Qualitative research)

Communication Strategy

For the first time, our role was to come up with a gender based approach on pleasure to reinforce our position amongst the female target and have a first close up with males. A new excuse for women pleasure seekers to identify with Magnum and an excuse for strengthening the engagement with Magnum's male target.

So in terms of message, the brief was to provoke pleasure seekers to express their personality through playful Pink or rational and assertive Black.

Bearing this in mind, we defined 3 objectives and tasks:

1. Broadcast: Impactful & visible awareness
2. Experience: Engagement & trial
3. Share: An always-on strategy to push WOM

Broadcast: Impactful & visible awareness

Create standout in category, through high reach channels and outstanding placements, and introduce innovation by dramatizing the opposite sides for each product.

Apart from the TVC, impactful POS and Outdoor were responsible for driving mass awareness and dramatizing the opposite sides.

Experience: Engagement & trial

Get consumers excited about the concept behind the campaign and experience through daily activities pushing trial.

Focusing in more targeted channels that allow interaction or content distribution.

Point of Sale and exclusive sampling activities would bring the new product experience and message to consumers and drive trial.

- UK activation and early listing and Valentine's promo at Tesco

Share: An always-on strategy to foment WOM

Drive the talkability and leverage the WOM to convert more Pleasure Seekers into Magnum consumers.

Markets anticipated their PR campaign before the great European launch to generate greater impact and more engagement.

- DACH: The world-class photographer Ellen von Unwerth staged the popular German Actress Josefine Preuss.

11 photos showed Josephine in playful pink and sophisticated black. More than a press conference, Magnum invited journalists and VIP to galleries in Berlin and Vienna to showcase the photos and celebrate the launch. Photos then toured around DACH.

- Portugal used Pink & Black as season starter through the Portuguese style icon Cristina Ferreira.

Pink & Black was launched in the Cannes Festival, starring top model Miranda Kerr. Cannes would become the big media moment that would leverage Magnum's key pleasure territories of fashion, film, celebrities and sociability.

Accompanying the big PR event, and in order to make Pleasure Seekers participate and define their personality, Magnum asked European consumers if they wanted to light up their city in Pink or in Black.

Media Allocation

Television: 55% Digital: 23%

Consumer Magazines: 4% Other: 18%

Specify: OOH

Commercial Communication Expenditure:

Euro 10m to under 15m

Creative Strategy

Our initial approach was easy, though not correct: Magnum Pink for girls, Magnum Black for boys.

However, we did not want to be so strict defining the target of these two variants. If the launch was about defining your personality, why should we predefine it? Wouldn't that be prescriptive and archaic?

Moving on from stereotypes

We needed consumers to freely identify with any of the products. Moreover, it has been consistently proven in research – both Qualitative and Quantitative - that men and women don't want to be told "for men" and "for women" in such a black and white manner. Moreover, gender association with Pink and Black is implied.

Reminder: Entrants will copy their answers into the entry form in the online entry area for judging purposes – this document will not be uploaded for judging. Use this form to draft your responses and collaborate with team members.

No girly girls, no macho men.

The men loved the Magnum pink; women didn't understand why they were left out of the black world.

As no gender differences needed to be shown, we needed to tackle the product launch from another angle. An angle that was inclusive, and enabled our Pleasure Seekers to freely identify with one ice cream or the other.

Consumer research revealed a human insight, based on personality, not gender, that we felt inspiring:

"None of us are the same person all the time.

We all have different sides to our personality that come out at different moments."

And this was spot on with our product: Two different ice creams, for two different moods.

This concept assumes the difference between the colours and personality of each ice cream, but highlights that depending on the day, the mood, the feeling, which one of the colours will fit better. And as moods depend on moments and moments depend on occasions, this concept helps the brand work on occasions too.

This concept also enables to delicately skip away from the sophisticated world of Magnum ice cream by introducing a more playful attitude. Every time we desire a Magnum we are not in a sophisticated mood, many of our Magnum moments are playful, and this was an opportunity to demonstrate it without losing sophistication.

Silky, delicate, pink raspberry Ice cream and sauce covered in a pearlescent pink layer of cracking Magnum Chocolate to bring out your playful side.

A ripple of intense black espresso coffee swirled in a smooth and creamy vanilla ice cream, all covered in a thick layer of dark Magnum cracking chocolate.

Giving birth to the concept

Magnum presents two new delicious ice creams to suit the different sides of your personality: Two different ice creams, for two different moments.

The world of pink: Fun, playful, light-hearted, flirty, exuberant, cheeky; but still sophisticated, upmarket, intelligent. The more frivolous and upbeat side of your personality.

The world of black: Sophisticated, elegant, cool, confident, assured; but still human, relatable, down to earth. The more refined and discerning side of your personality.

The idea was brought to life through a TVC; 'Sliding Floors' successfully brings to life the contrast between two different but equally appealing worlds, that relate to contrasting sides of our persona.

(Source: Nielsen Pre-briefing Qualitative research.)

(Source: Firefish, Qualitative copy test UK, TK, MX, 2012)

Additional Information

There was no on-pack promotion. We did print unique codes on the sticks, but in the end we did not use them for promotions. Price offs (and coupons) were part of the program. Overview of the value sold on deal for the key markets.

In terms of distribution, DACH countries worked on a fast distribution build-up to achieve objectives. However this fast distribution was in line with distribution deployment in previous Magnum campaigns.

Reminder: Entrants will copy their answers into the entry form in the online entry area for judging purposes – this document will not be uploaded for judging. Use this form to draft your responses and collaborate with team members.

Application Workshop

Throughout this book, you will have formal application workshops and exercises with supportive tools to help you apply the information from each chapter to your particular case or assignment. You will also have access to lists of key decisions to be made or capabilities that you need to have in place at each step of the shopper marketing planning process.

For this final chapter, the workshop will focus on the globalization of shopper marketing through a case study.

Global Brand and Global Shopper Marketing: Fuel Up for Battle with Mountain Dew and Doritos

We have selected the global brands Mountain Dew and Doritos, and the campaign ran in multiple countries:

- http://www.pepsico.com/live/story/fuel-up-for-battle-with-mountain-dew-and-doritos082120141555
- https://www.bevnet.com/news/2015/mountain-dew-and-doritos-kick-off-fuel-up-for-battle-campaign

Read about what they executed.

Study the culture of two of the countries where the game has been executed. One country can be Canada, and then select a second of your choice.

Here's some information on the Canadian and US version:

- https://charlieintel.com/2015/09/25/mtn-dewdoritos-fuel-up-for-battle-promo-starts-oct-5th-at-12pm-et-2xp-in-zombies-available-on-all-platforms/
- https://www.se7ensins.com/forums/threads/advanced-warfare-fuel-up-for-battle-dew-and-doritos-usa-canadian-promotion-code-request.1221082/

Here's some information on other countries and their versions of the game:

- https://charlieintel.com/2015/08/06/monster-energy-announces-promotion-with-black-ops-3-for-europe-get-zombies-2xp/

Here is a video to obtain additional information:

- https://www.youtube.com/watch?v=VM4c2Mqr8r8

From your reading and viewing do the following:

- Identify the top three cultural differences between the two countries.
- For each country, provide your opinion on the following regarding Pepsi:
    - Did Pepsi choose the proper shopper target? Why? Why not?
    - Was it focused on the proper changes of purchase behavior for this shopper target? Why? Why not?
    - Did it select the appropriate consumer promotion techniques? Why? Why not?
    - Did it formulate a proper offer? Why? Why not?
    - Did it have the proper campaign message and the proper creative execution? Why? Why not?
- Overall, how would you rate the apparent effectiveness of this campaign in terms of integrating the cultural characteristics that you have identified before?
- Between the two countries, which one do you think had the best shopper marketing? Why?

Answers can be found at https://drive.google.com/file/d/1u9XtzNGKmv8RKIL2Gv1ZUM46u6rRjzRl/view?usp=sharing.

Conclusion

Globalization of brands is on the rise and is expected to continue. Shopper marketing, as a way to keep a brand top of mind for the entire shopping journey, plays an important role in marketing in countries around the world. It is, however, challenging to sell internationally and support marketing initiatives with powerful shopper marketing campaigns, based on significant variations among countries in terms of culture, infrastructure, and the legal/regulatory framework.

(1) Sales Promotion by Tony Yeshin Apr 15, 2006

Credit Lines

Fig. 1.1: Source:
http://ebm.cmail.dickblick.com/c/tag/hBZuTnpB8hV5pB9gC1YAAhtonKM/doc.html?t_params=bfLWH8cgeMIO5 5kjP0OQXcCzdbN7iAF5yeTdd4a80dCGTAVSs7oof7nGxVzwQU2N-6w-QftMU32kO5Owi0RXeI-SvLyiCUmMBZUtldIBfFlfca7Pq7iDHLFdfRO.

Fig. 1.2: Source: http://thepomoblog.com/index.php/borrell-big-spike-in-promotions-spending/.

Fig. 1.3: Source: http://cadentcg.com/wp-content/uploads/2017-Marketing-Spending-Study.pdf .

Fig. 1.4: Source: The Beauty Consumer - US - March 2016 (Sources of Information).

Fig. 1.5: Source: http://www.emarketer.com/Chart/Most-Trusted-Sources-of-Information-Making-Purchase-Decisions-According-Internet-Users-North-America-July-2015-of-respondents/182209 .

Fig. 1.6: Source: https://www.l2inc.com/daily-insights/vlogger-influence-to-reign-strong-in-2016.

Fig. 1.7: Source: Beauty Retailing - US - January 2016.

Fig. 1.8: Source: https://www.emarketer.com/Chart/US-Total-Media-Ad-Spending-by-Media-2016-2021-billions/205099.

Fig. 1.9: Source: http://www.emarketer.com/Chart/Areas-Which-US-Marketing-Executives-Use-Marketing-Analytics-Make-Decisions-Aug-2015-Feb-2016-Aug-2016-of-respondents/196703.

"Say It With Pepsi," pp. 1-12. Copyright © 2017 by Effie Worldwide, Inc. Reprinted with permission.

Fig. 2.1: Copyright © 2009 by Factoryjoe, (CC BY-SA 3.0) at
https://commons.wikimedia.org/wiki/File:Maslow%27s_Hierarchy_of_Needs.svg.

Fig. 2.2: Source: https://listeningtostories.files.wordpress.com/2014/12/purchasefish.png.

Fig. 2.3: Source: https://www.emarketer.com/Chart/Sources-Used-Research-ProductBrand-Before-Purchase-According-US-Internet-Users-by-Generation-May-2016-of-respondents-each-group/193030.

Fig. 2.4: Source: http://totalaccess.emarketer.com/chart.aspx?r=190179.

Fig. 2.5: Source: http://totalaccess.emarketer.com/chart.aspx?r=206490.

Fig. 2.6: Source: http://totalaccess.emarketer.com/chart.aspx?r=207657.

Fig. 2.7: Source: Smart Insights.

"Sour Patch Watermelon Slurpee Campaign," pp. 1-6. Copyright © 2016 by Effie Worldwide, Inc. Reprinted with permission.

Fig. 3.1: Source: http://totalaccess.emarketer.com/chart.aspx?r=211310.

Fig. 3.2: Source: http://totalaccess.emarketer.com/chart.aspx?r=196278.

Fig. 3.3: Source: http://totalaccess.emarketer.com/chart.aspx?r=206490.

Fig. 3.4: Source: http://www.pewresearch.org/fact-tank/2016/01/29/us-smartphone-use/ft_01-27-16_smartphoneactivities_640/.

Fig. 3.5: Source: http://www.smartinsights.com/wp-content/uploads/2015/07/percent-time-spent-on-mobile-apps-2016.png.

Fig. 3.6: Source: https://scanova.io/blog/blog/2016/02/12/why-custom-qr-codes/.

Fig. 3.7: Source: http://totalaccess.emarketer.com/chart.aspx?r=209161.

Fig. 3.8: Source: https://s3.amazonaws.com/effie_assets/cases/2017/SME_2017_E-123-611/2017_SME_2017_E-123-611_hero_2.jpg.

"National Toilet Paper Day," pp. 1-7. Copyright © 2017 by Effie Worldwide, Inc. Reprinted with permission.

"FLONASE Allergy Relief Over-the-Counter Launch," pp. 1-7. Copyright © 2016 by Effie Worldwide, Inc. Reprinted with permission.

Fig. 5.1: "Save $1.00 Off Any Two Ortega Products." Copyright © 2018 by Ortega.

Fig. 5.2: "Avanquest $10 Mail-In Rebate." Copyright © by Avanquest USA.

Fig. 5.3: "Price Chopper 40 cents off per Gallon." Copyright © 2014 by Price Chopper.

Fig. 5.4: "Marks & Spencer Buy One Get One 50% off." Copyright © by Marks & Spencer.

Fig. 5.5: "Buy One Holiday Beverage, Get One Free." Copyright © 2014 by Starbucks.

Fig. 5.6: Source: https://www.nchmarketing.com/Valassis-2016-Coupon-Savings-Report-Summary/.

Fig. 5.7: Source: https://lh3.googleusercontent.com/G5CbLSU_elliOj2v2SxVL-sEYh0qyDhUnsxsmZ6FUBB4Swgz6Fq4ZAkf7clqZlXXP60S=s126.

Fig. 5.8: Source: https://lh3.googleusercontent.com/Z9pY-QsBnaf_rJloCQtAUDt3Se1M8KYnd3HesfKnSvZHkNS8W0AZjRnGacvUZy2hmoU9Ug=s128.

Fig. 5.9: Fig. 5.9: Source: https://addicted2savings4u.blogspot.com/.

Fig. 5.10: Source: http://www.mikescandywrappers.com/reesepbcup_bonus1102.html.

Fig. 5.11: "Johnson's Baby Wash Bonus Packs." Copyright © 2011 by Totally Target.

Fig. 5.12: Source: https://images.samsclubresources.com/is/image/samsclub/0003700085447_A?$img_size_380x380$.

Fig. 5.13: Source: http://cincyshopper.com/wp-content/uploads/2013/07/coppertone2.jpg.

Fig. 5.14: Source: https://i.pinimg.com/736x/f0/e4/ab/f0e4abadebfe7dc450cc21f5e44aeef3--sugar-free-gum-teeth.jpg.

Fig. 5.15: "Turtle Wax Complete Car Care Gift Pack." Copyright © 2017 by Walmart.

Fig. 5.16: "Diet Coke Karl Lagerfelds Limited Edition Bottles." Copyright © 2011 by Coca Cola.

Fig. 5.17: "Coca Cola Light Marc Jacobs Limited Edition Cans." Copyright © 2013 by Coca Cola.

Fig. 5.18: "Charmin Ultra Strong Double Rolls 36 Count Packages - Bonus Pack." Copyright © 2015 by Target.

Fig. 5.19: Source: https://www.geek.com/wp-content/uploads/2016/02/Galaxy-and-GEar-625x350.jpg.

Fig. 5.20: Source: https://lh3.googleusercontent.com/0cY8Fnf6ZGuHAurOdrDCdUYbm-z749F2uUz9Sf3FsOk3r1P_EKoEdm47KdctvrnwbRoizg=s113.

Fig. 5.21: "Office Depot Launches Facebook Sweepstakes." Copyright © 2011 by Office Depot.

Fig. 5.22: "Kelloggs Instant Win Game." Copyright © by Kelloggs.

Fig. 5.23: "Jimmy Dean Sweepstakes." Copyright © by Jimmy Dean.

Fig. 5.24: "Discovery Match & Win Sweepstakes." Copyright © 2015 by Princess Cruises.

Fig. 5.25: "Discovery Match & Win Sweepstakes." Copyright © 2015 by Princess Cruises.

Fig. 5.26: "Discovery Match & Win Sweepstakes." Copyright © 2015 by Princess Cruises.

Fig. 5.27: Source: https://s3.amazonaws.com/effie_assets/cases/2013/NA_2013_7327/2013_NA_2013_7327_hero_2.jpg.

Fig. 5.28: Source: https://s3.amazonaws.com/effie_assets/cases/2013/NA_2013_7327/2013_NA_2013_7327_hero_3.jpg.

Fig. 5.29: "Growth of Cause Sponsorship." Copyright © 2017 by IEG.

Fig. 5.30: Source: https://s3.amazonaws.com/effie_assets/cases/2015/SME_2015_10289/2015_SME_2015_10289_hero_1.jpg.

Fig. 5.31: Source: https://s3.amazonaws.com/effie_assets/cases/2015/SME_2015_10289/2015_SME_2015_10289_hero_2.jpg.

Fig. 5.32: Source: https://s3.amazonaws.com/effie_assets/cases/2015/SME_2015_10289/2015_SME_2015_10289_hero_2.jpg.

Fig. 5.33: Source: https://images.csmonitor.com/csm/2013/09/0912rewardscards.jpg?alias=standard_600x400.

Fig. 5.34: "Panera Frequent Customer Card." Copyright © 2017 by Panera.

Fig. 5.35: "Starbucks Rewards Program." Copyright © 2017 by Starbucks.

Fig. 5.36: "Dunkin' Donuts Rewards Program." Copyright © by Dunkin' Donuts.

Fig. 5.37: "Aetna Rewards Program." Copyright © 2017 by Aetna.

Fig. 5.38: "Burlington Coat Factory Sweepstakes." Copyright © 2011 by Burlington Coat Factory.

Fig. 5.39: "TD Ameritrade - Zombie Trader Game." Copyright © by TD Ameritrade.

Fig. 5.40: "#NutellaPancakeSweeps." Copyright © 2015 by Nutella.

Fig. 6.1: Source: http://cadentcg.com/wp-content/uploads/2017-Marketing-Spending-Study.pdf.

Fig. 6.2: "$1 Off with Purchase of Spongebob." Copyright © by Nickelodeon.

Fig. 6.3: "Target coupon." Copyright © 2010 by Target.

Fig. 6.4: "Victorious "Lights, Camera and Fashion" Sweepstakes." Copyright © 2010 by Nickelodeon - Kids Choice Award.

Fig. 6.5: Source: https://lh3.googleusercontent.com/bhpDYOAbo_q7jssiapWbiadB3zmxLayD1UnWJIpG8tl_D-60BafFAPlxE_CoM0eyoQf2tg=s106.

Fig. 6.6: Source: https://s3.amazonaws.com/effie_assets/cases/2017/SME_2017_E-31-973/2017_SME_2017_E-31-973_hero_1.jpg.

Fig. 6.7: Source: https://s3.amazonaws.com/effie_assets/cases/2017/SME_2017_E-31-973/2017_SME_2017_E-31-973_hero_2.jpg.

"ShopRite Mix-In Matchmaker Program," pp. 1-4. Copyright © 2017 by Effie Worldwide, Inc. Reprinted with permission.

Fig. 7.1: Source: https://www.ncsolutions.com/wp-content/uploads/2016/09/Multimedia-CPG-Benchmarks.pdf.

Fig. 7.2: Source: https://www.ncsolutions.com/wp-content/uploads/2016/09/Multimedia-CPG-Benchmarks.pdf.

Fig. 7.3: Source: https://s3.amazonaws.com/effie_assets/cases/2017/SME_2017_E-76-921/2017_SME_2017_E-76-921_hero_2.jpg.

"Say Thank You With M," pp. 1-7. Copyright © 2017 by Effie Worldwide, Inc. Reprinted with permission.

Fig. 8.3: Source: https://www.slideshare.net/Smart-Insights/integrated-marketing-2014.

Fig. 8.4: Source: https://www.lightpetal.com/vouchercodes-persona-decals-and-cards/.

Fig. 8.5: Copyright © 2015 by 7 Eleven.

Fig. 8.6: Copyright © 2015 by 7 Eleven.

Fig. 8.7: Copyright © 2015 by Sally Beauty.

Fig. 8.8: Copyright © 2015 by Sally Beauty.

Fig. 8.9: Copyright © 2015 by Publix.

Fig. 8.10: Copyright © 2015 by Publix.

Fig. 8.11: Source: https://s3.amazonaws.com/effie_assets/cases/2015/SME_2015_9516/2015_SME_2015_9516_hero_1.jpg.

"Coca-Cola Share It Forward," pp. 1-6. Copyright © 2015 by Effie Worldwide, Inc. Reprinted with permission.

Fig. 9.1: Source: http://www.business-to-you.com/international-business-strategy/ .

Fig. 9.2: Source: https://www.boston.com/culture/travel/2014/06/30/dunkin-donuts-you-cant-get-in-america .

Fig. 9.3: Source: https://www.boston.com/culture/travel/2014/06/30/dunkin-donuts-you-cant-get-in-america.

Fig. 9.4: Source: https://www.boston.com/culture/travel/2014/06/30/dunkin-donuts-you-cant-get-in-america .

Fig. 9.5: Source: https://www.boston.com/culture/travel/2014/06/30/dunkin-donuts-you-cant-get-in-america.

Fig. 9.6: Source: https://www.slideshare.net/aaalm/the-luxury-global-s .

Fig. 9.7: Source: https://www.effie.org/case_database/case/EU_2016_1004.

Fig. 9.8: Source: https://www.effie.org/case_database/case/EU_2016_1004.

Printed in the USA
CPSIA information can be obtained
at www.ICGtesting.com
LVHW082039220823
755991LV00004B/55